THE VALOR OF IGNORANCE

THE VALOR
OF IGNORANCE

BY

HOMER LEA

Including a short life entitled
THE VALOR OF HOMER LEA
by CLARE BOOTHE

With Specially Prepared Maps

NEW YORK AND LONDON
HARPER & BROTHERS PUBLISHERS

This book is complete and unabridged
in contents, and is manufactured in strict
conformity with Government regulations
for saving paper.

TO
THE HON. ELIHU ROOT

LIST OF CHARTS

THE VALOR OF HOMER LEA

By Clare Boothe

"To free a nation from error is to enlighten the individual, and only to the degree that the individual will be receptive of truth can a nation be free from that vanity which ends with national ruin."—Homer Lea

I FIRST heard his name in early October, 1941, in Manila. I was dining with several officers of the Philippine Department in their quarters built on top of the ancient Spanish walls of old Fort Santiago, which also housed the headquarters of General Douglas MacArthur's "Usaffe." It was still the rainy season. A sudden tropical downpour drummed loudly on the flimsy tin roof of the mess hall. Outside, the curtains of the deluge blotted out the lights of Dewey Boulevard and the twin red stars high on the steel radio towers at near-by Cavite. It was a melancholy, stifling night, but in the bright dry room, one talked, as every visitor in Manila did in those days, lightly enough of the possibility of a Japanese invasion of the Philippines.

"If it comes, where will they strike first?" I asked.

Colonel Charles Willoughby drew a deft map of Luzon on the Major's tablecloth. "The main attacks will probably come here, at Lingayen Gulf," he said, making an arrow, "and then here—at Polillo Bight. Ye olde pincer movement."

"You're not giving away military secrets?"

The officers all laughed. Colonel Willoughby pocketed his pencil. "No," he said. "Just quoting military gospel—according to Homer Lea."

"Who is Homer Lea?"

"Tell you a funny story," the Colonel said. "When I first came out here, about a year ago, some nimble wit in Military Intelligence had just hauled in a 'spy.' Young college-bred Filipino. Seems he had written a letter to a pal, complete with rough maps, analyzing the Jap plans for invading Luzon.

The pal turned it over to G 2, who had the boy on the mat. His maps, and his analysis corresponded rather too well with the Department's. The terrified kid swore he'd gotten the whole thing right out of an old book he'd taken out of the library. 'Son, have you by any chance been reading Homer Lea?' I asked. When he produced a library card which showed he had, we let him go . . . You see," the Colonel said, "thirty-five years ago, a strange young man who called himself 'General' Homer Lea, wrote a book about a war to come between America and Japan. In it he described, in minutest details the Jap campaigns against the Philippines, Hawaii, Alaska and California."

"A sort of American Nostradamus?"

The Colonel said, "Not at all. Homer Lea was neither a mystic nor a prophet. He was a scientist. He studied the science of war—the fundamental laws of which are as immutable as those of any other science. He also sought to analyze the causes of war and diagnose the symptoms of an approaching conflict. And, having proven, at least to his own satisfaction, that great causes of war existed between the U. S. and Japan, that the symptoms of the approaching conflict were apparent to all but fools or wishful-thinkers, he proceeded to set forth the tactical course that war would take."

The Major said, "I read him at West Point. Damned convincing militarily—if you accepted his political premise—that our democracy wouldn't get ready in time to lick the Japs."

"Is America ready?" the Colonel asked of nobody in particular.

"From which dismal question," I said, "am I to assume that you, like Homer Lea, doubt for a moment we could lick the Japs, *even* if they attacked tomorrow?" (It was no military secret, in the Philippines, in October, that the U. S. was racing against time to build up its defenses in the Far Pacific.)

The Colonel said, "Don't jump to conclusions. First, Lea wrote over thirty years ago. Since then, there have been revolutionary changes, not in the science, but in the instruments of warfare. Second, like all scientists, he did not make enough allowance for that forever inexact science: the science of the

human soul. There are two things—and only two things—
having to do with the defense of these Islands which Lea did
not, could not, foresee. One was the courage and genius of a
man called MacArthur. The other was a machine called the
airplane. If these omissions are decisive factors—Lea's analysis, that these Islands cannot be held will be proven wrong."

"Are they decisive factors?"

"Well, I hope to God they are!" the Major said fervently.

"Amen," said Colonel Willoughby. "But in any case, next
month, when you get home—brush up on the General."

I thought no more of Homer Lea until that first newspaper
map appeared, with its sinister little arrows which showed
where the Japs were landing—at Lingayen. Then suddenly I
remembered Colonel Willoughby's "military gospel according
to Homer Lea."

My bookshop had never heard of author Homer Lea. In
the end, I carried not one, but two books away from the New
York Public Library.

The first book was called, *The Valor of Ignorance*. On its
warped, faded blue covers were the arms of our Republic,
emblazoned in gold that time and dust had tarnished. The
pages were yellowed—but clean. It had not been "popular"
reading: The library card showed that it had been drawn out
only three times since it was published by Harpers, in 1909.
Quickly I flipped through it until I came to the text surrounding the invasion map of the Island of Luzon (page 175) the
same text, the same map no doubt the Colonel's Filipino 'spy'
had copied.

The conquest of these Islands by Japan will be less of a
military undertaking than was the seizure of Cuba by the
United States . . .

As I read the description of that conquest, so accurate in broad
strategic outline, my heart grew heavy.

Here was the prediction that Manila would be forced to
surrender in three weeks. It was occupied by the Japs twenty-

six days after the opening of hostilities. Here was the very picture of the convergent attack at right angles—the pincer movement—from Lingayen Gulf and Polillo Bight before which MacArthur's valiant troops fell back to entrench them-selves on Bataan Peninsula. And here the prophecy that should the 21,000 white and native troops, stationed on the Islands in 1909, be doubled, or even trebled in the future, this would merely result in the doubling of the Japanese forces. In 1941, MacArthur's 55,000 white and native defenders met a Jap army of 200,000. Here, above all, was a solemn warning against putting undue faith in "impregnable forts" in Manila Harbor (Corregidor, Il Caballo, El Fraile), unless they formed the base of a great fleet, equal to Japan's, or were de-fended by a great mobile army. Admiral Thomas Hart's Asi-atic Squadron, consisting of a handful of cruisers, overage destroyers, and submarines based on near-by, inadequately equipped Cavite, retired to the Netherlands East Indies thirty days after the Invasion. Here is a bitter warning of "the vul-nerability of permanent fortifications and the old fallacy of their making." Inveighing thirty-five years ago against all Maginots, Lea said, "These stone castles of nations are but the dream castles of their vanity."

No, Lea had not foreseen the gallantry and genius of Mac-Arthur, nor the invention of the fighter and bombing plane. But all that he wrote on the development of a Japanese cam-paign against the Philippines, implied that no man nor thing could do more than delay the end—improvise heroic varia-tions on the dark theme of defeat in the Philippines. That defeat itself, Lea said, was inherent in a national policy which left the Islands' defense—and America's—to the "shifts of unforeseen combat."

Turning the pages of this book, while the very war the author predicted is raging about us, one finds few words of comfort. The cloth is being cut much too close to the author's pattern:

"This Republic and Japan are approaching, careless on the

one hand, predetermined on the other, that point of contact, which is war . . .

"We exaggerate, not Japan's capacity to make war, but our capacity to defend ourselves . . .

"When Japan declares war, one of two naval conditions will be existent: Either the American Navy will be divided between the Pacific and the Atlantic, or the whole of it will be in the latter. Either condition will insure instant Japanese naval supremacy. A division of the American navy means the destruction of those portions in the Pacific; while the fleets in the Atlantic will have no effect upon this conflict . . .

"The question that now rises naturally in the thoughts of the reader is, 'What will the U. S. be doing during (the first) three months?' Instantly the mind is crowded, not alone with the speculations of victory, but with the vague grandeur of a nation's hope. The Old Lamp is rubbed and vast armies are suddenly mobilized; armaments are brought out of hidden recesses. Great Generals are made in the twinkling of an eye; then winged . . . take their flight . . . West. But what will actually take place in the Republic after war is declared is well known . . . confusion, ignorance, peculation, and a complete lack of every form of military preparation, armaments, supplies or means of securing them. . . ."

Nor is this dread apocalyptic vision all that *The Valor of Ignorance* holds to depress a modern reader. Clearly foreshadowed is another threat . . . the threat of a war on a second front waged on us by Germany.

Writing eight years before the outbreak of World War I, twenty-nine years before the Japanese invasion of Manchuria, thirty-three years before the outbreak of World War II, Homer Lea states, as militarily axiomatic, that all these dire events—including the surprise attack on Hawaii—would be in time and space, inevitable. Why? Because:

"No state is ever destroyed except through those avertible conditions that mankind dreads to contemplate. Yet nations prefer to perish rather than to master the single lesson taught by the washing away of those that have gone before them. In their indifference, and *in the valor of ignorance*, they depart, together with their monuments and their constitutions . . ."

That single lesson is vigilance, the eternal price of liberty.

. . . .

The Valor of Ignorance is charged with the bitterest apothegms ever penned against Isolationism and Pacifism. It explodes with florid and savage indictments of the smugness and conceit that lead fat rich contented nations to disarm while encouraging tough frugal hungry nations to attack them. Like a battle drum it beats the need of militant patriotism in times of peace—so that times of war may be avoided. Like the blast of a reveille bugle, it seeks to shatter "our mock heroism of dreams," and our "valor of the rostrum."

. . . .

The Day of the Saxon, the second book by Lea, is equally prophetic—and equally gloomy. Published in 1912, its thesis is also stark and simple: The British Empire (the Kingdom of the Saxon) shows certain specific military defects which leave it vulnerable to German aggression. Lea predicted that if the British Empire continued to rely solely on commercialism and sea power, if it could not, in short, quickly form a *lasting* military alliance with a great friendly land army power—it was doomed by the ever resurgent armies of Germany. But nowhere on the teeming greedy earth, except in the Western hemisphere, where America alone among all the great powers neither feared Great Britain, nor desired what was hers, could Homer Lea, in 1912, find for the Empire a "great land army" ally. And despairful that the United States would ever see—*in time*—"that the British Navy—not the Monroe Doctrine is this Republic's true protection," he foretold that "the day of the Saxon" was drawing to a close, and that on a hundred fields of battle—in Belgium, France, Holland, Russia, and Egypt, the day of the Teuton was dawning. And, bitterest prophecy of all: Great Britain at long last, exhausted by her perhaps "victorious" Germanic wars, would then lose her Empire to Japan and Russia.

. . . .

Who was this man who, thirty-five years ago, announced as though they were already accomplished facts, the multiple Armageddons that now face ourselves and the British? What were his spiritual, his intellectual and military credentials?

The frontispiece of the book shows a plain-faced boy, certainly in his early twenties, with a hard, wide mouth, intense wide eyes, a wide brow with long lank hair parted unevenly in the middle. The boy is wearing the gold epauleted uniform of a three-star general, and his breast is covered with medals. A great coat drops nonchalantly from one shoulder, and an extraordinarily long and delicate hand plays with the brass buttons of his tunic in a very Napoleonic manner. But, one discovers with a sudden shock—this is not an American uniform. It is a foreign uniform of some sort. This is strange, because there is nothing "foreign" about that strong young American face, or the name boldly written in a boyish scrawl beneath it. Let us see if the two prefaces in *The Valor of Ignorance* cast any light on the background of this young "General." The first is by Lieutenant General Adna R. Chaffee, a former U. S. Chief of Staff. It is a professional soldier's idea of a "rave notice." But not a word about who Homer was, or how he got to be a three-star "general." The second introduction, by Major General J. P. Story is equally ecstatic. But neither does he tell us whence this genius sprang, or on what field he won those fabulous decorations.

. . . .

I returned to the Library. No, there was no biography of Lea. No, he was not in the 1941 *Encyclopedia Britannica*. I sought *Who's Who* for 1912, the year his last book was published. He was there:

"Lea, Homer, author, soldier, b. Denver, Nov. 17, 1876 . . ."

And with this as a clue, to other clues, in old newspaper

files, in the course of a long month of research, I finally came upon one of the strangest, most adventurous and significant stories that America ever knew . . . and had ever forgotten—the story of a little cripple who longed to be a military giant, of a boy who gave his frail young life for China—and how that gift helped to change the course of the Chinese Empire in such a way that today China is able to help change the course of America and the British Empire. It is the story of the Valor of Homer Lea.

·   ·   ·   ·   ·   ·   ·

In the early days of the Civil War, Alfred Erskine Lea, fourteen-year-old son of a Tennessee doctor, living in Missouri, had made his way alone, through the bloody border states, in a mule-drawn covered wagon to the West. A few days after Alfred left, Dr. Lea, a rebel sympathizer, was murdered by border raiders. In Colorado, Alfred Lea mined at Cripple Creek, prospered mildly, married Hersa Coberly who bore him a son, Homer, and two daughters, engaged in "abstracting titles," and finally in 1892, moved to Los Angeles. There Homer attended the public high school for two years. A teacher recalls that he was a "brilliant though erratic student." The school records show there was nothing "erratic" about his marks. In Latin, Greek, French, history and mathematics he averaged for both terms well over 90. Maybe it was a strange ambition of little Homer's, which made him seem "erratic" in adult eyes. He wanted to be a soldier. And it was so very plain he could never be. He was a hunchback child, and after he was twelve years old and five feet tall, he never grew. As he approached boyhood a curvature of the spine grew more and more pronounced until it earned him the unhappy nickname of "Little Scrunch-neck" among his classmates. But "Little Scrunch-neck," nothing daunted even in school resolutely played soldier. Two childhood friends, the late Harry Carr of the Los Angeles *Times* and Marco Newmark, recalled that after hours "he drilled the kids with broomsticks and laid out campaigns in his backyard." His sister once wrote a friend that on Fourths of July Homer wasn't content just to set off firecrackers like other brothers; he insisted on staging maneuvers on the lawn, using the firecrackers as artillery to blast his little sisters out of the "untenable positions" he had entrenched them in behind trees and bushes. Why his sisters and his schoolmates meekly took orders from the frail hunchback, whose manner was always gentle and whose voice was always soft, they could never quite explain. Years later, a Chinese who had been with him on the field of battle said, "He had eyes that could bury you nine feet under the ground, if you disobeyed him."

In 1894, Lea entered Occidental College continuing to specialize in classical languages and history, but his extra-curricular interest in military matters continued unabated. Now, to the increasing annoyance of his classmates who had outgrown their adolescent interest in "playing soldier," Homer spouted the campaigns of Caesar, Hannibal, Alexander, Turenne and Napoleon, which he knew far better than they knew their football and baseball scores. To this, he added another idiosyncrasy: a tendency to talk Chinese. Newmark says he picked it up from the family cook, a pigtailed Chinaman, who had captured the boy's imagination with violent tales about his turbulent far-off native land. Carr said that Homer once confided to him that his interest in China was the result of a strange series of dreams, in which at last in a blare of Chinese trumpets, he saw himself revealed as the reincarnation of a great historic Chinese warrior called "The Martial Monk," marching at the head of his army to defend China. The true dreams of a small sick body, or the "daydreams" of a sensitive boy who felt his physical inferiority keenly, or simply the imaginative reflection of the interest all political-minded Californians had in the "Chinese problem" in those days, the fact remains that by the time Lea entered Leland Stanford in 1895, to study law, his main preoccupations were all things military and all things Chinese.

Although still popular, as cripples are always "popular," most of his college classmates thought him a full-fledged "nut." Wallace Irwin, the writer, and a fellow student, wrote of him, "he was a quiet little chap . . . and talked rather

large . . . bombastic, you might say, but there was an earnest-
ness about him that impressed one, just the same. . . ." A
gifted talker, with a rich low voice, Lea orated incessantly
on what he had now come to call "the forthcoming sack of
America by the expanding and predatory powers." He had
astonishing notions about vast "hemispheric wars between the
nations." Other fellows hung pictures of girls or baseball stars
on their walls. Lea hung huge maps, and on these maps, he
waged with colored pins a great world war, between the
Japanese and the Germans on one side, and on the other, China
and the U. S. A. Or sometimes the war was between Russia
and Great Britain, and India was the prize. "Witness," he
would say, "how India, the keystone of the Empire, is being
remorselessly pried loose by the screwjack, Russia!" On days
when Great Britain or the U.S.A. was ahead, Lea was in fine
spirits and acted, according to a classmate, "very exhilarated,
like he might be old Napoleon himself." But most days he was
depressed, because (he said) "things being the way they were
with the people, the politicians, the pacifists, the clericalists,
the feminists and the isolationists, 'The Republic' (as he always called it) and the Empire had to be behind." The one
thing on which Wallace Irwin and all his fellow "froshs"
agreed was that Homer played the "coolest, cagiest poker
game" on the campus.

Naturally, the little cripple could not go in for sports. But
he did take up fencing, and until the severe headaches from
which he had suffered as a child, and an eye ailment, aggra-
vated by this exercise, caused him to abandon it, he held his
own against all but the best campus swordsmen. His mon-
strously long arms gave him an advantage of reach over even
much taller men. The only fellows on the campus he was really
"pally" with were several young Chinese students. After a
time, he began to disappear at nights with his young Oriental
friends into San Francisco's murky Chinatown. It was there
that he first came into touch with the members of the Po-
Wong-Wui, a secret society of educated young Chinese dedi-
cated to working for the Reform of the Manchu Throne.
Now, on the maps of the walls of his room, when he returned

late at night and—according to some—a little drunk on Chinese wine, Lea waged a civil war against the armies of the tyrannical "Old Buddha," the Manchu Dowager Empress, TsuHsi, who sat, like a fierce old spider weaving murderous plots, on China's Dragon Throne.

On two of Stanford's faculty he made a definite impression. Ray Lyman Wilbur (now its President) "very much admired his mind." "He was very intelligent," said Wilbur, "he was one of those men who always question professors. He always wanted to know 'why'? 'why'? 'why'?" On the other hand, Dr. David Starr Jordan—then President of Stanford—did not admire Lea's mind at all. This was understandable. From 1890 to the very outbreak of World War I, Dr. Jordan was one of America's most vociferous Pacifists, and a profound believer in the power of International Arbitration to avert war. At some point in the course of that first university year, the tiny cripple, who violently disbelieved in both, and the big eminent doctor, probably crossed verbal swords. No doubt Lea, who knew his history thoroughly, pointed out to the kindly doctor, to use his own words, that, "From the 15th century before Christ until the present time, a cycle of 3400 years, there have been fewer than 234 years of peace on earth. . . . Disputes or disagreements between nations, instead of being the source or cause of war, are nothing more or less than the first manifestations of approaching combat. . . . To remove them by arbitration is at best but procrastination. . . ." And he may have added his favorite admonition, "All great nations are born of the sword, and all nations no matter how 'great,' if undefended, die of the sword."

Dr. Jordan found this young man "vulgar, loud-mouthed, excessively warlike . . ." Lea's quarrel with the pacifist Dr. Jordan as to the incidence or inevitability of wars might have continued to the end of his college career, if both quarrel and career had not been interrupted by the Spanish-American War. It was a bitter moment for warrior-student Lea, when according to Wallace Irwin, "many Stanford boys left for the Front, but the little hunchback could not go." Nevertheless, Irwin said, Lea joined a college "cavalry-troop that included a thousand freaks—the lame, the halt and the blind." To a greater extent than any knew, Lea was all three. At the end of his sophomore year, a return of his old eye ailment sent him to a sanatorium, where he caught smallpox.

He did not know, although it might further have persuaded him of his mystic belief that he was a child of Destiny, that the Chinese of the nineteenth century viewed a case of small-pox as an "auspicious omen from heaven," particularly if the disease progressed favorably.

When he recovered, with no scars on his strange intense young face, the war was over. Lea could bear college no longer. To Harry Carr he said, "All great careers are carved out by the sword. Mine, too, I shall carve that way." And when Carr gently reminded him of his deformity, Lea cited the example of club-footed Byron in Greece. "China shall be my Greece," he told Carr. When Newmark said, "You'll get your head cut off in China," the hunchback responded, "For-tunately, they'll have a hard time finding my neck." His sisters pled with him not to think of undertaking such a trip in his frail health. With that strange sense of predestination that comes to Destiny's children, Lea replied, "A man never dies until his work is done." In years to come, this was always his stock answer to pleas that he must "save his ever-failing strength."

When his father stopped his $300-a-month allowance, to prevent his sailing, Lea simply announced that he had already secured financial backing for his venture: he had prevailed upon the China Reform Association to raise funds to send him as "secret military agent" to China.

Harry Carr thinks that the young Chinese patriots took Lea to their bosom because there is a superstition in China that hunchbacks are lucky. Irwin thought that it was because Homer had told them—a pure fiction—that his grandfather was General Robert E. Lee—and that he had inherited his Honorable Ancestor's military genius.

After a little splurge of publicity in the San Francisco papers, planted, it seems, by the talkative Lea himself, the "secret military agent" sailed in July, 1899. To his campus friends he made a remarkable farewell speech. He said, "I go to topple the Manchus from their ancient Dragon Throne." What made the speech most remarkable is that he said it, according to Newmark, as coolly as he had been wont to say "And—*I* hold four aces."

On his way to China, Lea passed through Hawaii, Guam, and the Philippines. All along what has now become the most troubled highway of American destiny, he made his careful maps; his lengthy notes on their possible defense, and probable attack. And everywhere, of soldiers in the Pacific, he asked over and over, "why?" "why?" "why?"

Arriving in Canton, he met according to plan, agents of the Po-Wong-Wui who gave him a letter to the Empress' Prime Minister, Kong Yu Wei in Peking. Under the very nose of the reactionary Empress Dowager, Kong was covertly working to raise a volunteer army, with which to overthrow her, and put on the throne her liberal nephew, Emperor Kwang Hsu, imprisoned by the Empress for advocating "Western ideas." Liberal forces within the Manchu Court still believed that if the Throne could be "Occidentalized," and China opened up to Western, material progress, as Japan had been, the prosperity and greatness long fled from China, would return. To this end, they conspired in daily peril of their lives. The crafty, tyrannical old Empress hated and feared "the white devils" and all their works for she knew that the "Westernization" of her court spelled the end of her long and ugly reign of power.

Traveling from Canton by palanquin through hundreds of miles of China, Homer Lea arrived in Peking secretly. In the Forbidden Palace itself, he kept a prearranged midnight rendezvous with the Prime Minister.

The Prime Minister was frankly surprised to see a crippled boy. "Why have you come? What can you do?" he asked.

"I have come," Lea said, "to help you save China from the old Tigress. To rescue Kwang Hsu. To lead your armies to victory!"

The Prime Minister smiled, "You are very young to do all that."

Homer Lea replied, "I am the same age Napoleon was at Rivoli."

The Prime Minister laughed, but he was impressed as even greater men were yet to be. In the end, he ordered Lea to proceed to Shensi, there to take over a body of volunteers. As Lea left, accompanied by only two palanquin bearers and a guide provided by the Prime Minister, a secret emissary accosted him with a small package and a scroll. It was the Star of the Order of Emperor Kwang Hsu—and a commission as Lieutenant General in the "Army of the Emperor." At least, this is Homer Lea's own version. This part of his story has often been violently denied—it has never been either definitely disproved or verified.

The Shensi troops which "General" Lea had been sent to command were three hundred miles inland. Within a hundred miles of his destination a runner brought him disastrous news. The Empress Dowager's palace spies and her eunuchs—who had long been the scandal of her court—had overheard the Prime Minister's interview with Homer Lea. She was at last aware that Kong was plotting against her. She instantly ordered the beheading of all his officers and sympathizers. But upon a whispered warning from a friend, the Prime Minister had fled the palace, with a price of twenty thousand dollars on his head. On the head of the missing "white devil" Homer Lea, the runner said the Empress had put a price of ten thousand dollars. The Viceroy of Shensi, an appointee of the Empress', had already been apprised of the plot. He had lured all the officers of "Lea's troops" into his palace, under pretext of surrendering the province to them. The next morning their heads had appeared in a grisly row on the city walls. "General" Lea sent the runner back with a message to the troops, telling them to retreat into the mountains, and coolly as though he still held four aces, proceeded on his way.

The Empress' evil hand had touched off the spark that started the hideous holocaust called, "The Boxer Rebellion," in which all Chinese "loyal to the Manchu Throne" vowed to "purge" China of the white men. There began throughout China a widespread pillage of all "white devil" homes and holdings, and a wholesale slaughter and torture of white doctors, missionaries, businessmen and soldiers; while the outraged Foreign Powers hastily raised troops to send to China to quell the rebellion.

Meanwhile back in the distant hills of Shensi, General Lea rallied the scattered remnants of Kong Yu Wei's Reform Volunteers. After several months, at the head of a few thousand pigtailed, ill-disciplined "Volunteers," the American began his long-planned march on the Palace of the Empress Dowager. He now wore the uniform of a general with massive gold epaulets, the gold star of the Emperor about his scrunch-neck, and a sword almost as tall as he was. When he arrived outside the gates of Peking, the Boxer Rebellion was reaching its hideous climax. The compounds and legations of the White Powers—with their white women and children—were under desperate and murderous siege, in which the Dowager's Imperial troops participated. It is certainly too much to say or even to suggest that Homer Lea and his Reform Volunteers raised that siege. But history records that, much to the mystification of the besieged white defenders, when the U. S. troops, commanded by Major General Adna Chaffee of the Philippine Department, marched into the city, there was with them a young white man, dressed as a Chinese General, commanding several thousand ragged Chinese, who had fought the Boxers with General Chaffee.

The Siege of Peking was lifted, the Rebellion put down. The Empress with her Court, and her Imperial Troops, fled. She was promptly pursued—not by the troops of the Allied White Powers—but by Homer Lea and his ragged army.

Waylaid by the Empress' rear guard, his outnumbered troops were killed or dispersed. Every captain and major and colonel fled. The little General was abandoned. He took refuge in a Buddhist Temple. There (again according to a story Lea was very fond of telling at patriotic Chinese banquets when he returned to America) a monk dressed a small wound in his arm and gave him food and drink. As he reached out his hand for the cup, the old monk said, "It is a small hand. But it is a great hand. You will yet lead armies and vanquish your

enemies." As the monk spoke, a little bird dropped dead off
a branch of a tree outside the temple door. In China, there is
a superstition that when a bird drops dead from a tree, a great
throne will fall.

In the days that followed, the Empress Dowager bought
peace from the eight Foreign Powers—for the price of further "concessions" in China, and a 300-million-dollar indem-
nity. Quiet seemed again to reign in The Flowery Kingdom.
The little-General-without-an-army made his disconsolate way
back alone to Hong Kong, hunted all the way by the Empress'
spies. To elude them, he disguised himself as a French missionary and resolutely spoke French whenever he opened his
mouth to friend or stranger.

In Hong Kong, a Chinese graduate of his Stanford days,
took him in and nursed him, soothed his wounded ego, told
him even, that he, too, had abandoned all hope of "reforming
the Throne." Then one day he told Homer Lea that he must
"meet a certain man," a man who also knew that it was "too
late" to reform the Manchu Court, to reform the Chinese
from the top down, a man who knew that China, to be saved,
must be reformed from the bottom up—"saved by the people."

This man, he said, was a foreign-educated Christian Chinese
medical student, only ten years older than Lea. He headed an
even greater and more powerful Society than the Po-Wong-
Wui, one which had thousands of fanatic members working
night and day all through China for the hour of revolution
and liberation. Its password was "thumbs up." (In his turgid
Chinese novel, *The Vermillion Pencil*, Homer Lea describes
a secret Revolutionary Society which he dubs "The Deluge."
He writes: "The call to battle is to hold the right hand with
the thumb pointing up. I know of nothing more terrifying than
this pointing up of thumbs to Heaven.")

The "great man" was Sun Yat-sen, known now to the whole
world as the George Washington of China. Dr. Sun in his
autobiography, describes that first meeting with Homer Lea:

"It was now that another important event happened to me.
I was speaking to a company of my fellows, when my eye fell
on a young man of slight physique. . . . His face was pale.

. . . Afterward he came to me and said: 'I would like to throw in my lot with you. I believe your ideas will succeed. . . .' He held out his hand. I took it and thanked him, wondering who he was. I thought he was a missionary student. After he had gone I asked, 'Who was that little hunchback?' 'That,' said the man who brought him, 'is Homer Lea, one of the most brilliant—perhaps the most brilliant military genius now alive. He is a perfect master of modern warfare.' I almost gasped in astonishment. 'And he has offered to throw in his lot with me!' The next morning I called on Homer Lea. I told him in case I should succeed and my countrymen gave me the power to do so, I would make him my chief military adviser."

" 'Make me that *now*,' Lea said, 'and you *will* succeed.' "

Homer Lea became Sun's "Chief of Staff." He also became that day, something more: a soldier of Democracy. But the hour had not come for either man. When forced to stop persecuting "white devils," the Empress Dowager, enraged and humiliated by the triumphant White Powers, redoubled her persecution of all her own progressive countrymen. In Canton, her agents of death quickly closed in on Dr. Sun and Lea. Together they fled to Japan. There they spent several months, trying to persuade influential officials of the "modernized" and "Westernized" Japanese government to give political and financial backing to Sun Yat-sen's party. Everywhere, in high places they met with evasions. And now Homer Lea discovered that it was the policy of a strong modern united Japan to keep its neighbor, China, weak, backward, disunited—in order, as Lea at once clearly understood, the better to dismember and conquer her when the day came it could do so safely. When would that day come? Homer Lea was not long in discovering —when the Western Powers became either apathetic or indifferent to Japan's aims in China and the Far Pacific—Or, even better, found their hands full with a European War.

Lea's close study during these months, of the imperialistic and warlike Japanese mind, and Japan's dynamic racial drive toward Chinese, British and American possessions in the Far East, combined with his almost intuitive understanding of the importance to America in securing a democratic ally in the great Chinese people, formed the background of his Japanese-American war theme in *The Valor of Ignorance*.

In 1901, two years after the unknown little Stanford student left home, he returned to Los Angeles sporting the garish uniform of a Chinese General. His friends were a little embarrassed. This was many years before the boulevards of Hollywood became the haunt of freaks and crackpots. And his "round unvarnished tales" of his Oriental adventures seemed to their incredulous ears covered with a pretty heavy Oriental lacquer. Casual acquaintances and strangers were openly skeptical and highly amused. Incredulity was somewhat tempered when Lea's house on the beach at Santa Monica suddenly assumed the status of a sort of Democratic Chinese White House in exile. Dr. Sun made it his official headquarters. In due course exiled Prime Minister Kong Yu Wei, who at Lea's persuasion had now thrown in his lot with Sun, arrived at Lea's door, wearing gorgeous Chinese robes, and obviously financially well to do. Later aristocratic Prince Liang Ki Chew, equally bedizened and even more in funds, took up his abode with the crippled boy. And all of them firmly referred all newsmen to "The General."

Now Dr. Sun began to travel the length and breadth of the United States and Europe to raise money for the Revolutionary Movement. Sun, himself, estimates that from China's "little people" abroad, he raised two and one-half million dollars.

In peaceful California, the martial spirit of Lea found a new outlet. He began to raise again an army. On the porch of his home, he lectured and taught a group of Chinese students the arts and sciences of modern warfare. In the canyons behind Santa Monica, and on the outskirts of San Francisco, he set about drilling groups of several hundred volunteers. His idea was to form a corps-elite—a sort of Chinese stormtrooper band which would one day return to China and take over the Revolutionary Movement. Ansel O'Banion, a tough Irish ex-Sergeant of the 4th U. S. Cavalry whom Lea had run across when O'Banion was Captain of the Philippine Constabulary, became the body to Lea's brain. "He could drill a troop or a tooth," Lea said, "with equal efficiency." O'Banion was as strong and loyal and kindhearted as he was apparently practical.

There was only one thing O'Banion would not do for Lea. At the many Chinese dinners they both naturally attended in this organizing period, O'Banion would not eat with chopsticks. After the first few angry attempts he simply held the bowl to his mouth and to Lea's disgust, shoveled in his rice with his great square fingers.

A friend describes one stirring scene of this organizing period. In a great meeting hall in San Francisco, at which Dr. Sun was the principal speaker 88-pound Homer Lea, sitting piggyback on O'Banion's shoulders, in order to dominate his hearers, so impassionedly harangued a crowd of 5,000 poor Chinese immigrants on the tyranny of the Manchu Dowager Empress that in the end, they all whipped out their pocket knives and to a man, cut off their long black cues—the immemorial sign of their servitude to the Manchus. This was the first mass bobbing of pigtails in the history of the Chinese Revolution.

In 1904, Lea went back to China, there briefly to take command of the "second Army Division." When he returned to Santa Monica a year later, he was older and wiser. China was not yet ready for a Martial Monk. The yeast of Revolution was working in that chaotic nation but it had not yet reached the point where armies could be united under one banner. Moreover Lea's eyes were steadily failing. And there was another thing: Lea had begun deeply to worry about another country —America. His travels in the Far East had given him a "world-view." Daily he saw our growing indifference to the predatory forces at work in the world, how more and more we were beginning to mistake greatness and prestige for *power* —by which Homer Lea meant quite simply armed strength.

Although wedded, as a born soldier always is to the theory that the sword is mightier than the pen, Lea was forced to turn to the pen. First limbering the muscles of his mind on a novel of Chinese life called, *The Vermillion Pencil* (Harper & Brothers, 1908), a strange and bloody romance of Manchu

China, and an unproduced play, probably about the Dowager Empress, called "The Crimson Spider," he made meanwhile notes for *The Valor of Ignorance*. In this labor, two people helped him: the loyal O'Banion, and a young Tennessee divorcée, Mrs. Ethel Bryant Powers, who had to come to California with her two small sons, to get work as a secretary. As O'Banion was Lea's body, Mrs. Powers became his eyes.

Lea's theory was that the Japs, if they could once "knock out" Manila and Hawaii, would descend on the California coast. He set out to explore that coast. Sometimes riding on a burro, called "Baby," sometimes carried in big O'Banion's arms, he dragged his sick little hunchback body up and down the two thousand miles of littoral exploring every beach, bay, canyon, and pass by which the Japanese might attack. He explored for seven months, the San Jacinto, San Bernardino, San Gabriel, and Tehachapi mountains, the Mojave and adjacent deserts.

His military findings on the utter defenselessness of the Pacific coast against the Japanese attack (which he carefully plotted for them in the maps which profusely illustrate *The Valor of Ignorance*) were so dire that had a Japanese Admiral said in 1906, what Admiral Yamamoto said in December, 1941: "I am looking forward to dictating peace to the United States in the White House at Washington"—Lea would have bitterly replied, "And pray what's to stop you?" Returning in 1907 from his unhappy explorations, he lay every day on a blazing Indian rug, in Westlake Park amid the flowers, making his notes, his weak eyes shielded from the strong sun by a black slouch campaign hat, a long black military cape with a red satin lining, slung over his shoulders. Later he dictated his text to the gentle Mrs. Powers. When the manuscript of *The Valor of Ignorance* was finished, Lea sent it to General Chaffee for criticism. Chaffee came at once to see him, and brought Major Story. Chaffee said: "I have not been able to sleep since I read it. I see no way . . . no way to defend ourselves against the Japanese attack, according to what you say is their plan . . . unless we begin to arm now." Story said: "There is no flaw in it. We have made a colossal mistake."

When the book finally appeared, in 1909, under the Harper imprint, it caused a mild furor. Pacifist and International Peace Movements of all sorts condemned it bitterly.

Had they known such words in 1909, his critics would have called Lea a Fascist and a totalitarian. In Lea's doubt that the martial spirit would ever flame in "naturalized Americans," his open bias in favor of Anglo-Saxon racial and intellectual superiority, his equally frank predictions of wars to come between the races, his definite dread of the "Russian Octopus" whose vulnerable belly was so hard to reach beyond its icy tentacles, today's critics may still find reasons for calling him America's First Fascist. Lea was neither a Fascist nor a totalitarian. His ardent championship of Chinese democracy proved that. He was first a militarist. All militarists seem to the civilian mind somewhat 'fascist' because they "believe in force." Few people realize the extent to which most militarists favor strong *unapplied* force, which is peace, over *applied* force, which is war. Secondly, Lea, the hunchback was a thwarted soldier. One sometimes suspects that he lost his country's wars on paper, partially because his deformity precluded all possibility of his helping to win them on the battlefield.

But thirdly and most important, Lea was a true patriot. He deliberately designed his blue print of defeat in order to challenge the true victorious spirit of America. Time and time again, in his harsh reasoning in *The Valor of Ignorance*, he stepped over the mark in order to force his countrymen "slothful with fat pride" to toe it.

Now Lea's old enemy, David Starr Jordan, missed no opportunity to quarrel with its thesis. Offering a perfect example of the very type of wishful thinking Lea sought to destroy, when *The Valor of Ignorance* appeared, he wrote to "Dear Mr. Lea:"

". . . the matter of peace has very little to do with military experts. If a great Nation like this decides it will live in peace . . . it will be let alone by other countries . . . So far as Japan is concerned, there is no likelihood, unless we flaunt the red rag for years, that any thought of . . . war will arise among her statesmen. Wars are mostly started by hoodlums, by those interested in causing military promotion . . . by yellow journals . . . Japan staggers under . . . approaching bankruptcy. . . .

"On the whole it would be better for any nation to be thrashed and pass over temporarily into control of another nation than to continue the monstrous expenditures now going on in England and Germany. . . ."

Just two years before the outbreak of the first World War reviewing *The Valor of Ignorance* in a World Peace Foundation Pamphlet under the title, *The Impudence of Charlatanism* Jordan called Lea an "ambitious romancer," and the book itself "mischievous," "worthless" and "nonsense."

The literary critics were apathetic or skeptical. "Entertaining reading," said the December 1909 *American Monthly*. "Written in an amazingly hifalutin' style, bristling with historical generalizations," said the *Independent*, rating it a "Minus." But the *Literary Digest*, then in its heyday, called it "a daring and startling book . . . which every American would do well to ponder."

For a while "every American" did ponder Homer Lea's book. Hearst seized upon *The Valor of Ignorance*, and reworking its thesis into circulation-getting yellow journalism, launched "The Yellow Peril." He did Lea a grievous disservice. Lea thought—and wrote in terms of decades and centuries. That "it is all coming true" only thirty-five years later would not have astonished him. Hearst's shrill headlines implied that Lea's Jap-American War would break in months, even days. When it didn't, the public grew bored both with Lea, and with Hearst's "Yellow Peril." When the first World War broke in 1914, and Japan, greedily eying Germany's possessions in Asia and the Far Pacific, became Great Britain's ally, Lea apparently discredited, was forgotten. Having sold 18,000 copies, *The Valor of Ignorance* went out of print altogether in 1922—just about the time Japan began to fortify the German islands around Wake and Guam which she had picked up at the Versailles Conference.

The indifference of the ignorant public, the violent reaction of professional pacifists and ivory tower littérateurs, might have made Lea bitter, but for another circumstance. He began to receive high letters of praise from important military men all over the world—and even a few statesmen. The Japanese militarists paid him a greater compliment. In Japan *The Valor of Ignorance* went into twenty-four editions in one month. The blurb on the jacket of the popular edition brought out by Hakubunkwan, Tokyo's foremost publishers, read, "excellent reading matter for all Oriental men with red blood in their veins." And the Japanese government made it required reading for officers in all the services. German and Russian military schools followed. The King of Italy sent a personally annotated copy to his Chief of Staff. But in Sandhurst and West Point, although the book was duly placed upon their shelves, the reading of it was optional.

Strangest compliment of all was paid to Lea twenty-odd years later by a man called Adolf Hitler. Given a copy, no doubt, by 'geo-political' Professor Haushofer, he cribbed several paragraphs on the apparent inability of the democratic form of government to defend itself in time, and inserted them into a book which he was writing in jail called, *Mein Kampf*.

Most interesting of all the letters was one from England's Field Marshal Lord Roberts, inviting this American apostle of war to come to London to consult with him on the defense of the Empire. In his first letter to Lea, Roberts wrote in longhand:

". . . when I read it I could not rest until I had finished it. So struck was I with your description of the unpreparedness . . . of the people in America with that of my own people, that my first thought was to get (your book) very generally read here. . . . I found that (Harper & Brothers) had only some half dozen copies . . . I carried off all the copies they had, and begged them to cable for more. . . ."

During the years that preceded the outbreak of World War I, the Field Marshal's efforts to warn the British people, like Churchill's before and after Munich, had earned him the title of Great Britain's foremost warmonger. Although greatly flattered, Lea refused "Bob's" invitation. First, he was under-going constant treatment for his eyes. Second, he was, for the moment, too contented. These had been happy days for him in his little Santa Monica home. He was surrounded by old friends and a few admiring new ones. Charles E. Van Loan, George Herriman (creator of "Krazy Kat"), Ambrose Bierce were among a company which included Chinese princes and revolutionaries. And there was Mrs. Powers, who now never left her invalid's side. Like black Othello of white Desdemona, explaining their strange affection, Lea might have said,

> She loved me for the dangers I had passed,
> And I loved her that she did pity them.

Mrs. Powers spent the afternoons reading to him aloud volumes of history, travel, Napoleonic and political memoirs. Her son Joshua Bryant Powers reports that other favorites at this time were Draper's *Intellectual Development of Europe*, Abbé Huc's *Travels in Tartary*, Borrow's *Lavengro* and *Romany Rye*. After the Oriental dinners he was so fond of, Lea staged poker parties again, with his old high school and Stanford cronies. Sometimes he even got a little drunk, though generally, stepson Joshua reported, he was really drunk on his own talk. His 'bombastic' manner had mellowed, but he still could brook no challenge of his military dicta. Carr tells of a conversation between Lea and a cocky cavalry major who had served in the Philippines. The cavalryman had presumed to dispute Lea's thesis that the Islands could not be held. Lea turned on him. "I am, as you know, a consulting strategist. In the event of war I will pick out a post for you. You will not command troops." He jabbed his incredibly long forefinger like a stiletto into the officer's broad chest. "*You* shall be a mule driver. But don't try to lead the mules. Your brain is not equal to the task. Just pick out a mule somewhere in the middle of the pack train—and leave all other decisions to the mule."

Meanwhile Lord Roberts continued to press Lea, even offering to send his own physician to accompany him on the voyage. And then when Lea received another letter, a personal invitation from Kaiser Wilhelm II, to witness the German war maneuvers of that year, he could no longer resist. In Europe he could: (1) Put pressure on the British and German governments to extend loans and political backing to Dr. Sun Yatsen's revolutionaries; (2) consult with a famous German oculist in Wiesbaden about his eyes; (3) evaluate for himself the strength of the German and British war machines; (4) gather firsthand material from the Kaiser and Field Marshal Roberts on *The Day of the Saxon*, for which he had already begun to make copious notes.

So that Mrs. Powers might share the triumphs which her collaboration had made possible, the frail cripple married his nurse and amanuensis, and they, accompanied by ex-Prime Minister Kong Yu Wei, sailed for Europe in the spring of 1910.

In a full dress uniform (probably of his own imaginative designing) he witnessed the German maneuvers from a carriage with high cushions, which the Kaiser (himself a cripple, with his shriveled arm) had especially ordered. All political and military doors in Germany were automatically opened to the "General" who had never been asked to enter the doors of the White House, or—as he would dearly have preferred—those of West Point. In spite of this flattering attention—or perhaps because of it—Lea's estimate of the essential German character remained so objective, that it holds good to this day.

Fresh and pertinent as though it had been written this morning are his findings on the "racial" character Germans insist on giving to their warmaking. In Lea's eyes the German ethos was permanently ungodly, brutal, and Bismarckian. Likewise, as true now as it was thirty-five years ago is Lea's bitter analysis of the "personal character the Saxon gives war"—our democratic preoccupation with the wickedness of individual leaders of an enemy state, which obscures to us a true estimate of the peoples who chose those leaders. Lea today would be saddened and fearful anew to hear so many asserting that "Hitler, not the German people is our enemy." He would warn that Hitler-hating is mere demonology, if not dangerous in war, certainly dangerous to the preservation of the peace that will follow Hitler's inevitable destruction. For "it is conditions, not individuals" which determine Germany's aggressive actions. He would most certainly insist (though all the kind-hearted and tolerant people in the world decried him) that to "lick Hitler," without destroying the German state, German armies and German resources, in short only to deal with the Fuehrer and the Nazi leaders—would simply be to leave Germany lying fallow for another Hitler.

In London, all through the late summer and early autumn of 1911, he consulted daily with Roberts on plans for the prevention of the invasion of England. His military findings which concern German military strategy against the Empire hold as good for this war as they did for the war that broke three years later upon an astonished England. Few can fail to see that Germany's failure in World War I to follow Lea's plan of the conquest of Denmark and Holland *first* may have cost them that war. Even in 1911 he wrote that "only by the invasion and investment of the British Isles themselves can Germany hope to destroy the Empire." And in 1911 he warned Germany against an attack on Russia. "A war between Russia and Germany, while resulting disastrously to the defeated nation, will in the end bring no gains to the victor commensurate with its expenditures . . . But the dismemberment of the British Empire, on the other hand, will result most advantageously to Germany, Russia, and Japan." This "unholy alliance" the thing that the Democracies feared most in 1940, mercifully did not happen. All militarists today are in accord with Lea's assertion of the folly of a German attack on Russia. Lea, who did not overrate Germany's military intelligence did, fortunately underrate her political stupidity.

After the German war maneuvers, Lea went to London to confer with Field Marshal Roberts. He had become the first, as he is perhaps the last, "world consulting strategist." But in the very midst of his conferences he began to make notes for a third book, which, he said would complete the modern world's military trilogy. He called it, in his notes, "The Swarming of the Slav." In the end, Lea believed, after a period of Napoleonic wars between Britain, Germany, America and Japan were done, the greatest and last war of the United States and Great Britain would come—their war against Russia. Some

of the material that unwritten book might have held is published in *The Day of the Saxon*. His evaluation of the Russian
character is no less astute (in martial terms) than his evaluation of the Germans. To the Americans of his day, Lea pointed
out what Americans today have recently discovered with surprise—and satisfaction, that "Russia in her progress is no
more concerned with the devastation of her wars (and her
appalling losses on the battlefields) than is Russian nature with
the havoc of her winters."

He predicted that the very defeats that Russia might suffer
at the hands of the "Teuton" would result in a "great awaken-
ing of the Slav to his own power," and that regardless of the
conditions a reawakened Russia might face in our times, she
would exert that power in expansion. If thwarted by a strong
Germany and Japan on her East or West, she would expand
through Persia and into India. If these pressures were removed, and a weakened Germany and Japan lay on her flanks,
she would then, again taking the path of least resistance, expand on the European continent, or sweep down into the Far
Pacific. Lea wrote not in terms of decades but of centuries . . .

Lea received a great piece of news in the early winter of
1911, from his Chinese agents in London. The Sun Yat-sen
movement, so long a disastrous series of sporadic mob out-
bursts in the provinces, had begun to assume true revolutionary
proportions. Lea decided that at long last the day had arrived.
He cabled to Sun, still in America, to join him at once. After
a brief argumentative exchange of cables, Dr. Sun came.

Over the protests of his doctor who warned him that this
voyage must cost him his life, Lea dropped his study of the
defenses of Great Britain and prepared to sail for China. The
creation of a great strong democratic China—was more important to him than all the British Empire, for with uncanny
vision, with a strategic insight that verged on mysticism, Lea
knew that his America would need an Asiatic ally in its inevitable war against Japan.

Lea and Sun sailed out of Marseilles in 1911, for Shanghai.
Again he gloried in his title of Lieutenant General of China's
armies. On the thirty-day voyage, Lea finished his book, and

completed his plans for his forthcoming "campaign," while Sun pondered the outlines of his "San-Min-Chu"—the "three people's principles" which had long before been so purely expressed by Abraham Lincoln, as "government of the people, by the people, for the people."

Homer Lea, borne in a palanquin, did lead an army of the Republic to victory. The crippled American boy had at long last made good his cool boast, "to topple the Manchus from their Dragon throne."

The rest is history. In Nanking in 1911, General Homer Lea saw Sun Yat-sen elected President of the New Chinese Republic, while a "foreign fashion" band played "Behold the Conquering Hero Comes," and—prophetically enough—"God be with you till we meet again." He was the only white man present at this occasion which was the birth of a democratic nation of 450 million people. In that birth he had played a singular and valorous part.

At the presidential reception he congratulated the President, and is supposed to have uttered a strange word of warning, in which he paraphrased his own written words:

"Now China," he said, "is a Republic. America, too, is a Republic. Your Republic, like ours, can only be preserved in its beauty and freedom by vigilant swords . . . China's enemies now are its historic pacifism and political corruption . . . and Japan. We have the same three enemies . . . I can do nothing for either of our two great countries. I am a dying man. I have warned America in my books. I now warn you, in words . . . Free China will yet perish unless there rises from your innermost bosom the militant spirit of another Martial Monk. If he does not come, Republic or no, the hour for this ancient kingdom has come. . . ."

Homer Lea had grown too blind perhaps, to see the face of a very young soldier who may have stood by Sun Yat-sen's side. Or was that young soldier looking too raptly on the face of the doctor's pretty little sister-in-law, Mai-ling Soong? At any rate, no one knows whether or not General Homer Lea saw or met that day a young soldier, whose name was Chiang Kai-shek.

In Nanking a stroke paralyzed his left side. Although he had always expressed a wish to have his ashes buried in China, now suddenly, Lea said he wanted to die in America. He was carried aboard the *Shinyo Maru* on a litter. In May, 1912, he reached California. *The Day of the Saxon* "finished on a field of recent battle," went to his publishers. Lea was far too ill to read the reviews. This was just as well, for the book which predicted so accurately World War I and II, was not well received. It sold altogether 7000 copies in English, and in the year Hitler came into power, went out of print and out of mind.

In his Santa Monica Beach cottage, on the first day of November in the first year of the Chinese Republic little Scrunchneck died. His poor broken body was laid out in his resplendent uniform, at its side the long sword, which he always dreamed as a boy of wielding boldly and brilliantly in his country's defense, still unstained by any man's blood.

In those last months of his illness, he had not been able to drill or instruct his Chinese students. Still, once or twice to please him, the students came, because they knew although he could not see them, he could hear their marching feet. He had always been so loyal to them, although even the more intelligent ones of them wondered why a man of such vaunting military ambition, who was, after all, primarily concerned with the greatness of America, had cared so violently about China's cause. What possible importance could poor, weak, far-far-off China—this "mysterious Orient"—have to a great country like America? They did not know that as Lea lay dying on his porch, looking out over the wide sunny Pacific which spread like a midnight plain before his sightless eyes, he nevertheless saw, as in a great white horrible light, the bombs bursting over Pearl Harbor . . . and the dawn coming up like thunder out of China, cross the way.

He had often said to Harry Carr in an agony of spirit, in those last days, "Must I die, not knowing if my work is finished?"

Much of the unfinished work of Homer Lea has yet to be finished by China and America. But it will be. Homer Lea were he alive today would be the first to deny the possibility of the very defeat he predicted. He would have noted with great hope how the scales have dropped from our eyes since Pearl Harbor; and he would have rejoiced, as few men, in our subsequent determination to preserve our freedom by "vigilant swords."

But he would also be the first to warn that in Victory, too, there is a "Valor of Ignorance"—the ignorance that may fall on our spirits again when the peace comes. Even when Japan and Germany are beaten, other trials will face us. For Lea realized that the beginning of wisdom is the acceptance of the fact that war and peace are forever indivisible. It is not as a gloomy forecast of defeat in 1942 that Lea should be read. It is as a still timely warning of Trials to come after Victory.

Homer Lea thought not in the decades of his time, but in our still unrounded twentieth century.

. . . .

PREFACE

THIS book was partially completed just subsequent to the signing of the Portsmouth Treaty. But it was put aside in order to allow sufficient time to verify or disprove its hypotheses and conclusions.

In all but inessential details it remains as originally written. Succeeding events have so confirmed the beliefs of that time that I now feel justified in giving the book to the public.

H. L.

March, 1909

INTRODUCTION

By LIEUTENANT-GENERAL ADNA R. CHAFFEE

Late Chief-of-Staff, United States Army

TO THE AUTHOR:

Hail!—The Valor of Ignorance!!

AFTER careful reading of the manuscript, we believe that when it is given publication it will greatly interest public officials, National and State, as well as the mass of intelligent citizens in private life, who have not hitherto had arranged for them a series of pictures equal in importance to the collection that is to be found in the twenty-one chapters of this book.

We do not know of any work in military literature published in the United States more deserving the attention of men who study the history of the United States and the Science of War than this—*The Valor of Ignorance.* And, as the government of the United States is "Of the people, for the people, and by the people," it is quite in order to invite citizens who control in military matters of the nation, as they do in other important national affairs, to "know thyself."

The popular belief that the United States is free of opportunities for invasion is all "tommy rot," if allowable to use an expression that we think more apt for our purpose than elegant in style. Briefly, and to the point—no nation offers more numerous opportunities for invasion by a foreign nation than does the United States whenever cause therefor is sufficiently great to induce preparations by any other nation that will beat aside our resistance on the sea. The world is a grand stage whereon are many players. In the game of cards called "poker," the straight flush, headed by the ace, is occasionally held by one player. It wins. In the course of time no one knows when or how soon, the family of nations may get to playing at cards, and beyond the sea, perhaps, will be found a "full hand" against our three "aces"—the Navy, Coast fortifications, and the Militia.

Our mobile Army is so ridiculously small in the World's War game that it amounts to nothing better than a discard! What will the Militia do under circumstances when, in the game of War, as in the game of poker, there is a call for show of hands—the very time in the game when "I. O. U." will not have the value of coin? Rush into the jaws of death? Let all who believe in the value of Militia for war turn to the preface you have chosen for Volume II. We quote it here, to save the trouble of doing so:

"Regular troops alone are equal to the exigencies of modern war, as well for defence as offence, and when a substitute is attempted, it must prove illusory and ruinous.

"No Militia will ever acquire the habits necessary to resist a regular force. The firmness requisite for the real business of fighting is only to be attained by constant course of discipline and service.

"I have never yet been a witness to a single instance that can justify a different opinion, and it is most earnestly to be wished that the liberties of America may no longer be trusted, in a material degree, to so precarious a defence.

"WASHINGTON."

It is with no lack of appreciation of the military enthusiasm and skin-deep experience which the organized Militia of the country has that we quote this passage from Washington, for every little effort helps. But who does not know that the sentiment for cohesion that enables the Militia organizations to "keep in the swim" is chiefly the social sort rather than the sterner sentiment—duty to the Nation? So, as Washington's observation had reference particularly to the condition of soldiery that results from a levy of volunteers, under our present system of raising armies for war purposes, we are justified in saying that his words are as true to-day as when penned.

They were true then and will be true until the time when the author of the sentiment shall be no longer affectionately regarded as a man who would not deceive his countrymen; as one who wisely advised of future dangers out of his great experience and his true appreciation of the natures of men.

We do not find that Washington was an advocate of coast-defence fortifications to anything like the fad of to-day. The few he had were useful then, just as the many we have now are useful, to divert the enemy to wayside landings—not very hard to find then, nor impossible to find now.

So when the enemy attempts to invade the United States he will land, for such is the power of nations now for the offensive, unless the Almighty who hath power greater than he to control the waves of the sea opposes relentlessly his efforts; and when that time comes, as come it may, nothing short of mobile armies, trained to discipline in service, can prevent an enemy's occupation of lines of supply and, as a result of such occupation, quick capitulation of any city of first rank in the United States, plus its fortified places; this, too, the fate of any such city in the world. Why, therefore, divert more millions of money to ineffectual use when we have enough coast-defence works now? Possibly one excuse for further construction may be, as was said by a military genius interested in the defence of his country: "Coast-defence fortifications served well two purposes:

"1. To preserve, and make progress from experience, the science of manufacturing large guns.
"2. For testing the skill of military engineers."

When we arrive at the conclusion that it is a mistake to rely upon untrained, undisciplined men for serious war operations (all our war history can be cited in proof that it is so), we have not far to look and find what seems to be the popular reason for such reliance since the Nation has become a grand factor in the world. It is because the Nation is wonderfully rich in natural resources and artificially made wealth—so great a Crœsus that it can afford to pay, at all events it seems willing to pay, for the extravagance in money and life which follows on occasions of war and left-handed business, as regularly as night follows day.

The popular belief in our country that money is the controlling factor in war needs to be materially shocked and greatly modified. The better sentiment would be—and it is a national harm that it is not so now—all men and women in love with military service, obligatory in peace and war!

The shades of night are not yet so dense as to shut from memory the recollection that certain states, having small treasury accounts and poor credit, fought near to bankruptcy wealth much superior to theirs. Thus, an example at our door where great wealth was no scarecrow to men of courage when long-standing causes (real or fancied) for war arose.

No Hague Conference could have stopped that conflict, based, as it was, on limitation in opposition to expansion of the rights of a race.

The second part of your Book I treats of problems provocative of war so evidently within the realm of exalted wisdom for correct solution that the citizen and state legislator will serve his country best by following the advice of statesmen charged with that vision which comprehendeth the American universe and its glory.

The best way to determine whether an apple is sweet or sour is to eat it. Only thus can one decide what at sight is a doubtful condition of the apple.

The several chapters of Book I we regard as in the category of "gradual approaches" to obtain view of the *Apple* to be found in Book II, which the reader should attentively examine and determine the flavor of, through close study of the text and maps.

It is quite probable, because of the very general indifference throughout the country for things military, which serves excellently to heighten the ignorance of the purpose for and value of armies to nations, many readers will find the apple to have a neutral flavor, and in the valor of their ignorance will answer your well-prepared practical demonstration of our actual and possible military situations in their usual way: "Just let 'em try it and you'll see what we can do."

The statesmen and the technically informed will more likely pass in review one of Napoleon's maxims: "The frontiers of states are either large rivers or chains of mountains or deserts. Of all these obstacles to the march of an army, the most difficult to overcome is the desert; mountains come next, and broad rivers occupy the third place."

We can think of nothing better suited with which to end this letter than the following quotation from a page of your book: "Nations, being but composite individuals, all that which moves or is part of an individual, in a larger sense, moves or is part of a nation.

"To free a nation from error is to enlighten the individual, and only to the degree that the individual will be receptive of truth can a nation be free from that vanity which ends with national ruin."

Yours truly,

ADNA R. CHAFFEE,
Lieutenant-General, U. S. A., Retired.

INTRODUCTION

By MAJOR-GENERAL J. P. STORY,
U. S. A., Retired

THE VALOR OF IGNORANCE is the striking title of a most remarkable book by Homer Lea. The title, however, does not indicate the scope of the undertaking, which is a military work that should be carefully read by every intelligent and patriotic citizen of the United States.

The book consists of two parts—the first made up of philosophical deductions, founded upon the unchanging elements of human nature as established by historical precedent.

Man in his evolution from primitive savagery has followed laws as immutable as the law of gravitation. No nation has long been permitted to enjoy the blessings of peace, unless able to safeguard such blessings by force of arms. The richer a nation may be in material resources, the more likely it has been to fall a prize to a more militant people. The continuous enjoyment of peace and national independence has always cost dear, but is well worth the price.

A few idealists may have visions that, with advancing civilization, war and its dreadful horrors will cease. Civilization has not changed human nature. The nature of man makes war inevitable. Armed strife will not disappear from the earth until after human nature changes. Words extolling peace are worthless for national defence, and a too clamorous gospel of peace may paralyze the best efforts to meet our military necessities.

The most persistent lovers of peace, since the historical period, have been the Chinese. China is now reaping the logical reward of "peace at any price." It is a subject nation, its destiny controlled by alien Manchus, and its fairest possessions ravished from its littoral.

The most Christian nations of Europe have for several centuries, in Asia and Africa, exacted tribute as mercilessly as did the robber barons of the Middle Ages.

A *Century of Dishonor* shows that the United States have seized from an unwilling people nearly every foot of their soil.

The United States, within ten years, have ruthlessly suppressed in the Philippines an insurrection better justified than was our Revolution of glorious memory. This insurrection was inspired, from the Philippine point of view, by a passionate aspiration to be freed from the domination of a people alien in language, customs, and religion; yet it was impossible for the United States, in honor, or in the interests of humanity, to avoid the action taken.

The second part of Mr. Lea's book consists in making a logical application of the principles deduced in the first part to the United States under its present conditions. If the data published by Mr. Lea be correct, and there seems to be no reason to question its substantial accuracy, Germany could, if it has sea supremacy in the Atlantic, land within two weeks two hundred and fifty thousand troops on our eastern coast.

Japan now has sea supremacy in the Pacific. In the event of war, that supremacy could not be challenged until after we had constructed a sufficient fleet of colliers. Japan can within three months land on the Pacific Coast four hundred thousand troops, and seize, with only insignificant resistance, Seattle, Portland, San Francisco, and Los Angeles.

A barrier of mountains and deserts makes the defence of the Pacific Slope an easy matter against attack from the East, and only from that direction could the United States hope to recapture its lost territory.

Never has there been on this earth so rich a prize, now so helpless to defend itself, as the Philippine and Hawaiian Islands, the Panama Canal, Alaska, and the States of the Pacific coast.

Mr. Lea has lived in the Orient and carefully studied it. He sees clearly the menace of the "Yellow Peril," yet it is less than sixty years since the United States went to the uncharted shores of Japan with an olive branch in one hand and in the other a naked sword. Then was removed the lid of Pandora's box with the enthusiastic approval of the American people.

It is very remarkable that the author should have so just a conception of the true value of coast fortifications in the general defence of the country. The sole function of such fortifications is to defend a port against direct naval attack. Against an enemy powerful enough to land, the coast fort has no defensive value, and may even prove an element of weakness, as did Port Arthur to Russia.

Not the least of Mr. Lea's service to the country is in his republication of the solemn warnings of George Washington against the employment of militia in war. Within the last one hundred and twenty-five years disaster and humiliation to our arms have fully confirmed Washington's judgment.

The system of organization in the militia is the cancer which destroys its usefulness. It is futile to hope the militia may by a change of name escape the curse of its inherent inefficiency.

Mr. Lea shows clearly that we are confronted by conditions which may imperil our national security, peace, and welfare. No candid mind, who carefully reads Mr. Lea's book, can draw any other conclusion.

It is to be hoped this book may arouse a public sentiment throughout the country which will lead to a full and serious consideration of a problem which should no longer be ignored.

J. P. STORY,
Major-General, U. S. A., Retired

Book I

THE DECLINE OF MILITANCY AND THE CONTROL OF THE WESTERN HEMISPHERE

"... *As a principle in which the rights and interests of the United States are involved ... the American continents ... are henceforth not to be considered as subject for future colonization by any European power. ... We owe it, therefore, to candor and to the amicable relations existing between the United States and those powers to declare that we should consider any attempt on their part to extend their system to any portion of this hemisphere as dangerous to our peace and safety.*

MONROE."

I

THE diversity of man's beliefs is as wide as the uncounted millions that have been or are now cluttered upon earth; enduring no longer than a second of time, yet in that brief and broken moment doubting, affirming, denying. It is this unstable, widening difference in the viewpoint of man that has filled the world with so much contention and error; the setting up and tearing down of so many transitory ideals, the making of fallible laws, constitutions, and gods.

Truth, outside of the exact sciences, can only be approximated. The degree to which that approximation approaches completeness depends upon the exactitude of empirical knowledge and freedom from error in deductions, which means, principally, a freedom from antipathies or attachments.

Under such limitations we are to write this book. So the reader, for the time being, must also put aside his hates and desires, since that which we are about to write will arouse his passions, support or rage according to his view-point. If he is not equitable his prejudices will distort these unwelcome truths and leave undiscovered the fount of their bitterness.

A man who wishes to be just or seeks after perfection has no immutable sentiments of his own, but will make, as far as possible, the mind of mankind his possession. Calmly he looks upon the world; upon all its transitory institutions, and his passions are aroused in no manner. He preserves for all mankind the same regard and consideration.

The just perusal of any work demands such a state of mind, and requires a temporary obliteration of such preconceived ideas as have, through their undisturbed sway over his mind, become prejudices or attachments.

In this book many conditions may be met that will appear im-

3

possible or unbelievable, since they are contrary to what has heretofore been held up as perfection. When certain beliefs, though false or dangerous, pass to the stage of national fetichism they often become invulnerable even to the shafts of truth itself.

Of the few virtues that appertain to or are emanations of mankind in the aggregate, patriotism is foremost in being universally impersonated and put to a wide variety of uses; turned to all degrees of roguery. When it becomes a national fetich, virtue goes out of it. Under its borrowed cloak crimes are not only committed, but nations betrayed and given over to pillage; hence the truth of the old statement, that in patriotism rogues find their final refuge.

Besides being the subterfuge of rogues, patriotism is divisible into three forms: two that are false and—common; one that is true and—rare. The commonest of the accepted forms, also the most erroneous, is to be found in uncompromising and general contempt for all nations, together with an inveterate prejudice against some one of them. The next ordinary and false form shows itself in vaingloriousness, whether over great deeds or greater crimes; the condoning of national faults or their concealment by the exaltation of this fetich worship.

True patriotism would rot away if its exemplification lay only in contempt or prejudice toward others.

To inspire pride it is not necessary to arouse hatred.

In peace, and not in war, is the time to judge the worth of a man's or a nation's patriotism. Those who are indifferent to their country's welfare in peace will be of no use to it in time of war: while those who make it a practice to rob the public exchequer of its virtues, as well as gold, or to condone such thievery, are, during warfare, so delinquent in patriotism as not to be removed from the sphere of negative treason.

Patriotism in its purity is a political virtue, and as such is the antithesis of commercial vanity. To boast of a nation's wealth, under the delusion that it is patriotic, is to commit a crime against patriotism.

To boast does not liquidate the debt of duty.

As patriotism does not hibernate in the time of peace, it is by no means difficult to discover the true patriot from the false. He is made noticeable by two characteristics causing him to stand out from among other men. And though he may be humble and unknown, yet these two virtues make him pre-eminent even among those who are vain of their honors and wealth.

To die for one's country, while not less patriotic than to live for it, is by no means as beneficial. But it is in this proposal to die in battle that cowards, rogues, and treasonable men find subterfuge befitting their evil practices. When, in peace, men postpone their patriotic activity to a time of war, their procrastination is only indicative of their worthlessness.

As it is impossible after death to distinguish the coward from the hero, so in national defeat distinctions cannot be made as to the cause of it. The world and the victor take no note of post-bellum explanations. For a nation to suffer defeat through unpreparedness is, to all practical purposes, as bad as though it were through cowardice on the field. In consequence, the man who opposes, in time of peace, suitable preparations for war, is as unpatriotic and detrimental to the nation as he who shirks his duty or deserts his post in time of battle.

To those who have within themselves the spirit of true patriotism, this book will appeal with a passion peculiarly its own, for it is not other than an emanation of their own thoughts. To those in whom it arouses wrath we would suggest that if they will look to the origin of their feelings they will find that what they have heretofore regarded as patriotism is not even the sham of it.

The third matter of importance that the reader should bear in mind as he makes his way through this book, attendant with many doubts and perhaps much passion, is not to set up the transitory fabrications of man against conditions that are eternal because such ephemeral works exist in his time.

National existence is not a haphazard passage of a people from an unknown beginning to an unforeseen end. It is not an erratic phantasm of dreams that has fallen upon the sleeping consciousness of a world; but is, on the other hand, a part of life itself, governed by the same immutable laws.

No state is destroyed except through those avertible conditions that mankind dreads to contemplate. Yet nations prefer to evade and perish rather than to master the single lesson taught by the washing-away of those that have gone down before them. In their indifference and in the valor of their ignorance they depart, together with their monuments and constitutions, their vanities and gods.

II

I<small>N THE</small> works of many philosophers, the birth, growth and decay of nations is made analogous to the life history of individuals, wherein they pass from the cradle to manhood, expanding in intellect, accumulating vigor and strength until, in due time, they grow old, die and are forgotten, down in the deep, vast ossuary of time.

This similarity in the lives of men and nations is in actuality true, although it should not be precisely so. As the body of man is made up of volitionless molecules allowing the natural course of age, disease and decay to destroy it, the body politic of a nation is an aggregation of rational beings, atoms supposedly possessed of the ability to reason, and who should, if they are obedient to laws governing national growth and deterioration, prolong the existence of a nation far beyond the years and greatness ordinarily allotted to it.

The analogy, however, contains this melancholy truth: that only so long as a man or nation continues to grow and expand do they nourish the vitality that wards off disease and decay. This continuous growth and expansion in human beings is their childhood, youth and manhood; the gradual cessation of it, old age or disease; its stoppage—death. But among nations, though the progress and consummation are identical, we take but little note of it and *name* it not at all.

As physical vigor constitutes health in the individual, so does it among nations, and it is exemplified by strength among them as in mankind. A brilliant mind, a skilful hand has nothing to do with the health or duration of life in the individual, so neither has mental brilliancy compositely taken, as in a nation of scholars, anything to do with the prolongation of national existence.

The duration of life in an individual is determined by his

power to combat against disease, age and his fellow-men, resulting in the gradual elimination of those possessed of least combative power and the survival of those in whom these qualities are best conserved. So it is with nations. So it has ever been from the first dawn, when protoplasmic cells floated about in a pallid ether devouring one another, and so in the last twilight shall these same cells, evoluted even beyond what man now conceives, pass into endless night.

The beginnings of political life are not hidden absolutely from us, and though there is no exactitude in our knowledge, we are nevertheless cognizant of the fact that at one time, when primitive man lived in continuous, individual strife, there occurred, somewhere in the sombre solitudes of a preglacial forest, what has proven to be to mankind a momentous combat. It was when the brawniest paleolithic man had killed or subdued all those who fought and roamed in his immediate thickets that he established the beginning of man's domination over man, and with it the beginnings of social order and its intervals of peace. When the last blow of his crude axe had fallen and he saw about him the dead and submissive, he beheld the first nation; in himself the first monarch; in his stone axe the first law, and by means of it the primitive process by which, through all succeeding ages, nations were to be created or destroyed.

Wars—Victory—a nation. Wars—Destruction—dissolution. Such is the melancholy epitome of national existence, and such has it been from the beginning of human association until to-day. From the time, six thousand years past, when the wild highlander rolled down from the mountains of Elam and moulded with sword and brawn the Turanian shepherds into the Chaldean Empire, until within the last decade, when the Samurai of Nippon rose out of their islands in the Eastern Sea and carved for themselves a new empire on the Continent of Asia, there has been no cessation nor deviation from this inexorable law governing the formation and extinction of national entities.

All kingdoms, empires, and nations that have existed on this earth have been born out of the womb of war and the delivery of them has occurred in the pain and labor of battle. So, too, have these same nations, with the same inevitable certainty, perished on like fields amid the wreckage and cinders of their defenceless possessions.

As physical vigor represents the strength of man in his struggle for existence, in the same sense military vigor constitutes the strength of nations: ideals, laws and constitutions are but temporary effulgences, and are existent only so long as this strength remains vital. As manhood marks the height of physical vigor among mankind, so the militant successes of a nation mark the zenith of its physical greatness. The decline of physical strength in the individual is significant of disease or old age, culminating in death. In the same manner deterioration of military strength or militant capacity in a nation marks its decline; and, if there comes not a national renascence of it, decay will set in and the consummation shall not be other than that sombre end which has overtaken the innumerable nations now no more, but who, in the vanity of their greatness, could conjecture the end of time yet not the downfall of their fragile edifices.

An analysis of the history of mankind shows that from the fifteenth century before Christ until the present time, a cycle of thirty-four hundred years, there have been less than two hundred and thirty-four years of peace. Nations succeeded one another with monotonous similarity in their rise, decline and fall. One and all of them were builded by architects who were generals, masons who were soldiers, trowels that were swords and out of stones that were the ruins of decadent states. Their periods of greatness were entirely coincident with their military prowess and with the expansion consequent upon it.

The zenith of these nations' greatness was reached when expansion ceased. As there is no stand-still in the life of an individual, so neither is there in the life of a nation. National existence is governed by this invariable law: that the boundaries of political units are never, other than for a moment of time, stationary—they must either expand or shrink. It is by this law of national expansion and shrinkage that we mark the rise and decline of nations.

Expansion culminates, or, in other words, nations begin to decline with the subordination of national to individual supremacy. When the debasement of this formative capacity of empires is complete, the state is given over to devitalizing elements —social and economic parasites. It is in these, valorous with fat pride, that the nation takes its final and inglorious departure, as did its predecessors, forever from mankind.

The hunt for old empires has now become the pastime of solitary men who find on the willow-fringed banks of rivers only a mud mound and a silence; in desert sands, a mummy and a pyramid; by the shores of seas, a temple and a song. The shattered signs of kingdoms are but few, for most of the vanished empires have in their departure remitted to posterity neither broken marbles, teopali, Alhambras, nor Druid stones. In the manner of nomads they have gone away and left no sign of habitation in the sands behind them.

Theorists, in contradiction of this view, with unconscious superficiality bring China out of the mists and mystery of her antiquity and present her as a nation created and enduring in endless peace. Such observations, unfortunately, only betray the profundity of their ignorance. The law of national expansion or shrinkage has governed the development of the Chinese Empire with the same inexorable invariability as it has that of nations in the West.

Not only does the history of the political development of China resemble the history of the remainder of mankind, but has, perhaps, within itself the solemn prophecy of the world's political future. China, from the obscure hour of its deep antiquity until modern times, has worked out its own advancement and civilization in no way benefited by other civilizations of the world. Yet China, in its political evolution and expansion, has been subject to all those elements, those periods of physical vigor and deterioration, such as have controlled the destinies of the separate successive nations that have thundered so loudly in the Occident. China, like every great empire, is made up of the cleavage and multiplication of political units, alternately decadent and renascent through the unnumbered years of its existence.

When the brawling Elamite mountaineers came down from their high places and founded the Chaldean Empire on the plains of Mesopotamia, there were, in what is now the Chinese Empire, a number of political units surrounded on the north, south, and west by less civilized peoples. The state upon which the present empire was founded was a small kingdom on the loess plains of Shensi. From this primitive state has been developed the vast empire we now watch crumbling and falling away from its former greatness in a manner wherein time is less the vandal than the childish vanity of man.

The cycles of decay and renascence that mark the development of this race have, in cause and effect, been homogeneous, though thousands of years have separated a portion of them. This homogeneous expansion can be compared to the still waters of a lake where a cast stone causes to extend outward in widening sphere a series of ripples with intervening spaces. In this manner has been marked the evolution of the Chinese race from the time a small splinter of them was cast thither by the hand of Panku. Each ripple marks a cycle of development, each depression a period of decadence, similar in every characteristic except their widening sphere.

The inexorable law of combat has governed in all its various phases the development of the Chinese Empire. Its political evolution, in a manner no different from that of European nations, has been through the battle-field. The edifice of its greatness has been builded by no other than those who have fought its wars. Of the twenty-five dynasties that have ruled over China, each was founded by a soldier and each in due time heard from surrounding armies the melancholy taps of its approaching end.

The reasons for and the conditions contributing to the long continuance of the Chinese Empire, while other kingdoms almost as great have survived the erosion of time but a generation in comparison to the ages through which it has passed and grown great, are apparently unknown in the West. The beliefs ordinarily expressed have nothing whatever to do with it. They are fanciful, speculative or otherwise, but worthless. The Chinese as a people, their laws or customs, have had nothing to do with the preservation of their nation against the wearing away by time or that wilfuller element—man.

The preservation of the Chinese race for these thousands of years has been due solely to the natural environment wherein the race began its national growth; an environment ramparted by inaccessible mountains, moated by uninhabitable deserts or seas as shipless as they were vast. On the north and northwest are the deserts of Gobi and Shamo; beyond these, the impenetrable forests of Siberia and steppes where rests a gloom that is white. On the southwest is the Roof of the World and the blue-black gorges of the Himalayas. On the south, jungles and the Indian Ocean. On the east is the vast and lonely Pacific, a purple solitude through which only a few years ago the ships of man found their way.

Until the nineteenth century China was as secure in her isolation as if illimitable space intervened between her borders and the nations of Europe. To the rest of mankind China was only the mythical Kingdom of Cathay, situated somewhere on the jewelled banks of Eastern seas.

The Chinese, therefore, and their system of government have had nothing to do with the preservation of their race. Isolation alone has been responsible for its continuation through the storms of more than fifty centuries. Had the Celestial Kingdom been surrounded by other powerful nationalities, as were European and Central Asian Empires, ancient and modern, it would have gone down in due time as they did and now be but a memory hidden away in the old tales of the tribes of man.

In six cycles of decadence China has fallen into such sick corruption and internal desolation that Xenophon's Ten Thousand could have conquered the whole of it. But, fortunately, when China sank into these periods of national decay there were none to attack her but the elements, her own hungers, or the Tartars tending their herds on her northern frontiers; a wild, snout-nosed race that lived without government or kings. Yet during every period of decadence and dynastic struggle China has been subject to attack by these frontier nomads. The greatest task incumbent upon succeeding dynasties during the beginning of each period of renascence was to drive back beyond the borders of the empire the yak-tail banners of these marauders.

To such a low plane of self-defence did the Chinese fall in the fourth and fifth cycles of decadence that we find the vast empire conquered by these desert tribes. And it is in relation to these two periods of national disintegration, during which China became a subject nation, that the present cycle must be considered, since conditions are basically the same. In these periods of decadence, during which occurred the destruction of the Sung Dynasty and the establishment of the Mongol Dynasty of Yuen, and later the dissolution of the Ming Dynasty and the enforcement of Manchu sovereignty, China had but to protect herself from the squat horsemen that screamed along her northern frontiers. To-day, in a period of national depression and decay that is in no degree removed from the defencelessness of the fourth and fifth cycles of disintegration, this race has now for the first time to face enemies, not alone on her northern borders, but also upon the east and south and west, nations whose morality of conquest is no different, no better than was that of the Mongol and Manchu tribes who made her ten thousand fields a barren tenure.

The Chinese people—not the government nor the dynasty, for dynasties and governments are but the playthings or temporary utensils of races—have now to confront the most critical period in all the ages that have been allotted to them since that dim morning when first they gathered themselves together and Fuki ruled over them on the plains of Shensi.

Shall the Chinese as a nation survive this old internal struggle now about to break forth and enter into the seventh cycle of their evolution, or shall they utter themselves, thunderously but with finality, into such oblivion as awaits the decadent nation? The Chinese people were in former times proportionately manyfold stronger and more capable of resisting foreign conquest by nomadic hordes than they are to-day able to resist the

European or Japanese powers that now so relentlessly hang upon all the borders of the empire.

Unless there rises out of the uttermost depths of her bosom the militancy of another Martial Monk[1] the still hour has come when this ancientest kingdom shall make its solemn salutation to mankind, indifferent in the noisy buzz of his diurnal flight.

[1] Hung-wu, founder of the Ming Dynasty.

III

THE contemplation of empires that have spluttered and flickered out on this windy earth is not without value. For as the ancients were able, after cycles of time, to predict with certainty lunar eclipses from no other knowledge than the inevitability of their recurrence, so we, by the recurrence of the same causes and effects, the same beginnings and ends, are able to understand those eternal phases that alternately cast their glare and darkness over the orbit wherein nations move.

It is in such a manner that we now come to consider the American commonwealth towering as it does so mightily among nations that to those who compose it and are part of it it appears a pyramid amid the sand-dunes of time. This national vanity is justifiable so long as the existence of the nation's vastness, its grandeur, and the part it has taken—as great as any other state—in the evolution of human society continues. We only propose to examine into the valor of that ignorance now endeavoring to destroy the true basis of national greatness and to replace it with a superstructure of papier-mâché, not unlike a Mardi-gras creation, around whose gilded and painted exterior the nation is asked to dance in boastful arrogance, neither beholding nor caring at all for the sham of it nor its weakness.

As an individual can form no conception of personal death, so neither can nations. While individuals readily realize the inevitability of death in the greatest of men or a world of them, they cannot comprehend their own extinction, though their hours be ever so pitifully few. So it is with nations; and though the most insignificant of them can complacently witness the death-throes of the greatest of world empires, they are utterly unable to comprehend the possibility of a similar fate.

The American commonwealth stands in no different relation

to time and the forces of time than any other nation that has ever existed. The same elements brought about its birth and the same causes will prolong or shorten its existence as prolonged or shortened theirs. Up to the present time the life history of this republic has varied only in the slightest degree from the elemental forces that brought all other nations into existence and governed the growth of their youth and manhood.

It is unnecessary to recall the battle-fields upon which this republic was born or the subsequent wars that have marked its growth and expansion, other than to recall the invariability of that universal law governing the beginnings and rise of nations. This country, as others that have gone before, has been built up from the spoils of combat and conquest of defenceless tribes. Its expansion has been no more merciful nor merciless than the expansion of any other nation. The same inexorable law of physical strength has governed it as all others. But its conquests have been over nations and aborigines so disproportionately weak and incapable of waging war on a basis of equality that its wars have been destructive rather than inculcative of equitable military conceptions. The very ease with which this commonwealth has expanded is responsible for the erroneous beliefs now prevalent concerning the true basis of its future greatness. The people have come to look upon themselves in a false though heroic manner, and upon other nations with the same indifference as they did the untutored savage whose sole defences were the solitudes of his swamps and forests and a God that thundered in vain.

This republic has forgotten that during the last few decades its relation to other countries has been completely altered, not only because the ripple of its expansion has, by a law of national growth, reached out to other portions of the earth, but that modern means of transportation and communication have reduced the whole world into a greater compactness than were the United States in 1830. To-day it takes less time to reach Washington from the most distant nations than it took senators from their respective states seventy years ago. No longer, therefore, has this nation to carve its way onward to further greatness by defeating kingdoms months from their base; by devouring uncouth republics and whole tribes of aborigines, or laying bare a skeleton that went forth to battle in no other manner than did the corpse of the Cid concealed in the robes of royalty.

The time of this nation's youthful achievements is past. Yet proportionately as defenceless as were the peoples it has conquered the republic goes on, heedless of its fate, complacently contemplating the restless shadow of vast armed forces to the east and west of it. Only perhaps in that inevitable hour when this bluster, tragic or otherwise, shall end will this republic understand the retribution of national vanity and become cognizant of the end issuing from the fiat of that inexorable law, a law that never hesitates nor in its application varies or is found wanting.

Why mankind remains age after age blind to this unchangeable and universal ordinance controlling the destiny of nations is because he believes that in his own myopic life rests the *raison d'être* of national existence. But never until he emerges from the petty traffic, from the hurrying crowds of the streets, and ascends those heights where its clamor finds no echo, can he hope to see the endless procession of nations as they move onward majestically, tragically to their predestined end. On the thoroughfares of life he sees only the particles that constitute his country, not the nation itself; he can only comprehend their ambition, their momentary struggle for gain, and takes no note of nor makes any effort to understand the noble or melancholy destiny of his fatherland as a whole. This is hidden from him in the dust and pitiable cries that reach, as he believes in his self-exaltation, to the ear of God; but do not in fact struggle upward higher than the roof-tops.

In considering the future of this Republic one must do so, not from the closets of its politicians, not from its alleyways with their frenzied crowds, not from theorists nor feminists, for these are but the feverish phantasms and sickly disorders of national life. It must be regarded from the heights of universal history and empirical knowledge which appertains to national existence. The transitory tribes of man are not for themselves worthy of momentary consideration. They can only be considered in the same light as are organic particles consti-tuting the body of an individual. As these molecules come into existence to perform their predetermined function, then die and are replaced by others, endlessly and without cessation until the body itself ceases to be, so is mankind in the body-politic of a nation, and as such must be considered.

The future life of this Republic has not only been predeter-mined by the primordial laws already mentioned, but it has blazed the way of the future by its acts of the past. This irre-pressible expansion will no longer bring it into contact with inferior nations, but with those whose expanding capacity and military ability are far in excess of this Republic. We have before called attention to the fact that modern transportation and communication has reduced the world to such compactness that no future ripple of national growth can expand without breaking against some similar ripple emanating from another nation. When this occurs, it is war.

If this Republic is to achieve the greatness and duration its founders hoped to secure for it; if it is to continue to spread abroad over the earth the principles of its constitutions or the equity of its laws and the hope it extends to the betterment of the human race, then it must realize that this can only be done by possessing an ability and potentiality to be supreme over those nations whose ambitions and expansion are convergent. Preparations for wars consequent upon the growing compact-ness of the world and increasing convergence of all the world powers must go on ceaselessly and in proportion to the in-crease of expansion and fulness of years.

In the life of most nations the era of decadence has been more or less proportionate, in time, to that of their growth and the consummation of their greatness. The deterioration of the military forces and the consequent destruction of the militant spirit has been concurrent with national decay. When this deterioration of armies and militant ideals was complete, the nation was destroyed. In the history of no country other than this Republic do we find militant deterioration progress-ing other than in accordance with conditions consonant to an environment naturally productive of militant decay. In this nation, however, we find that the natural disintegration of militancy is artificially increased, not only by the indifference of the people to military enterprise, but by organized efforts to destroy not only the Republic's armament, but its militant potentiality.

High or low, the ambitions of the heterogeneous masses that now riot and revel within the confines of this Republic only regard it in a parasitical sense, as a land to batten on and grow big in, whose resources are not to be developed and conserved for the furtherance of the Republic's greatness, but only to satisfy the larval greed of those who subsist upon its fatness.

If there is any patriotism worth having it belongs alone to the primitive principles of the Republic, to the militant patriotism of those who in simple, persistent valor laid with their swords the foundation of this national edifice and who after seven years of labor cemented with their own blood the thirteen blocks of its foundation. The continuation of this building, and the endless extension of the Republic, the maintenance of its ideals and the consummation, in a world-wide sense, of the aspirations of its founders, constitutes the only pure patriotism to which an American can lay claim or, in defence of, lay down his life.

What we have said, or what we will say, as regards commercialism should not be misunderstood. If, in the development of the industries and potential wealth of the land, industrialism is regarded as incidental to national progress and not the goal of national greatness, then it is in its proper sphere. Industrialism is only a means to an end and not an end in itself. As the human body is nourished by food, so is a nation nourished by its industries. Man does not live to eat, but secures food that his body may be sustained while he struggles forward to the consummation of his desires. In such relation does industrialism stand to the state. It is sustenance, a food that builds up the nation and gives it strength to preserve its ideals; to work out its career among the other nations of the world; to become superior to them or to go down before them. Never can industrialism, without national destruction, be taken from this subordinate place. When a man has no aspirations, no object to attain during life, but simply lives to eat, he excites our loathing and contempt. So when a country makes industrialism the end it becomes a glutton among nations, vulgar, swinish, arrogant, whose kingdom lasts proportionately no longer than life remains to the swine among men. It is this purposeless gluttony, the outgrowth of national industry, that is commercialism. The difference between national industry and commercialism is that while industry is the labor of a people to supply the needs of mankind, commercialism utilizes this industry for the gratification of individual avarice. Commercialism might be defined, not as an *octopus vulgaris*, which is self-existent, but as a parasite of the *genus terrubia*, a fungoid growth that is the product of industrial degeneration. It is this commercialism that, having seized hold of the American people, overshadows and tends to destroy not only the aspirations and worldwide career open to the nation, but the Republic.

On the other hand, we do not consider military activity as something in itself. It is a condition of national life in the same sense as industrialism, but with this difference: though military development and industrialism are both factors subordinate to the ultimate aim of national existence, the militant spirit is a primordial element in the formative process and ultimate consummation of the nation's existence; while industrialism, in its normal function, is national alimentation, and the only other part it ever plays in national life is where, by degenerating into commercialism, it brings about the final corruption of the state.

Commercialism is only a protoplasmic gormandization and retching that vanishes utterly when the element that sustains it is no more. Military or national development, on the other hand, is not only responsible for the formation of all nations on earth, but for their consequent evolution and the peace of mankind. It makes that which is dearest to man—his life—no dearer than principle or loyalty for which he yields it, while commercialism sacrifices without the slightest compunction every principle and honor to gain the basest and paltriest possession of which man can boast.

Whenever a nation becomes excessively opulent and arrogant, at the same time being without military power to defend its opulence or support its arrogance, it is in a dangerous position. Whenever the wealth and luxury of a nation stand in inverse ratio to its military strength, the hour of its desolation, if not at hand, approaches. When the opulence and unmartial qualities of one nation stand in inverse ratio to the poverty and the military prowess of another, while their expansion is convergent, then results those inevitable wars wherein the commercial nation collapses and departs from the activities of mankind forever.

IV

LAWS governing national growth are as simple as they are immutable. The increasing wisdom of man and the varying conditions of his political existence give but an altered utterance to these changes. The political boundaries of nations continue to expand only as their military capacity is superior to the countries whose interests are convergent or whose frontiers are in common; while nations whose ambitions conflict with those of stronger powers or whose frontiers stand in the way of their expansion will, as in former ages, be overcome and absorbed by them.

The political frontiers of nations are never other than momentarily quiescent; shrinking on the sides exposed to more powerful military nations and expanding on frontiers where they come in contact with weaker states. This expansion of military powers and the shrinkage or extinction of those less capable of withstanding them is determined by their hungers and ambitions, by the supply and demand of natural resources and that immeasurable, theoremless ambition of man as a nation.

The older the world grows and the more compact it becomes through man's inventions, the more strenuous and continuous becomes this struggle. No longer is it possible for any Great Power to expect the expansion of its geographical area at the expense of aboriginal tribes or petty kingdoms alone, for they have now fallen within the sphere of some greater nation.

It was the recognition of these ordinances that led Monroe to enunciate his doctrine providing for the inviolability of the Western Continents. By removing them from the sphere of

European expansion he hoped to prevent the widening boundaries of these militant powers from coming in contact with
the natural growth of the Republic. No doctrine proclaimed
by any statesman of this nation or of the Old World ever portrayed truer insight into the nature of national life.

In the time of Monroe, it was impossible to foresee the
changes mechanical inventions were to make in the political
development of the world after his time. While human nature
is no different from what it was then and will remain un-
altered eons yet to come, this world has been whittled down
to a small ball and time has been scoffed at. No longer, as in
Monroe's time, does a vast Atlantic Ocean separate this continent from Europe. Man's ingenuity has reduced it to a small
stream across which the fleets of European Powers can cross
in less time than it took Monroe to post from Washington to
Boston. No longer is the Pacific hidden in the purple solitudes
of illimitable vastness nor do its waters splash on toy shores
of porcelain and green tea. The smiling mists and mysteries
of these Oriental lands have not only been cleared away, but
their very fields have been ploughed up and harrowed by the
bayonets of Western Nations. In their lust for the Golden
Fleece they have sown over them the teeth of the Twin Sleeping Dragons from which have sprung up vast and terrible
armies, warships as swift and ruthless as the swooping Kite
that is the symbol of their valor.

Monroe could not perceive the possibilities of such changes;
and while his doctrine is as correct in principle as when enunciated by him, it has, unprovided with such ordinances as would
make it effective, been handed down to the present age nullified
by man's new means of transportation and the changed military as well as political conditions that now govern international intercourse. But to the average American, as to Monroe,
the Atlantic and Pacific are still such vast seas that no enemy
will have the temerity to cross them, hence this nation, without
armies and without navies proportionate to its new responsibilities and their concomitant dangers, hopes to remain secure
and immune, without effort, from foreign invasion. It is this

vanity, which can be called the Valor of Distance, that will be considered in this chapter.

In a military or naval sense, distance is not measured by miles. Napoleon found all the capitals of Europe closer to Paris than the sea-coasts of England. On the other hand, in the Boer War, the English discovered that the five thousand miles from Portsmouth to Cape Town were shorter than a few hundred miles from Cape Town to Pretoria.

Distance from a base in a military sense is measured by the time, ease and capacity it takes to move bodies of troops and munitions to a secondary base in the theatre of war or to armies in the field. The space lying between an army and its base, instead of being measured by miles, is determined by the speed of the means of transportation, the immunity of the lines of communication from attack, and the number of lines converging from the main base to the theatre of war.

Two places a thousand miles apart, but connected by a railroad, are closer together than two places only one hundred miles apart with no other means of communication than a country road. The sea, when free from the enemy's warships, offers the best means of communication, not only on account of the speed of modern steamers and their carrying capacity, but from the fact that their lines are immutable and can be as numerous as are the ports controlled on the enemy's seaboard.

Those who hold to the belief that the remoteness of the United States from Europe renders it inaccessible to attack point to Napoleon's Moscow campaign and the defeat of the Russians in the Japanese War as failures resulting from the conduct of a war at great distances. The truth is that distance in these two distinct campaigns was not responsible for the disasters consequent upon them. The Moscow campaign, moreover, has nothing whatever to do with modern or future conditions of warfare or with the military relation Europe now bears to the United States. It required several months for troops to march from Paris to Moscow or for supplies to be transported over this distance; while Washington, New York, or Boston are but seven days distant from the capitals of Europe. The transport by sea of Japanese troops to America would involve that nation in no greater difficulties than did the carrying of them to Manchuria.

The campaigns of Gustavus Adolphus, of Frederick the Great, and numerous other great captains were conducted many weeks from their main bases. The campaigns of Napoleon in Italy, Spain, Austria, and Germany were carried on in the heart of an enemy's country, many weeks and in some instances months, from his base. In the war with Mexico the forces of the United States operated several months from their source of supplies, while in the Civil War, Union armies conducted campaigns and operated many weeks from their depots: as Grant in his Vicksburg campaign; Burnside advancing from Louisville to Knoxville; Sherman in his march from Chattanooga to Atlanta, thence to the north; as General Banks' advance in Texas and Sherman's march across the State of Mississippi. The Union Army in New Orleans drew its supplies, even its beef, from New York City, thirty-six hundred miles away.

The significance of these statements belongs to the comparison between them and the distances that separate the United States from European bases of operation, which in no instance exceeds ten days.

Grant, in the state of Mississippi, was twenty days marching from Brunes-burgh to Vicksburg. To-day an army of the same size could be embarked at Bremen, carried across the Atlantic and debarked on the seaboard of this Republic in one half the time.

When in 1865 the Fourth Army Corps of the Union Army was transported from Carter's Station to Nashville, three hundred and seventy-three miles, it required fourteen hundred and ninety-eight cars. An army corps of the same size, together with all necessary equipment, could be transported from Germany to the United States on five steamers of the Hamburg-American or Norddeutscher Lloyd. Twenty-five of these steamers could transport from Germany to the American seacoast seventy-five thousand troops, together with their equipment, in less time than it would have taken Grant to march the same number of men from Washington to Appomattox.

Germany can transport to the United States a quarter of a million soldiers in a fortnight.[1]

In the Virginia campaign in 1864, the supply train for General Grant's army of one hundred and twenty-five thousand men consisted of forty-eight hundred wagons drawn by some twenty-five thousand mules and horses. This train transported twenty thousand tons of supplies. The entire tonnage could be transported from Europe to America in the *Deutschland*, *Amerika*, *Kaiser Wilhelm* or any other one vessel of the same class in less time than Grant's train could have traversed the distance from the southern bank of the Rapidan to the northern bank of the James, unhindered by the vicissitudes of war and delays of battle.

Such is the isolation of this Republic, a condition that does not exist. The only isolation of which this nation can afford to boast is that rendered by fleets of battleships and mobile armies. When they do not exist or are inferior or are destroyed, the defence of the Republic has been thrown down.

To maintain national isolation it is necessary to possess fleets not less than twice the size of any European navy and a standing army not less than one-half the size of the largest standing army in Europe or Asia. At the present time England alone can array against the American navy in the Atlantic fleets three times greater, while at the same time British warships will be ten times more numerous in the Pacific. Both Germany and France could place in the Pacific a fleet four times greater than the American Pacific squadrons and at the same time maintain a sufficient number of ships in the Atlantic to prohibit the departure of a single American battleship from their Atlantic stations. This can be comprehended more clearly by considering a state of war, under present naval and military conditions, between any one of these powers and the United States. England, France, or Germany not only possess territory, but naval stations, docks, and troops in the Orient. Initiating a war, any of these nations could previously mobilize in the Pacific a fleet as many times greater than the American squadrons as would insure their destruction. The

[1] German General Staff.

American fleet could not be reinforced from the Atlantic without reducing the Atlantic squadrons to a state of inutility and exposing the remainder to destruction by an overwhelming attack from the enemy's Atlantic fleets. Since the time necessary to reinforce the American fleets in either ocean is not less than four months, it allows the enemy, based only six days distant from the Atlantic coast, to seize by land attack the American harbors and naval bases and thus prevent the return of the American fleets to the Atlantic should they attempt the relief of the Pacific.

With the destruction of the American Pacific fleet the Philippines, Hawaii, Samoa, and Alaska would pass into the hands of the enemy. The towns along the seaboard of the Pacific coast would be destroyed and the American flag would no longer be seen loitering over the wide waters of this sea.

To such a small area has man's ingenuity pared down this once vast world that nations can now conduct war on any portion of it, no matter how remote, as measured by miles, the theatre of combat may be from their base. The difficulties of transportation are reduced to a minimum. Oceans no longer prevent the successful invasion of distant lands, but on the other hand make such attack possible.

To march a body of troops two hundred and fifty miles, together with their train and general impedimenta, has never been considered in warfare other than an insignificant undertaking. But Germany or France or England can land a similar force on the American shores in no longer time. Japan could land an army in California in less time than a force could march from Los Angeles to San Francisco.

Within a given time a single vessel of the *Mauretania* or *Deutschland* class could transport more troops from Europe to the American shores than could all the fleets of England have done at the time of the Revolution or War of 1812. Vessels of this class will carry a brigade, together with all of its equipment, from Europe to the United States in six days. The entire merchant marine of Germany and Japan can be converted into transports immediately upon declaration of war and land within a month more than a quarter of a million men on either shore.

Nations lulled into somnolent security because they are separated by wide expanses of water from the vast armaments of these Powers will find that their airy bastions of space will fall down about them and their resistance will be measured only by weeks or months; the end of the year shall see their battle flags furled and laid away to rot dryly in ignominious dusk.

A knot added to the speed of a transatlantic steamer and the width of the sea grows less and the armed frontiers of Europe brought closer to these shores. When the vessel's size or carrying capacity is increased, the ocean shrinks again and the armies of distant nations draw nearer.

The great rampart of ocean has utterly vanished, only the delusion of it still remains. Its illusionary defence and the dreams of peace born out of it must give way to that which belongs to man in his combats, the blood and iron of military preparation proportionate to the dangers and difficulties that surround American sovereignty in the Western Hemisphere.

No longer, as in Monroe's time, does the passage of the seas require weeks or months. No longer are the ships buffeted about by unruly winds, nor drawn hither and thither by uncharted currents. Straight and unswerving are these enormous steel vessels hurled through seas, timed as accurately as the movement of the constellations overhead. No longer do fragile craft, with the destiny of a nation in their cargo of souls and shot, drift unknown, unspoken, over an abyss of stormy seas. The very winds that once shrieked through their broken rigging now mutter with man's speech or scream with the commands of monarchs three thousand miles away.

V

THIS Republic has not only been foremost in the utilization of scientific discoveries, but from its activities have come the most important of modern inventions. The economic phases of its career have been altered; its social and political fabric changed through the advance of science and general knowledge. But in its military system there has been no progress. In this regard the altered conditions of human society and international relationship have passed over the nation as clouds hurrying through the azure heavens, leaving no deeper imprint upon it than is possible from the erosion of fleeting shadows.

The modern American's conception of military efficiency is but a succession of heroics culminating in victory. This heroism of dreams, this valor of the rostrum, is based, not upon the real history of past military achievements, but upon the illusions of them. Like bubbles these fragilest of militant deeds are tinctured with an iridescence that does not belong to them.

This nation, denying in a practical manner the fact that military science is subject to change and evolution, as all other phases of human activity, still clings with the tenacity of evasion to the *laissez-faire* military system of Colonial days, or rather to the skeleton of it, for that which made it vigorous and effective, the militancy of the individual, has now all but departed, naturally and in accordance with the laws that govern the preservation or destruction of national militancy during the career of a state and the evolution of its society.

As the social and industrial, ethical and political organism of this nation becomes more and more complex, absorbing or diverting the activities of the people from national to individual achievements, the self-deception of the people as regards their inherent military capacity becomes more dominant and unreasonable. It is this national self-deception now so rampant in the Republic that we will consider in this chapter and show that natural laws govern, as they do all other forms of human progression, the growth and decay of national militancy.

If no provision is made by a nation for enforced military service among its inhabitants, the militant capacity of a race or state decreases proportionately as is increased the complexity of its social organism and the diversity of its economic activities.

The self-deception of a nation concerning its true militant strength increases at the same ratio as its actual militant capacity decreases.

We find that the uttermost limits of national self-beguilement, in relation to military capacity, are reached when the social, political and economic phases have become so intangibly complex that the ideals of the people, ceasing to be national—have become individual. While this condition is the antithesis of militancy, yet we discover in it—strange as it may seem—the maturity of military conceit. At this stage national decomposition sets in and patriotism rots serenely.

The first and most difficult task of statesmen is the preservation of the national or militant instinct intact in the virtues of the people. However disagreeable the thought may be, militancy is alone responsible for the creation of every state and the preservation of it through manifold disasters. Only when this militancy deteriorates is the state doomed.

By the formation of political entities the evolution of mankind has been made possible. All human progress, together with individual freedom, has been hewn out from man by the very agencies that so many to-day labor to destroy, agencies that, so long as man gathers himself together in separate states, will never cease to determine the greatness of a race, or by the lack of it the ushering into the Infinite Past of a whole people and their institutions.

Military strength or incapacity is never constant, but varies almost from hour to hour as does the thermometer in registering the heat and chills of the passing hours. It is relative to innumerable conditions; not more of man with his hungers and loud noises than the seas and rocks and the winds that blow over them and the unpanned dust that hides in their clefts and fissures.

The heights and depths of theatres of war, their topography and climate, the militancy of hostile peoples, their armaments and science, as well as innumerable other conditions that enter into the transient phases of human conflict, determine the continuous and consistent readjustment of military forces in numbers, armament, discipline, tactics and logistics; conforming concurrently with new mechanical inventions and scientific discoveries that each year alter to a greater or less degree the conduct of war. A nation with an inflexible military system, determined by a national constitution and controlled by civilian politicians, will soon end by having no military forces, spirit or capacity.

Warfare, either ancient or modern, has never been nor will ever be mechanical. There is no such possibility as the combat of instruments. It is the soldier that brings about victory or defeat. The knowledge of commanders and the involuntary comprehension and obedience to orders is what determines the issue of battles. An army controlled by more than one mind is as many times useless as are numbered the minds that direct it. But what mankind does not take cognizance of is that, in the alteration of modes of combat by mechanical and scientific inventions, there must be a psychological readjustment of the militant spirit of the combatant. As the instruments of warfare become more intricate, the discipline and *esprit de corps* must be increased accordingly. Because of this fact volunteer forces become more and more useless as the science of warfare progresses.

The causes of militant degeneration in a race or nation are not generally understood. In primitive times militancy was conditioned by necessity, and as this necessity passed the militancy dependent upon it deteriorated. This necessity might return to the race or nation at any subsequent moment, but militancy could not return simultaneously with it. Hence it is that nations having reached such military greatness and commanding position as to appear to themselves impregnable, the military spirit is allowed to degenerate. When this decadence reaches a certain point the nation, regardless of its wealth, area and population, is destroyed by, perhaps, an insignificant though warlike race.

Laws that govern the militancy of a people are not laws of man's framing, but belong to the primitive ordinances of Nature and govern all forms of life from a single protozoa awash in the sea to the empires of man.

We divide militancy into three distinct phases:

(1) The militancy of the struggle to survive.

(2) The militancy of conquest.

(3) The militancy of supremacy or preservation of ownership.

It is in the first, the struggle to survive, that the military genius of a people reaches its height, for it is that militancy which is common to all forms of life. Moreover, we find that the harder the struggle for a race or tribe to survive in its combats both with man and the elements, the more highly developed becomes their military spirit. It is because of this that we find conquerors rising up out of desolate wastes or rocky islands.

Success in the struggle for survival is followed by the second degree of militancy, that of conquest, in whch militancy becomes a positive instead of a negative factor. It is in this metamorphosis, out of this red chrysalis, that the race rises upward on the pinions of an eagle.

In the third stage the natural militancy of a nation declines. This going to pieces is hastened by the institution of new ideals. Commercialism grows as militancy deteriorates, since it is in itself a form of strife, though a debased one—a combat that is without honor or heroism. The relegation of the militant ideal to a secondary place in national activity is succeeded by accumulative ignorance concerning military efficiency, while the spirit of it—that intuitive perception of what constitutes militancy—vanishes utterly, and to most nations that have reached this dwelling-point of fraud it returns not again forever.

Only when a nation endeavors to return to militant ideals, and battles for self-preservation, does it realize the gulf that separates it from such a possibility. Few are they that have recrossed this wide abyss of their neglect and scorn. This final period of militant decay is succeeded by an age of subterfuge, an era of evasion, that ends in national dissolution.

In attempting to determine the probability of an effective national uprising to repel an invasion of this Republic by a foreign Power it is necessary to consider it from two sources only: first, by an examination into circumstances analogous to this probability as they have existed in other countries; second, by deductions made from actual conditions existent in this nation.

From the beginning of the formation of national entities until the present time, the idea of popular uprisings to repulse foreign invaders has ever been a universal conceit, an indelible vanity that neither the erosion of ages has erased nor the deluges of blood issuing from them have washed away. Yet, while there exists not an age nor a nation that has not resounded with the triumphant hoof-beats of invading armies, the truth is there is not a single instance in the whole military history of the world where the mobile armies of a warlike race have been destroyed or defeated by the popular uprisings of a militantly decadent state. Such warring multitudes have been but the wild windstorms of human beings that, without direction or intelligence, have passed by in no long period of time.

In the wars of mankind, popular uprisings, in the full meaning of the phrase, are only possible to a primitive despotism. The more diffused national civilization becomes with the political elevation and liberty of the individual, the less probable is a unified resistance. The idea of repelling invasion has always found a prominent place in popular superstitions—the myths of man's credulity and vanity. Such uprisings were possible only in primitive times, ceasing with the establishment of armies that required training and cohesion: diminishing proportionately as science entered more and more into the conduct of war. Modern warfare is the conversion of the nation's potential military resources into actual power and its consequent utilization in a unified and predetermined manner by men more scientifically trained than lawyers, doctors or engineers.

To repel an invasion of this nation ideals remote from those that now litter and ferment abroad over this land must be created. The soldier spirit, that spark, illuminating not alone the abysses wherein nations move, but those chambers of souls ordinarily dark and forgotten, must be struck. This requires not months but years. Whole armies of men must be animated to this by discipline and exalted by the quest of idealistic honor, such as distinguishes them from those enriched by trade or those who are able to purchase with gold all but that which alone is bought by blood.

This preparation now belongs to the time of peace.

Once a country is invaded the machinery of government, which determines unity of effort, is thrown down and the entire arsenal of national strength is strewn fragmentary over the whole land. Like the ignition of scattered grains of loose powder, resistance is reduced to a sporadic flaring-up, a sickly sputtering of small flames and much smoke, sulphuric and bitter.

No one is justified in saying that there would be no defence of this Republic in event of invasion: such a statement would be manifestly untrue. But the defence would be no greater nor worse than that heretofore made by nations heterogeneous and opulent as this Republic: a defence, in innumerable instances, Alamodian, heroic, even Gracchian, but in the end proving to be no more stable than a defence of tumble-weeds and loud noises.

Why public confidence in the infallibility of volunteer forces still survives in this Republic would be a military enigma were it not known that such is the case in every nation where man's aspirations are measured by the ephemeral and immaterial.

Volunteers are purely a mediæval institution, effective only in those ages when weapons of warfare differed little or not at all from those used by men during times of peace: when, in fact, the mechanism of war was crude and the science of it was no science other than to kill or be killed in the simplest and most natural hand-to-hand manner.

The weapons used in American wars up to a time subsequent to the Civil War were the same used during peace by men struggling through forests or over plains, shooting, hunting, killing. In times of war these men were formed into regiments and went on hunting and killing, but, instead of fowls and beasts, they hunted their fellow-men, no better armed nor trained, nor more valorous than they. So it is not strange to hear men who are in truth patriots by right of blood and deed proclaim that in the event of invasion they will seize from their nooks and mantel-pieces such arms as hang or repose there and go forth to the slaughter of the invader. We doubt not that such would be their actions; but how far would they go, these stern and uncompromising patriots? The nobility of patriotism will not, unfortunately, increase the initial velocity of antiquated weapons; and armaments change so rapidly in modern times that a soldier of one generation is more or less worthless in a war of a succeeding period.

Battles are no longer the spectacular heroics of the past. The army of to-day and to-morrow is a sombre, gigantic machine devoid of all melodramatic heroics, but in itself all-heroic, silent and terrible: a machine that requires years to form its separate parts, years to assemble them together, and other years to make them work smoothly and irresistibly. Then, when it is set in motion, naught shall stop it but a similar machine stronger and better.

Battles are now fought, won or lost on wide, deserted fields, and no combatants are seen, only here and there small blue clouds and distant noises mark the dumb heroism of modern armies. Volunteers, patriotic, heroic as the mind of man can make them, are of no use in this mile-away war, since they know nothing of its science. They are led forward into death nullahs by officers who never saw an army in the field, and whose military knowledge is only reminiscent of Bunker Hill and the Minute-men of Concord. Who shall blame them if they scamper off on all fours to the rear when the pilfering bullets, dropping from heaven itself, begin to loot whole squads and companies of their souls?

It is the hour and terror of helpless death.

The time of volunteer forces has forever passed. Nations that expect to make war in the future with hastily raised levies of volunteers against standing armies are doomed to disaster.

It is natural that both the North and South should preserve out of the four years of battles and night-marches only that which is heroic and noble. But this glamour does not obscure within its brilliancy some dark spots, such spots as men love not to dwell upon, howsoever beneficial their contemplation may be. So the most valuable lessons taught by the Civil War have been buried as the dead were buried in graves not again to be opened. We will not commit this sacrilege, though it were for the good and just cause of tempering down the crude, fragile valor of this nation.

The history of the volunteer in the Civil War ends as soon as the war enters upon its serious phase; thence come enormous bounties, drafts, conscripts, riots and incipient rebellions. We will only make two statements as regards these volunteers in the Union Army, but in these rest volumes of foreboding facts. In the Union Army from 1861 to 1865 there were more officers discharged and cashiered for dishonor and incapacity than were killed on the field of battle; more discharged "without stated reasons" than died during that time from disease. In other words, the casualties of dishonor and incapacity among officers during these years were greater than that of the battle-field and disease.

Who is there that will make out that sad roster of the unnamed ten thousand dead among enlisted men that these incompetent officers led about to die? Yet we lay no blame upon their shoulders. Their crimes were the crimes, not of themselves, but of the ignorance and worthlessness of the military system still extant.

Snatched suddenly, as they were, out of the peaceful round of civil life, with its orderless, undisciplined equality, they knew nothing concerning the duties that devolve upon military officers. Skilled as these men might be in every phase of human activity, yet they knew not the primary principles of the end-less technique that belongs to the vast science of war; a science that is alone the relentless determinant, not only in the creation of nations, but the length of their duration, their greatness or littleness upon earth, and in the hour of their desolation to be the inexorable umpire of their unfitness.

An army possesses a heart and brain as does every other living organism. This heart and brain of an army is made up of the officers composing it, while the soul of it is the spirit that inspires them. The worth of an army must be measured primarily by the character of this soul. In volunteer armies it is little more than embryonic, and in its absence armies are but mobs. It is immaterial how numerous they may be, how vast their armament, or how perfect their utensils of war, these things shall avail them not at all.

The soul of the soldier can only be developed by discipline, by honor and martial deeds. It cannot be constructed to order or dressed up with false shoulders in twenty-four days by uni-forming a civilian volunteer or by commissioning and spurring him with purchased valor or the transient glory of loud-mouthed multitudes. The creation of this martial soul necessi-tates year after year of sternest labor and toil that callouses not alone the hands and wrings sweat from the brow, but also callouses the weakness inherent in man and wrings sweat from his heart. It is moulded by Regulusian discipline, and lives are thrown carelessly away, mechanically, almost irrationally. In the lessons of these years they learn that in warfare a relentless absorption of individuality must supervene, an annihilation of all personality. Only then can they reach that pinnacle of human greatness, to seek glory in death.

The second fact that it is our duty to record in determin-ing the efficiency of American volunteers as well as the valor and loyalty of those who, we are assured, would rise en masse against invading armies, causes us again to revert to the rec-ords of the Civil War, wherein we find that from 1861 to 1865 there were nearly two hundred thousand deserters from the Union Army—one-fifth the size of the army at the close of the war. One man out of every twelve who enlisted was a deserter. The Union Army lost nearly four times as many men from desertion as were killed on the field. To this melancholy intelligence, annotations or commentaries would be superfluous. But it will be well for the people of this Republic to think of the solemn portent of these facts when the braggart spirit steals upon them, when imaginary hosts of unarmed patriots rise up and destroy this mighty and sadly turbulent world.

When science entered into warfare, volunteers made their exit. They become soldiers only after they cease to be volunteers, at the end of the second or third year; while militia are made into soldiers only after they have had their minds freed from the tangled skein of false notions, which takes a year longer than a raw recruit.

To hit a bull's-eye in a shooting-gallery or a quail on the wing does not constitute military marksmanship. The hunter of animals who kills at two and three hundred yards has no relationship to the hunter of men who kills at ranges exceeding a thousand yards. The former is practice, the latter science. The military marksman must be able to calculate distance under varying atmospheric and topographical conditions. At a range exceeding a thousand yards he must make calculations for temperature, wind and humidity. If his rifle has an initial velocity of two thousand feet, and the wind is blowing a dozen miles an hour, he must allow a deviation of eighteen feet for the bullet. For every degree of temperature he must allow one inch deviation; and fourteen inches for every fifteen degrees of humidity. But marksmanship alone does not constitute, in any degree whatsoever, a soldier, and it can be said that it affects in no manner the issue of modern battles, if the other primary elements that go to make up an efficient and powerful army are absent.

Rifle, pistol and all other similar civilian associations are not only negatively but positively harmful to the nation, inasmuch as they produce an erroneous conception of the knowledge and duties necessary to a modern soldier. After three years' service in a regular army not more than twenty-five per cent. of the men can be qualified as military marksmen. To believe that the scatter-gun marksmanship of civil life is a factor in warfare is not other than a yellow-flamed *ignis fatuus*, starting up out of the Dismal Swamp of ignorance and national vanity.

Before the final hour is tolled over this careless and somnolent nation it should realize that in the performance of military duty there must be no substitution of the immaterial for that which is essential; no evasion of responsibility nor subterfuge.

A vast population and great numbers of civilian marksmen can be counted as assets in the combative potentiality of a nation as are coal and iron ore in the depths of its mountains, but they are, *per se*, worthless until put to effective use. This Republic, drunk only with the vanity of its resources, will not differentiate between them and actual power. Japan, with infinitely less resources, is militarily forty times more powerful. Germany, France or Japan can each mobilize in one month more troops, scientifically trained by educated officers, than this Republic could gather together in three years. In the Franco-Prussian War, Germany mobilized in the field, ready for battle, over half a million soldiers, more than one hundred and fifty thousand horses and twelve hundred pieces of artillery in five days. The United States could not mobilize for active service a similar force in three years. A modern war will seldom endure longer than this.

Not only has this nation no army, but it has no military system. It has neither arms nor equipment. No preparation for war is made. No organization, no staffs, no plans for feeding, supplying or transporting forces; while the militancy of the nation has been washed away in the most transient and fouling of summer floods.

The spirit of militancy is born in a man, but a soldier is made. Not, however, machine-made, nor hand-made, nor tailor-made, nor put together in twenty-four hours. A soldier cannot be created by a formula of speech nor by the vanity of valor. It takes not less than a dozen men six-and-thirty long months to hammer and temper him into the image of his maker and fit him for the performance of his duties.

A man who enlists in an army has the right to demand that those who are his leaders shall know to the fullest extent the duties appertaining to their office. Lives unnumbered are placed in their hands, but they are offered upon the altar of their country and not to satisfy the vanity of individuals; they are in the field to fight the enemy, not disease: if they must perish, let it be by the kindly singing bullets and not by the ignorance of their commanders.

In civil life a butcher is not called upon to exercise the skill of an oculist nor to remove a cataract from the dulled eye; barbers do not perform the operation of laparotomy; nor farmers navigate sea-going vessels, nor stone-masons try cases at the bar, nor sailors determine the value of mines, nor clerks perform the functions of civil-engineers. Yet, in the time of war in this Republic, these same men, together with all other varieties of humanity, go forth in the capacity of volunteer officers to be learned by the end of one-and-thirty days in the most varied of all sciences, the science of war.

The most promiscuous murderer in the world is an ignorant military officer. He slaughters his men by bullets, by disease, by neglect; he starves them, he makes cowards of them and deserters and criminals. The dead are hecatombs of his ignorance; the survivors, melancholy spectres of his incompetence.

VI

BELIEF in the potency of gold is not new; it is as old as the Jews and prevails wherever wealth constitutes power in civil life and forms the highest consummation of individual effort. In any nation where wealth is the source of political power, the criterion of rank and the mark of social eminence, it becomes impossible for the people not to see in it also a complete source of military strength. People that can turn patriotism into cash and their gods into profit could not believe otherwise.

A nation that is rich, vain, and at the same time unprotected, provokes wars and hastens its own ruin. This is a law so old and invariable that man thinks no more of it than he does of the forces of gravity, the tides of the sea or the inevitability of death. Neither does he realize that a nation never becomes opulent that it does not become arrogant, nor opulent and arrogant that it does not become defenceless. And no nation, as we have heretofore stated, ever becomes defenceless that it does not sooner or later suffer the penalty of its deterioration. Opulence, instead of being a foundation of national strength, is liable to be the most potent factor in its destruction. Instead of adding power to a nation, it simply increases the responsibility of its rulers and necessitates a greater diligence for defence. National opulence is a source of danger instead of power, for the arrogance that comes of it is only Hebraic, hence trade, ducats, and mortgages are regarded as far greater assets and sources of power than armies or navies. It produces national effeminacy and effeteness, hence there spring up whole tribes of theorists, feminists and, in fact, all the necrophagan of opulent decadence. When wealth forms the criterion of all human ambitions, justice, emoluments, nay, of worth itself, then corruption sets in and patriotism departs.

To reason analogically is oftentimes erroneous. In fact, it can be said that analogy is a source of innumerable misconceptions, and whoever makes deductions or attempts to construct universal axioms solely from analogical reasoning will sooner or later land in a quagmire of untruthfulness. Analogy can only form true and irrefutable conclusions when it deals with identical causes producing under various and widely divergent conditions the same results. Thus, it is possible to state, more or less accurately, that a volcano upheaves its ashes and molten lava in a more or less constant and identical manner, whether in Italy or Java, in ancient or modern times. These volcanic causes and effects, identical at all times, though occurring under widely separated geographical or chronological conditions, differ little from the periodical eruptions of the elemental scoria of mankind.

But only so long as the elemental characteristics of mankind form in themselves the basis of analogical reasoning can analogy be considered reliable or a source of truth when dealing with man, his institutions or customs. Each succeeding age regards itself as infinitely wiser than the age that has preceded, though in fact it may be a dark and villainous affair, as were the Middle Ages, and even recent times, in comparison to the antique Greek and Roman, Indian and Chinese civilizations. Each succeeding religion, likewise, regards the efforts of its predecessor as futile, and that it alone hath the ear of God. Each age regards its customs alone sensible, and those that have gone before ridiculous; its morality more pure, its equity more perfect, and so on, *ad infinitum*, through the whole list of transient vanities that are as mutable as though written on fluxing sands that the veriest froth waves, rolling in from the illimitable oceans of time, toss into confusion and nothingness.

Only in the ever-recurring tracing on the sands and obliteration thereof do we discern human characteristics that are immutable; characteristics that bring about the formation of the human race into political entities, and in due time their inevitable dissolution. These characteristics are of themselves the elemental instincts of the human race, instincts that as a whole are but momentarily affected by the transient caprices of theories or morals, styles or religions. It is in these ever-recurring forces innate in mankind that we alone reason analogically concerning the present and the future; not so much from the sand-dunes of the past as from the inevitable tides that form and shatter them.

So while, within the brevity of this work, it is impossible to take up each nation and deal minutely with the causes of its formation, its decay and melancholy end, the reader can determine for himself, with no great amount of exertion, the exact part and proportion wealth has contributed to their strength and duration, or to what degree it has undermined their foundations and rotted the great beams of their edifices.

Unlike theories and moral codes, religions and customs, the part wealth has played in national existence has never been sporadic nor transient, nor the political exudence of a single period or race, nor varied one jot in any age on any portion of earth nor among any people. Its effect has been invariable, whether applied to the Empire of the Pharaohs or to Korea, to China or Rome, to India or Spain; and likewise, with the same inevitability will it lay its heavy hand upon this nation. The law of its application is inexorable.

The wealth of a nation, as a factor in warfare, possesses certain potential but entirely subordinate capabilities, which appear in themselves as actual conquering forces of warfare, though the truth is otherwise. War between wealth and militant energy has but one end, the old doom of the Purple Persian. Such a conflict is only a contest between the hollow panoply of warfare and an actual combatant; the plumed cadaver of a Cid against a live Moor; thunder and smoke on one side, lightning and fire on the other. The Battle of Issus, the Sack of Rome, Marengo, Sedan, Liaou Yang—such are the endless epitaphs of gold against steel, corpulence against muscle, pomposity against discipline.

Not unlike Midas, nations succumbing to the excess of gold soon come to beg deliverance from it. But not unto them is it given that they may turn to the waters of Pactolus for the washing away of it. The cleansing of their folly belongs only to those streams that drain down from the hearts of nations.

Wealth in the time of war, no matter how limitless, can do no more than provide arms and munitions, pay the salaries of soldiers, provide their subsistence, clothing and transportation. Gold illimitable cannot buy them valor, nor self-sacrifice, nor endurance, nor discipline nor military knowledge. Gold-purchased heroism is a conception only possible to a nation sunk in the lowest depths of commercialism. In fact, no heroic action has ever, in all the turbulency of the human race, been conceived and executed with ducats before and behind it. Gold may harness men for war, but it has never been able to make them conquer when opposed to those whose discipline has been kneaded into the marrow of their bones and the inner chambers of their hearts.

The expense of conducting a war is not, simultaneously, the same with any two nations, notwithstanding the fact that the price of armaments may be identical to all of them. War expenditures are in proportion to the wealth of the nation itself. The cost of a war carried on by England or this Republic is manifold greater than if waged by any other nation. Should the United States to-day be obliged to place in the field the same number of men, for the same length of time, under the same conditions, as did the Japanese in their war with Russia, the salaries alone would nearly equal the entire war expense of the Japanese; while the total expense would equal a sum as proportionately greater as is the wealth of this Republic greater than that of Japan, plus its concomitant corruption.

In the Civil War of the United States, nearly two hundred millions were alone expended in bounties. Taking into consideration the increased values now prevailing in this country as compared to the values of that period, bounties would, under this head, be treble, or alone equalling the entire expenditure of Japan in the war with Russia. In addition to this, the non-American population at that time was comparatively insignificant, hence patriotism stood in proportionately high ratio, while to-day the heterogeneity of population is over fifty per cent. How much gold, therefore, would now be required to enlist these people into the pain and sacrifice of war—to coax them from their rich labors to die for a land they regard only as the wide, fat fields of the harvest moon?

The cost of prosecuting a war is not only proportionate to the wealth of the nation, but the actual maintenance of the individual soldier stands in ratio to the cost of living and rate of wages. The wage of a stone-mason, which is high or low according to the opulence or the frugality of a nation, is in the United States from four to five dollars a day; in Japan, forty-five cents; in Europe, about ninety cents, and other labor in like proportion. The high cost of living that prevails in an opulent nation not only necessitates high wages, but this in turn brings about an increase, perhaps proportionate, perhaps excessive as inflated by trusts, in the price of all materials, foodstuffs, and munitions used in war as well as in peace.

Thus, European nations in time of peace maintain armies from three hundred and fifty thousand to five hundred thousand men and officers, together with reserves of regulars varying from two to five million, with a proportionate number of horses and guns, for the same money that the United States is obliged to expend to maintain fifty thousand troops with no reserve of regulars. Japan could support a standing peace army exceeding one million men for the same amount of money this Republic now spends on fifty thousand. This proportion, which exists in time of peace, becomes even more excessive in time of war; for whenever war involves a country there exists in all preparation an extravagance that is also proportionate to the wealth of the nation.

During the last few years of peace, from 1901 to 1907, the United States Government has expended on the army and navy over fourteen hundred million dollars: a sum exceeding the combined cost to Japan of the Chinese War and the Russian War, as well as the entire maintenance of her forces during the intervening years of peace. Yet to-day the United States possesses no army, while the navy is only one-half the size it should be to defend its shores.

Poverty never begets extravagance, and frugality is never the offspring of wealth. Poverty is productive of every human exertion, while wealth is the parent of every form of corruption. The richer a nation is in time of peace, the poorer it is in time of war.

Corruption exists in direct ratio to the wealth of a nation, or, if the nation is in a decadent state, as India, China, and Spain, it is extant in vaster proportions. Though the wealth of a nation may decline, corruption remains constant in ratio to the maximum wealth of the past.

A nation can become so rich that its wealth will bankrupt it in a war with a country poor but frugal and warlike.

Excessive national wealth is responsible for another factor that even in itself is productive of utter incapacity to execute warlike measures or even to prevent the collapse of a nation in war—the enervation through luxury, feminism, theorism, or the decay of martial inclination and military capacity. This sooner or later begins to show itself in every phase of life, from National Assemblies to Debating Societies, Communism, Idealism, Universalism, and innumerable other bright, fantastic tapestries that the ingenuity of man weaves through woof and warp of human hopes and their follies.

Wealth is a factor in the naval and military strength of a nation only so long as it is regarded in its true and subordinate capacity: to build battleships, but not to fight them; to buy arms, not valor; to manufacture powder, not patriotism. But when wealth becomes so paramount in a nation's life that it forms the chief ambition of individual efforts, then the factors that constitute military strength fall away.

The only poverty from which a nation suffers in war is poverty resulting from the excesses of opulence.

Only so long as national wealth remains entirely subordinate to public honors and aspirations can it be utilized to increase the greatness of a nation; and only so long as the chivalry and virtue of a people are held aloof from it can the country be considered as either free or rich. When wealth, however, becomes the master, no words can fitly describe the poverty of the state.

The contemplation of the inutility of wealth to defend itself is not without bitterness, hence it is that man and whole nations of men shrink from the knowledge of its impotency. The sad

sophistry of commercialism points to vast cities adorned by
every accessory of luxury and art, to factories, crafts and sciences innumerable; to education, the hum of industry, millionaires, constitution and statistics as illustrative of the power and
resources of riches. How, therefore, for in such manner do
men reason, can any nation or body of men lacking in these
capabilities, these apparently illimitable potentialities of civilization and power, contemplate other than annihilation in war?

How pitiable is all this! Yet it has ever been that man wil-
fully hides, not alone from those whom they would deceive, but
from themselves, the fact that the forces of war are not identical with those of peace. What is necessary to one has nothing
to do with the other. The genius of battle has no more to do
with that of peace than have the tides of the sea to do with the
building of the sand-dunes they wash away; or lightning with
the growth of the century-old oak that it blasts forever in a
second of time.

Commercial acumen is necessary to accumulate wealth, but
that capacity possesses not the slightest ability to prevent the
destruction of its edifices or accumulations. Nay, more, wealth
so benumbs man's ability to comprehend its limitations that,
unless both combatants are simultaneously suffering from the
same green sickness of this misconception, it is self-destructive
and its riches only add to the splendor of its sarcophagus.

Who were there among the marble cities of Greece, or
within the purple empires of Darius, Egypt or India, with their
wealth, scholars, merchants, theorists, commerce and gold-
studded soldiery, that could conceive of a beardless youth
coming down from the wild highlands of Epirus, from the
bleak hillsides of Macedonia, to conquer, not one, but all of
them?

Who, in the luxurious kingdoms of Asia, feared the skin-
robed Hun; who, in Rome, dreaded the canine-toothed Goths
and Vandals whose wealth did not exceed the skins that clothed
them or the spear-heads and swords in their hands; whose
revenues were no more than the leaves of forest trees, the thunder of heaven, the flints of earth?

Who, some thirteen centuries ago, could surmise that a melancholy epileptic would find in the rocks and sands and wandering tribes of Arabia a force to grind into small dust the most powerful empires in the world; and from India to France destroy governments, alter laws, customs and religions? Yet these things happened, and the fragile edifices of wealth crumbled in a day, and through his roaring funnel balance sheets of trade vanished like so much waste paper.

Who, in the fabulously rich empires of China, India, Persia and the whole Asian world, as well as that of Europe, contemplated the issuance of the Scourge of God from the semi-mythical depths of Tartary? Yet this also came about one sombre day when, on the desolate banks of the Orkhan, Genghis gathered together his cow-tail banners from the nine desolate wastes of Shamo and swooped down upon the world. His numbers were fewer than the cities he razed; while his revenues were but his genius, his horsemen's valor and the milk of his desert mares.

A century ago, Europe watched complacently the self-devastation of France. The monarchy had been murdered; the nobility guillotined; commerce ruined; manufactures destroyed; the country-side was a tangled thicket presided over by a half-starved and tattered people. The wealth of the nation had gone up in the bonfire of the Republic. Suddenly, a little sallow man took hold of these famished people, this nation devoid of commerce, manufactures or revenues, and with its poverty conquered the whole of incredulous Europe.

Only a few years since, on some mountainous islands, a people little known fought among themselves with weapons as primitive as those of the siege of Troy. Their entire revenues were less than an American city, the cultivable land of the whole empire less than one-half the area of Illinois. Suddenly they also rose up, and, with the perennial power of poverty, in less than one decade disembowelled the two vainest and vastest empires on earth, causing the whole world to whisper in old and stale wonder at this New Sun that rose, with the suddenness of an unknown comet, out of the Eastern Sea.

In these widely separated incidents of history we perceive how futile it is to consider wealth in the remotest degree a factor of military prowess. Every age with its diversity of weapons, every sociological and ethnological phase of humanity, whether in the Orient or the Occident, past or present, proves the invariability of these conclusions. The truth of this lies in the fact that wealth, no matter how vast, can never supply a nation with what constitutes the true material of warfare. All the riches of the world cannot supply national unity nor that perseverance which is unappalled by disaster. Yet unity of action and fearlessness of purpose has never, nor ever will, be lacking in whatever resources are necessary to carry on their conquests.

In a nation ruled by opulence, men and the souls of men are not only the valets of wealth, but the nation itself is obsequious to it. The government pursues its course through a labyrinthine way: the interests of countless individuals are paramount to those of state, and national ambition ceases to exist. The commonwealth in protecting individual interests resorts to expedients that are as temporary as the lives of those who make them. Yet to these transitory acts the integrity of national greatness is sacrificed. When war falls upon such a nation it becomes disunited. In the same myriad-minded manner that it carried on the mercantile projects of peace it attempts the conduct of a war; then disintegration, disaster and destruction ensue.

On the other hand, in a military power where individuals are considered only as instruments of its greatness, the dreadful intentness of its aims knows no discouragement, the straightforwardness of its progress no hesitation, the terribleness of its energy no fatigue. Neither property nor mankind disturb its calculations. It is systematic, simple in design, relentless in prosecution. Theories of finance carry with them no awe; revenues and commerce it takes as it finds them; millionaires and economists strike no terror to its heart, for the excise and stamp duties it levies are not on material resources, but on the souls and passions and ambitions of men. These resources are exhaustless, and so long as nations conceal these facts from themselves, so long must they suffer and be vanquished and die.

VII

IN THE history and biography of national life, from remote periods to the present era, there are certain immutable elements that are characteristic of the life of political entities, regardless of their smallness or greatness, their barbarity or civilization; and while the means and manner of both the birth and dissolution of them change with every age, the formative processes are the same and the causes of deterioration identical.

In states and nations, as in all other phases of life wherein man desires to act as a reformative agent, he invariably attaches his own transitory and changeful characteristics to elemental forces, forces that are immutable to all but endless eons of time. The judgments of men are formed not from facts as they are, but as they wish them to be. They root through tons of good wheat to find three pieces of chaff, if the chaff lends weight to their belief and argument. It is not that they want others to know the truth, but to have them believe as they do. Beyond this they do not care. The conceit of man ordinarily forms his criterion of truth. His judgment is contemporaneously governed by the most trivial exteriors; a live militia general is infinitely greater than a dead Cæsar, and the dictum of a complacent bourgeois in frock-coat and top-hat is not to be gainsaid.

Elemental forces from which are derived all the acts of man are few in number and are only imperceptibly altered through long periods of time. While climatic and topographical conditions, degrees and kinds of civilization, laws, customs and innumerable other local and transitory phases of life may give infinitely varied expressions to the portrayal of these forces, the tendency of mankind is to base his judgments on the most trivial of their expressions and regard them as fundamental, though they are no more enduring than the plumage of a summer or the roosting-place of a few seasons. Nevertheless, the elemental characteristics of the human race are considered changed and the empirical knowledge of ages passes as naught.

Mankind will probably never realize how useless is his antlike diligence and labor to fill up with his formulas and ordinances the fissures of this world. Yet his conceit is such that he lays on to this task with the utmost nonchalance, as if it were the most petty of affairs. As he indifferently commanded the sun to stand awhile upon Gibeon, so again he would set nature at naught by the application of his formulas to those forces governing the rise and fall of the tides of nations, that they may be checked and tideless as the Dead Sea, and so remain through eons yet to come.

The utmost that man can do individually or nationally is to exist in obedience to the laws that govern him. To live as free as possible from pain, to better his condition and to postpone the inevitable hour of final dissolution. To exist thus, individually or as a nation, man must ceaselessly endeavor, not to thwart, but to comprehend and live in accordance with those laws that know not of him nor his vain progeny.

It is through empirical knowledge alone that man is able to ascertain what laws do or do not regulate his activities. Inventors do not invent; they only apply in a new manner laws and forces that have existed from the beginning of time. Chemists do not create; they only make known the presence of elements and conditions existent already in nature. Thus it is that sophists and theorists and all that category have not left to mankind, throughout the ages of the human race, one single substantial legacy, and for no other reason than that they try to invent out of airy nothings that which the laws and forces governing the world deny; or labor to create, out of the nebulosity of their own sick brains, elements unknown to nature. As far as the world is concerned they might as well be a louse on the back of a wild duck as it wings its way through the stormy night.

It is in relationship to these forces that govern the formation, duration, and dissolution of political entities, that International Arbitration and Disarmament are to be considered.
Not that they themselves are worth even a passing word, but
for the fact of the mischief that their illusive ideas are capable
of bringing about, especially in this Republic, where education
is so prevalent, while knowledge and capacity to discern between what is true and what is superficial is proportionately
absent. No people are so visionary and none hang more persistently onto the coat-tails of false gods as those who have
enough education to read but not enough learning to be able
to distinguish between what is false and what is true. It is on
account of the prevalency of this smattering of education in the
United States that every ism has its followers, every form of
religious dementia its sanctuary and apostles, every visionary
his devotees; and it matters in no way from what depths of
absurdity they may come up, they have their adherents. Usually these delusions are harmful only to the individual, and
as such are not worthy of concern, but when the hallucination
is apt to become so widespread as to affect the welfare of the
nation, then it is time to point out the mockery of their hopes
and the quicksands into which their aspirations have led them.
In this class of visionaries we place International Arbitrationists and Disarmamentists, who are so persistently striving
through subservient politicians, through feminism, clericalism,
sophism and other such toilers to drag this already much de-
luded Republic into that Brobdingnagian swamp from whose
deadly gases there is no escape.

It has been shown, in the fore part of this work, how irrev-
ocably national entities, in their birth, activities and death,
are controlled by the same laws that govern all life, plant,
animal or national; the Law of Struggle, the Law of Survival.
These laws, so universal as regards life and time, so unalterable in causation and consummation, are only variable in the
duration of national existence as the knowledge of and obedience to them is proportionately true or false. Plans to thwart
them, to short-cut them, to circumvent, to cozen, to deny, to
scorn and violate is folly such as man's conceit alone makes

possible. Never has this been tried—and man is ever at it—but what the end has been gangrenous and fatal.

In theory International Arbitration denies the inexorability of natural laws and would substitute for them the veriest Cagliostroic formulas, or would, with the vanity of Canute, sit down on the ocean-side of life and command the ebb and flow of its tides to cease.

The idea of International Arbitration as a substitute for natural laws that govern the existence of political entities arises not only from a denial of their fiats and an ignorance of their application, but from a total misconception of war, its causes and its meaning.

All nations experience at one time or another the same internal phases of fiery activity or a smouldering-out of it, and though no two of them may ever be subjected simultaneously to this internal rumbling and tendency to belch forth masses of mankind with their residue of scoria and trail of cinders, nevertheless war will result whenever such causative conditions occur within the body politic of a single state. The source or origin of war must always be searched for, not in disputes between states, but deep down in the bowels of one or all of them. There alone will be heard those bruised noises, political, industrial or revolutionary, sooner or later to end in that eruption of mankind called—war.

International Arbitration not only does not differentiate between the source or origin of all wars and their precipitating causes, but ever misconstrues the latter to be the sulphurous smoke of quarrels and disputes that flutter about between the crater-tops and heaven.

War is not the result of disputes *per se*. International disagreements are, on the other hand, themselves the result of the primordial conditions that sooner or later cause war. Disputes or disagreements between nations, instead of being the source or cause of war, are nothing more nor less than the first manifestations of approaching combat, or are the preliminaries thereto. To remove them by arbitration, or any other means, is at best but procrastination.

The possibility of settling international disputes is propor-

tionately great or small as is distant or at hand the hour for
ushering in a successive period of national expansion on the
part of one or the other nation: a crisis or crucial moment in
their evolution such as is marked by war. Sometimes disputes
may arise when the time of war is so far away that they hardly
cause a passing notice and give no thought to the need of arbitration. At other times disputes between two or more powers
may take place so near the outbreak of war that they merge
imperceptibly into that inevitable hour when it is declared—
hence, in history, are considered the cause of it.

The sources of war are basic, not ephemeral. They are not
the passing of cyclonic storms of human passion, but are the
ever-recurring manifestations, violent as they may appear to
be, of national evolution. They mark, in the life of political
entities, the successive periods of their greatness or vicissitudes.

Nations in their nature are transitory; the laws that govern
them everlasting. What laws man wishes for his own regula-
tion he may change and shift from day to day as he pleases;
but to those decrees issuing from nature, illimitable and eternal, he must bow down. The laws of man are only the expedients of a day, illusive, fleeting, transitory; those of nature
predetermined, imperishable. Yet International Arbitration
means nothing more nor less than the reversal of these conditions: the substitution of the ephemeral for the everlasting and
the erratic phantasms of human hope for the majestic grandeur of unchangeable law.

International Arbitration deals, and only can deal, with effects or causes of war. It can never touch, even remotely, the
primordial elements that bring it about. Hence it is that International Arbitration is only brought into action when the results of the causes of war are being felt by the nations
involved. Disputes may take place between two nations, but
not be derivable from those inherent causes that terminate in
warfare, and will, as is customary, with much smoke and noise
pass away of their own accord.

It is upon these ephemeral controversies that International
Arbitration bases the premises of its *raison d'être* and its

policy of universal quietude by unrestricted loquacity. With quixotic valor they lay on most industriously, and charge not windmills, nay, only the terrifying shadows that thresh themselves about upon earth.

If we admit the cause of warfare to be the result—as Arbitrationists wish us to believe—of the secondary effects of elementary conditions, and concede the events that usher in a war, or occur just prior to its commencement, to be the cause thereof, then we find that International Arbitration is involved in even greater impossibilities. Investigation shows that whenever two nations have become engaged in warfare they have been for decades, and perhaps centuries, advancing on converging lines of self-interest and aggrandizement. When the contact takes place, the struggle for supremacy, or even survival, is at hand. As these lines approach one another, difficulties due to increasing proximity of interests arise between the countries and result in disagreements, the seriousness and frequency of which stand in inverse ratio to the distance at which they take place from the point of contact. When these lines meet, war ensues. This inevitable hour is approximately fixed and determined by the angles of convergence plus the sum of the relative speed by which the nations are moving along their respective lines. Thus it is that, when the angle of convergence of both or even one of the nations is acute and the speed or progress along one or both of the converging lines correspondingly great, war results in a few years or decades. If, on the other hand, the angles of convergence are obtuse and the speed correspondingly slow, centuries may pass before the nations are involved in a struggle for domination or survival.

No two nations or tribes of men move on parallel lines, though they may for centuries have the appearance of so doing. Circumstances and conditions, changing from age to age, or from decade to decade, alter imperceptibly the angle of the line and accelerate or retard the speed of the advancing power. When a nation enters into a decadent state and ceases to advance along any line, but in deterioration recedes along the line it has formerly traversed, the convergence of surrounding nations at once becomes acute and their speed accelerated proportionately and in direct ratio to the increasing defencelessness of the decadent country.

As these converging lines of advancement have their beginnings in the body-politic of a single state, so within the body-politic of the nation itself is determined the angle of convergence and their rate of speed. The people, their wants and their needs, the various phases of their internal political economy or decay, the ascendency of militancy or commercialism, the centralization or decentralization of their government, as well as innumerable other factors, determine these angles' convergence and the speed by which nations thunder or creep toward the goal of their ideals and the summit of their greatness.

Arbitration, to do away with war, must prevent the contact of these converging lines along which all nations ever have and ever will continue to move. Shall they, then, with their colossal lever—not unlike the hypothetical lever of Archimedes—pry these lines of national advancement into a state of parallelism by placing their fulcrum at the angle of their source or not far distant from the point of contact, somewhere in fact between the first embroilment and the final outburst that culminates in war? Arbitration, denying the elementary origin and purpose of combat, declares that its prevention can take place at the latter point and always in the angle of contact. With their great lever they would, at the last moment, prevent these lines from meeting, and by no other means than attempting the cessation of extraneous disagreements and international troubles that the proximity of converging national interests bring about.

It is apparent that even if it were possible to pry apart or block the converging paths of national interests, such success would be less than temporary, and not more than procrastination. By settling disputes—in themselves more or less trivial—that arise between states and increase in intensity and frequency as nations draw toward a common point, they do not stop the advance of a nation nor their evolution, nor have they anything to do with the *raison d'être* of national progress.

War is but a composite exemplification of the struggle of man upward: the multiplication of his individual efforts into one, and the aspirations of his diurnal strife turned toward a greater and nobler end, not of himself but of his race. War cannot be averted by mollifying those extraneous embroilments that take place as nations in their advancement converge upon a common objective—an objective that is necessary to the future growth of both of them or to the duration of their existence as a dominant political entity. This objective may be political, geographical, commercial or ethical; but, whatever it is, once its acquisition or control is deemed necessary by more than one nation, then do they converge upon it, and those international disagreements that eventually take place are only the manifestations of the approach of their conflicting interests. But so vain is man and so blind is he in his vanity that he refuses to believe, until it is too late, that these disputes are the premonitory growls of an approaching struggle.

So it has been left to this age and to arbitration to discover that it is only necessary to mollify these growls. It does not matter if the causes that give vent to them continue to exist, and the fangs that are wetted and drooling with human passion draw nearer. The growls have been stilled, and signboards admonishing peace have been tacked up along the roads of nations!

Yet we are unable to deny this primitive and eminently self-satisfying philosophy of arbitration. It is based on the credulous timidity of man, which causes him to tremble more at thunder than lightning; more at the smoke as it rolls out of the windows than the fire; more at the fall of volcanic dust that obscures the heavens than the molten lava seething within the crater. If these resultant terrors can be done away with, even though it is temporary, mankind should not be troubled at the causes thereof and burrow down into the cavernous depths where they abide.

We do not dispute these things, for we recognize only too well that the labors of arbitration are but human and inspired by human hope. They are the expedients of a single day. Temporarily, they care naught for laws that are changeless and which are in no manner cognizant of them. Transitory and fleeting, momentary and full of faith, they do not seek to comprehend in any manner the immutable.

Nevertheless, paradoxical as it may appear, while man cannot arbitrate peace into the world, he can lengthen the periods of peace by preparation for war: by recognizing and acting in accordance with those invariable laws that govern not a portion of the human race, but the whole of it; not applicable only for yesterday and to-day, but for all time, forever unto the end; by being cognizant of the fact that the control of such laws over nations differs from that over individuals and even lower forms of animal life only in duration of time and manner of application.

Arbitration denies, however, the orderly sequence that follows and is part of the application of natural laws. Besides being vain even beyond the vanity of man, it is arbitrary in due proportion as the name implies. Not only would it substitute its dictum for laws not of man's making, but would controvert the application of laws man himself has been forced to make and uphold and recognize the necessity of their enforcement.

Arbitration is a denial of the application of dynamic force in the control of human affairs as they stand in relation to one another internationally: that whenever those difficulties—mentioned herein as rising out of the increasing proximation of their several interests—shall be settled by formula, then the final outburst, resulting from a direct contact of these converging lines, may be settled in a similar manner. In failing to comprehend that the origin of war is in the evolution of a political entity, and not the result of it, Arbitrationists fail to differentiate between the disputes and disagreements that take place afar from the point of contact and near to it. They fail to understand that in a republic, or in any government where the popular voice is listened to, the nearer these disputes take place to the point of contact the less do they come within the sphere and control of statesmen, and the less are they subject to reason, either in the abstract or in the practical. When these disputes arise within the acute angle of convergence they take on a new phase wherein all the passions that actuate individuals in stress or anger dominate the actions of the state.

The morality of any nation whose people have electoral rights is no greater than the morality of its people. No republic can be free from any of the motives, passions, ambitions, hate or delinquencies to which the majority of its people are subject. And the ability to substitute arbitration without the use of dynamic force in dealing with international affairs must first be substituted in the nation itself for all laws whose enforcement depends upon might.

Whenever the time comes that nations are not obliged to enforce their own laws with a power superior to that of individuals and communities, then and then only can they hope to substitute International Arbitration for the power of armies. But from whence and when will that devoutly wished-for day come wherein states may discard the use of power in enforcing justice and in exacting obedience to their laws? When will that Golden Age be ushered in upon this unhappy earth, and arbitration between individuals substituted for law and dynamic force in which it originates and ends? When will laws made by man for the government of man, together with his courts, his penal institutions, be put aside and voluntary arbitration between man and man take their place?

Only when arbitration is able to unravel the tangled skein of crime and hypocrisy among individuals can it be extended to communities and nations. Thence will International Arbitration come of its own accord as the natural outgrowth of national evolution through the individual. As nations are only man in the aggregate, they are the aggregate of his crimes and deception and depravity, and so long as these constitute the basis of individual impulse, so long will they control the acts of nations.

When, therefore, the merchant arbitrates with the customer he is about to cheat; when trusts arbitrate with the people they are about to fleece; when the bulls and bears arbitrate with the lambs they are about to shear; when the thief arbitrates with the man he is about to rob, or the murderer with his victim, and so on throughout the category of crime, then will communities be able to dispense with laws, and international thievery and deception, shearing and murder, resort to arbitration. But crimes of individuals—hence nations—stand in inverse ratio to the power of the state to enforce law. Thus in 1906 in the United States there were one hundred and eighteen murders to each million of population; in England less than nine, in Germany less than five.

All law presupposes the exercise of force in its execution; hence we find that crime increases proportionately as this power deteriorates.

So completely do Arbitrationists misconstrue the application of force by a nation in dealing with other states that they do not differentiate between the means and the power itself.

VIII

IT IS strange a belief should prevail that standing armies are a menace to the world's quietude, while it has only been due to the formation of permanent military forces that intervals of peace have been lengthened. This misconception of modern peace is responsible for the theory of national disarmament.

To attribute to the utensils of combat the cause of war is the same as saying that man is not responsible for his good deeds nor guilty of his crimes; that he has no self-initiative and is only the will-less creature of some inanimate instruments that happen to be in his possession.

Modern civilization began with the invention of gunpowder. As these black grains were scattered about, not other than as tiny acorns over the earth, there sprang up oaks of national strength in the form of armaments under which, protected from the vicissitudes and storms that previously assailed national life as well as individual existence, the arts and sciences of mankind flourished.

Prior to the introduction of gunpowder into Europe no large standing armies existed and no practical peace. All men were considered soldiers, and, excepting the priesthood, held themselves ready at all times to respond to their leaders' call. Instead of a small fraction of the male population being on war footing, the whole nation was so constituted; instead of being the profession of a few men, it was the business of them all. Each possessed weapons inexpensive and requiring little or no skill in their use, so that not only were they ready for combat at any time, but so long as military duties were shared by all, instead of by a small portion of the nation, the avocations of peace were of secondary importance and that of war primary, not to a few, but to the entire population.

No continuity marked the pursuit of peaceful industry, for men were, at all times, liable to be dragged away from their occupations to that of war. There was no certainty in the duration of their labors, no stability nor permanence nor incentive. Consequently nations could not develop their resources, or the skill or the intellectuality of their people, or the arts and sciences that come of them.

The invention of gunpowder weapons for its use necessitated the organization by the state of permanent armies, since the weapons required were not only too expensive for the people to purchase individually, but their use demanded a skill that was not only the result of personal knowledge, but collective training. When, therefore, nations were obliged to provide weapons for their troops and to assemble them together for training, they created a separate institution. No longer could they assemble raw levies at a day's notice and hurry them into combat. The entire people, except those especially employed in the profession of arms, now turned their attention to the occupations of peace with the assurance that there was ever ready a fraction of the population especially trained for their protection. Industries and the products of their skill and genius now thrived with new vigor. Diligently they went about their work, no longer perturbed with the thought of being dragged out in the middle of the night or from their half-completed labor to march and fight and starve or to die from the innumerable diseases that afflicted their unorganized hordes. Once again orderly civilization and progress came to man.

So, in due time, all nations changed, and most happily, from a condition of disarmament and national militia to armament and conscription. Forever and gladly should they pay the expense of it, for the returns are the civilization and advancement of mankind. Only by such means can men pursue with continuity and cumulative returns industries that bring them not only wealth, but happiness and wisdom, individually and collectively, over and above all that which they are called upon to pay.

In the history of nations it will be found that the growth of their higher civilization is subsequent to the utilization of permanent armaments, a complete segregation of the militant forces from the industrial.

Disarmament of standing armies means the armament of the whole nation. Instead of training to a high degree of efficiency an insignificant fraction of the people to protect the whole, the entire male population is called upon to defend no greater interests. The number of men required to undertake successfully any military enterprise stands in inverse ratio to the skill and efficiency of their training. A most insignificant people can, by a high degree of military capacity, force the entire male population of a vast non-militant country into the field and then destroy them.

Means of self-protection, advancement in all phases of life, or domination are comparative. So in nations, armaments are great or small, effective or worthless as they stand in relation to the armaments of other states with whom their interests come in contact.

The first introduction of gunpowder caused a complete segregation of the military forces from ordinary civil life and necessitated standing armies, but, as the manufacture of these new weapons grew apace, they became cheaper, commoner, and eventually found their way into each household. For a considerable period there again existed very little difference between weapons of chase and warfare, so that, especially in new countries where the struggle against aborigines and wild beasts was constant, there was a return, in a certain degree, to that state of universal militarism or dependence upon the entire male population to carry on war, instead of standing armaments proportionate to the need of the time.

The Napoleonic wars were followed by two phases of national activity that lengthened the periods of peace between nations and reduced the number of wars. First, the introduction by Schornhorst of conscription in times of peace. Second, the absorption and unification into large political entities of smaller states, as the unification of Germany, Italy, and the Austrian Empire; the supremacy of the Federal power in the United States; and the absorption into the British Empire of innumerable petty potentates and decadent principalities.

The amalgamation of small states into great political entities is the reason for the diminution in number and frequency of wars, a lessening of international conflict that has nothing to do with the so-called increasing morality of man. International wars can only be proportionate to the number of separate political entities into which mankind is divided. As this absorption goes on by the might of the strongest state, so wars, while concurrent with this unification, will in the end diminish. Therefore, as nations grow less in number the greater must be their armaments. Wars will diminish numerically, but the effects will be proportionately greater.

Modern science has, with its inventions, brought about another cycle in warfare, new as regards means, but not in cause and effect. The invention of modern military instruments and mechanical contrivances has produced the same condition, in relation to the nation as a whole, as existed some hundreds of years ago just subsequent to the invention of gunpowder— i.e., a complete segregation of the military from civil life, doing away with militarism, its dangers and evils.

As the single introduction of gunpowder into warfare caused nations to establish permanent forces of men trained in its uses, so each new science, as it is introduced into war, requires more and more special training on the part of officers and men in the army. The more science enters into warfare, the more perfect must be the training of the men who handle the machine of combat—the army.

Therefore, it will be found that in proportion to the complexity of the sciences and mechanical inventions employed in war, the longer and more perfect must be the training and construction of national armaments. So, instead of the disarmament of nations becoming possible through increased civilization, it becomes more and more impossible as science increases the number of inventions, not only of those appertaining directly to war, but in all other phases of human activity. To the science of war belongs, or is utilized in one way or another, every science and invention of mankind. It is the utilization of them for the purpose of war that will constitute the strength of nations in the future. Therefore, armies must have long and minute training in those sciences that are in warfare interdependent. They must act harmoniously or the result will be a chaotic condition wherein the ignorant application of a single part will cause the inefficiency of the whole. This knowledge can be acquired by the nation in but one way—the unification of the sciences appertaining to war and by a knowledge of their practical application. It, therefore, can be considered an axiom, that as the complexity of science and mechanical invention increases and enters more fully into the conduct of war, the less difference which exists between the peace and war armaments of a nation, the greater will be its chances of success.

Science to-day has reached that point in the conduct of war wherein the use of volunteers or militia as against regular troops has become impossible. And the time is not far distant when nations will be forced to increase the size of their standing armies, constituting them only of long-serviced men, and do away with those ex-regular, short-serviced troops that now constitute their reserves.

The use by a nation of reserves against regular troops in the future will only end in defeat, the dangers of which increase proportionately each year, while the use of volunteers and militia drawn from civil life means complete annihilation to whatever nation attempts their use.

As the weakest link in a chain determines the strength of the chain, so the efficiency and size of the armament of a single great power determines the proportionate size and efficiency of all other nations, according to the part they do or expect to play in the affairs of the world. Thus, to urge the reduction of the armament of one's country while that of other powers increases or remains stationary, invites the destruction of the government and the subordination of the fatherland. The need of armaments must not only be proportionate to the importance of the state in the comity of nations and increase proportionately, but the difference between the peace and war footing must diminish as civilization with its science and inventions progresses. The demands of the future will be, not for less but for greater armament in all dominant powers.

It has been shown in the earlier part of this work how man's inventive genius in the means of transportation and communication has reduced the size of the world to less than the size of the United States two generations ago. No longer, therefore, can nations consider themselves safe behind their moats of space. The peoples of the whole world are now elbowed together with all their racial antipathies and convergent ambitions to struggle and war in a theatre of action no greater than that in which European nations only a few years ago sweated and strove for supremacy. On the one hand, while the causes of war have diminished by the elimination and unification of innumerable smaller nations, on the other the shrinkage of the world by man's inventions has brought the remaining nations, different not only in race, but in civilization, ideals and purposes, so closely together and with so little hope of amalgamation that we cannot say that the possibilities of war have in the sum total decreased. The peace of the future must be, as in the past, an armed peace.

There is one element we have not yet considered in relation to disarmament, *viz.*, the so-called economic—the eventual impoverishment of nations by the burden of armament and diversion of a large proportion of the population into the class of non-producers.

It seems most pitiable that men will, in their fruitless endeavor to find support for their arguments, reduce the sublime to the ridiculous, so that by getting it down to their level they can better demolish that which, in its original form, is beyond them. In this manner of attack calculators excel all others. They have succeeded in reducing the evolution of nations to dollars and cents; the sum totals of which are cataclysms or utopias according to the object they have in view. Thus these economists, piling up the figures of yearly budgets, crying abroad that nations are impoverishing themselves by the burden of their armaments, would have us regard a nation in the same light as a spendthrift individual who scatters his wealth until poverty is upon him.

It was thought many years ago that Adam Smith had put an effective quietus on this kind of reasoning, though evidently it will not down, but, not unlike Banquo's ghost, seems doomed to haunt a certain species of pretenders even unto the end.

The truth is, if the amount of money expended by a nation on its army were increased a thousandfold, the wealth of the nation would not be diminished one iota, nor would it be impoverished one cent. Budgets are but the sums total of the symbols of wealth. Whether they are great or small, the wealth of the nation varies not one potato. An individual measures his wealth by coinage, but a nation only by that which coinage represents. As a man squanders his money, he becomes impoverished; but it is only when the resources and means of producing that which money represents is destroyed or diminished that the wealth of a nation is lessened. The armament of a nation, instead of being indicative of its impoverishment, is rather an indication of its capacity. In a single soldier is represented the various gradations of its wealth; instead of being prophetic of its destruction, he stands in no other relation than its protector.

The wealth of a nation, what it produces, is dependent on the natural resources of its territorial possessions, on the intelligence of its people, the means they employ, and, lastly, the size of the population. Thus the wealth of France with thirty-eight million people is infinitely greater than that of India with two hundred million.

It is in consideration of these facts, wherein the statement that national armaments impoverish nations by withdrawing a large number of men from its productive energy, becomes preposterous. Under the ordinary definition given by Disarmamentists two-thirds of the world's population can be classed as non-producers.

The German Empire possesses the greatest armament of any nation proportionate to its population; yet the entire army —considered as non-producers—consists of only 1.17 per cent. of the population, the other 98.83 per cent. carrying on their customary vocations. While 1.17 per cent. of Germany's population is in military service, man's inventive genius during the last generation has increased the productive energy of the remaining portion of the population more than a thousand per cent. It is on account of this increasing productivity of man, due to the use of mechanical inventions, that nations will suffer in the future, not from under but over developed industrialism.

The law of diminishing returns applies only to the natural resources of the territorial possessions of a nation. These possessions are great or small, permanent or temporary, capable of systematic exploitation or a surface rummaging, in ratio to the strength or weakness of the nation. On the other hand, the law of productive energy increases in geometrical ratio to the increase of civilization. The task in the future will not be to find men to exploit the natural resources of a country, but natural resources for the utilization of their inventions and labor-saving devices. The number of men a state can withdraw from productive occupations is proportionate to the intelligence of the remainder in their utilization of mechanical inventions and the diminishing of natural resources.

A law of national progress might be stated as follows: A nation, in order to preserve an equilibrium between over-industrial production and under-political development, should withdraw from industrial occupations for military purposes a proportion of the male population that is (1) not greater than what labor-saving inventions can, by being substituted therefor, more than replace the productive energy lost by the withdrawal of men from industrial production; (2) the number of men so withdrawn not to be more nor less than that number which is deemed imperative to acquire or to hold whatever additional natural resources are necessary for the increasing productive energy of the nation.

In other words, while the productive energy of a nation increases in geometrical ratio to the increase of civilization, the resources of the country diminish in inverse ratio to the increase of both population and productive energy. So the nation destined to survive above all others and to absorb them will be the sovereign country that maintains this equilibrium. Natural resources, therefore, that come with territorial possessions are to be in the future the first requisite of national greatness.

In the first portion of this work is enunciated the law that the boundaries of nations are never, other than momentarily, at rest; and that there are two phases to this state of agitation, expansion or shrinkage. Expansion of a nation's boundaries is indicative, not only of its external growth, but of the virility of its internal constitution; the shrinkage of its boundaries, the external exemplification of its internal decay. Both growth and decay have their origin, not along the rims of national boundaries, but within the very heart of the state itself, and are governed by those laws to which we have just given expression. These laws are not and could not be new, for they are of man and are as old as the rise and fall of the first nations. Modern conditions of life can in no manner affect them. The primitiveness of this truth and its material proof is the rise of the German and Japanese empires. A few decades ago Japan was almost a myth and the German Empire only a geographical possibility. To-day they are considered equal, and in many respects superior, in strength and greatness to the other powers of the world, and for no other reason than that they have not become top-heavy with industrialism, but have, from Bismarck's time until the present, recognized the immutability of these laws and have maintained and are continually preparing to maintain in the future the equilibrium between their industrial expansion and political development. Should Germany on the one hand and Japan on the other continue to adhere rigorously to these laws, resisting the deteriorating influence of industrialism, feminism, and political quackery, they will, in due time, by the erosive action of these elements on other nations, divide the world between them.

Economic disarmamentists propose that all nations mutually exploit the resources of the world in harmonious and equal division, for by so doing armies would be disposed of and more men added to the productive energy of mankind. We have heretofore shown the impossibility of this proposal in that political entities are not other than collections of individuals, and their governments only the expression of their ideals. Changes in government for good or bad originate in the people. What the people are, so is the state, together with all their passions, wants, hates and struggles; and whatever their ideals are, they are exemplified in the conduct of the government. When, therefore, individuals voluntarily do away with ideas of possession, so that complete socialism and harmonious anarchy prevail, then only will it be possible for such ideals to be extended to the conduct of international affairs so that the nations of the world may dwell peacefully and happily together in a condition of international communism.

IX

THE military preparation of a nation must be determined by its relationship to the balance of the world geographically, politically and racially. If the United States were geographically situated in a sphere of its own, removed from the pathway of foreign expansion and economic interests, its foreign policy non-assertive and ductile to the demands of other nations, the attitude of the populace politically and sociologically so constituted that they would not involve the government in disputes and entanglements with the people of other powers, then armies and navies for the Republic might be dispensed with. Otherwise, its armament and military preparation must be proportionately as great as the above hypotheses are categorically untrue.

Geographically, the territorial possessions of a nation are provocative of war when they possess a positive valuation to other nations under three separate heads—commercial, strategic and racial.

The territorial dominions of the United States are not only those possessions governed by its laws, but that vast region of Mexico, the West Indies, Central and South America, which, as far as being causative of war, are as much under the political sovereignty of the United States as are the states of the Union. The preservation of the Constitution is not more vital than the inviolability of the Monroe Doctrine.

It is, however, necessary in considering these questions not to regard the world in the old sense of distance by area or miles, but only in the modern sense of distance by time. Not many years ago it took six months to cross from New York to California; at present it requires four days; consequently, to the people in all their practical activities the size of the United

States is less than one-fortieth what it was fifty years ago. The world, on account of modern means of communication, is more compact, as far as the intercourse and conflict of man is concerned, than were the dominions of Cæsar or the kingdoms over which Napoleon cast his shadow.

The possessions of the United States, therefore, owing to this shrinkage of the world, concern the great powers geographically, strategically and politically in as vital a sense as did those territories concern Cæsar that finally constituted his dominions, or the kingdoms of Europe that made up Napoleon's empires, or the states that constitute this Union; hence, we must consider them in such light and in no manner removed from their spheres of activity, whether it is commercial, political or military.

Europe, having within its borders the greatest nations of the world and nearly a quarter of its population, consists of less than one-twelfth of the world's land. Japan, greater in population than the United Kingdom, possesses only one-two-hundred-and-fiftieth part of the earth's surface; while the suzerainty of the United States extends over one-fourth.

Of the world's territory that comes under the political jurisdiction of the Republic, two-thirds is covered by Mexico, Central and South America, capable of supporting three times as many empires as now divide Europe. This vast and fabulously rich continent, practically uninhabited, lies midway between Europe and Asia and is less distant from Europe than Poland was from France at the beginning of the nineteenth century, while the people of Japan and China can reach its western seaboard in less time than it took travellers not many years ago to pass from Prussia to Portugal.

In, however, considering the exploitation of the Western Hemisphere by the crowded populations overflowing from Europe on the East and Asia on the West, innumerable modern factors not only hasten but increase beyond computation the need by nations of virgin territory. Not only is the knowledge of the wealth of every portion of the world now common to all of mankind through the rapidity and universality of intercommunication, but improvements in the arts and sciences extend more or less over the entire world, resulting in a com· mon demand by all nations for the primitive materials that enter into the fabrication of modern arts and sciences.

Accompanying the augmented needs of civilized man for the almost limitless necessities and luxuries that modern science has created, but have nevertheless their origin in natural resources, is the demand for unexploited territory. This is not in proportion to the increase of the population, but is due to that intense cumulative demand brought about by science and invention, both in consumption and in the means of exploitation. Formerly, the increased production of necessities and luxuries was dependent more directly upon the increase of population. That condition no longer exists. The increase of production due to increase of population is insignificant when compared to that due to science and invention. The very machines that the ingenuity of man has contrived have become in themselves monstrous consumers. The inanimate has been given teeth and bowels and a hunger that knoweth not satiety. Man, in order to meet this ever-increasing thousandfold-by-day consumption of the world's resources, has turned to science and invention to improve the efficiency and augment the capacity of exploitation.

While, therefore, the resources of the world are governed in their exploitation by the law of diminishing returns, and the population of mankind goes on increasing by the law of nature, there is no law of nature nor of man that regulates the increase and consumption of the devouring, tireless machines by which man now furrows and devastates the earth in quest of those things that whole nations to-day and to-morrow demand. There is no end to this universal thievery, and the earth continues to be rooted and drilled and sucked. Day is not time enough, and night glares and resounds with monstrous throbbing. Pathways of cinders mark its surface and mountains of tailings rise upon it. Man and nations of men go on struggling even more madly and deliriously to gain new lands whither their engines may whistle and scream in Frankenstein delight as they claw and rend and prod the virgin earth.

How unreasonable is it, therefore, to expect that the combined nations of Europe, with all their military strength, shall remain restricted to one-twelfth of this world's land, burrowed into and hewn over for the last thousand years, while this Republic, without armies, shall maintain dominion over one-half the unexploited lands of the world! Or that Japan, possessed of two-thirds the population of this nation and a military organization fifty-fold greater, shall continue to exist on her rocky isles that are, inclusive of Korea, but one-two-hundred-and-fiftieth of the earth's lands, while an undefended one-half lies under the guns of her battleships!

What prevents the occupation of this vast and rich continent by powers having military capacity? The defensive ability of the Latin republics is, proportionately, no greater against European or future Asiatic military aggression than was the defensive capacity of the aborigines against the first European conquerors. Ordinarily, it is believed that the dictum of this Republic, the Monroe Doctrine, has been responsible for their immunity against foreign aggression. Nothing could be further from the truth.

There have been five separate causes productive of Mexican, Central and South American exemption from foreign conquest:

(1) Inadequacy of transportation and communication.
(2) Adjustment of European political conditions.
(3) Duration of the pre-inventive or non-mechanical period.
(4) A correspondingly low demand for natural resources.
(5) The seclusion of the Oriental races.

One by one we have seen these sources of immunity vanish and antithetic conditions imperceptibly take their place, increasing each year in cumulative intensity. Herein lies the inevitability of war between this Republic and European as well as Asiatic nations, or a complete repudiation of the Monroe Doctrine. In the history of mankind never before has one nation attempted to support so comprehensive a doctrine as to extend its political suzerainty over two continents comprising a fourth of the habitable earth and one-half of its unexploited wealth, in direct defiance of the whole world, and without the slightest semblance of military power, nor possessing any right to regulate the domestic or foreign policy of numerous and irresponsible political entities that simmer and sweat within two-thirds of its suzerainty.

The Monroe Doctrine is Promethean in conception, but not so in execution. It was proclaimed in order to avoid wars; now it invites them. This great statesman fully realized the inevitable conclusions of his doctrine though he could not comprehend that, in the vital hour of its need, the militant power necessary to its enforcement would all but have vanished in a quagmire of sophistry.

The Republic was at that time separated by vast oceans from European nations, across which small wooden craft struggled over their unmapped currents, and against winds that blew down from the mysterious regions of an unknown world. Had Monroe been able to foresee that science and invention would, in a few generations, bring both continents within less distance of Europe than, during his life, separated Virginia from New England, that the armies of five European nations would exceed the population of the thirteen colonies, and that beyond the Western, mystic ocean would suddenly emerge out of impenetrable mists even greater empires to struggle and war for the possessions encompassed by his proclamation, how much more insistent would he have been upon the strict and inviolable maintenance of it! How careful would he have been to command the augmentation of military force proportionate to the increasing probability of its violation.

The Monroe Doctrine, if not supported by naval and military power sufficient to enforce its observance by all nations, singly and in coalition, becomes a factor more provocative of war than any other national policy ever attempted in modern or ancient times. Yet it is given to us, in this swift-ebbing age, to witness the sad spectacle of this great national doctrine slowly but surely vanishing in a slough of national self-beguilement, an all-encompassing mud-puddle of mediocrity. Societies, religions, unions, business men and politicians, on the one hand, spare no effort to debase every militant instinct and military efficiency or preparation necessary for its enforcement, while, on the other, they demand that the Chief Executive shall assert to the entire world this Republic's intention to maintain, by the force of arms if necessary, this most warlike and encompassing policy ever enunciated by man or nation.

The Old World smiles at this childish credulity as it goes calmly on ploughing the fields of the world with its fire-breathing, brazen teams, sowing the teeth of dragons, reaping the harvest of warriors, and in due time to gain by this husbandry the golden fleece of the Western Hemisphere.

The possessions that come within the jurisdiction of the Monroe Doctrine are not, however, the only territories under the political sovereignty of this Republic that are geographically so located as to be considered provocative of war. We divide these foreign possessions into three groups: (1) the Caribbean Sea; (2) the Central Pacific; (3) the Asiatic. While these islands are not a source of war commercially, they are strategically. The value of all possessions is as much determined by the control of the intervening lines of communication as by their intrinsic wealth. The oceans, constituting seventy-three per cent. of the globe, are the main lines of trade between nations, and to the extent that these ways of commerce are controlled does a nation or group of nations, so commanding them, possess the wealth of the world. If the United States controlled the ways from Europe and Asia to this hemisphere, neither Europe nor Asia could gain possessions in North or South America. If, on the other hand, the Atlantic and Pacific are controlled by the European and Asiatic nations, respectively, then the United States is powerless not only to enforce the Monroe Doctrine, but to protect its insular possessions or the commerce of the Union.

In order for a nation or coalition of nations to gain control over lines of communication, whether on land or sea, it is first necessary to secure points of vantage; in other words, territorial possessions for strategic purposes only. Napoleon declared the intent of war to be a struggle for position. All great wars are preceded by these conflicts. The possession by a nation of highly strategic points is, unless defended beyond a question of doubt, even more provocative of war than territories sought after on account of their intrinsic wealth. The possession of strategic positions determines to a greater extent than any other factor the issue of an international conflict. Hence, there must come in due time those inevitable struggles for position which will precede all wars for conquest of the unexploited territories of the Western Hemisphere by the nations of Europe and Asia.

In the Atlantic, the future theatre of war in which to secure strategic position will be the Caribbean Sea. No one locality in or bordering on the Atlantic possesses such strategic possibilities as does the control of this sea. Whatever powers gain undisputed command over it will gain supremacy over one-half the Western Hemisphere. We divide its strategic possibilities under four heads:

(1) The command of the Panama Canal and Central America.

(2) The command of the Gulf of Mexico and the Atlantic seaboard of Mexico.

(3) The command of the Atlantic seaboard from Cape Hatteras to Key West.

(4) The command of the Atlantic seaboard of South America.

The control of the Panama Canal is the most important factor of these four divisions, since it belongs only to the nation that militarily commands its approaches; who builds it is immaterial. Should any nation expend in the same period of time an equivalent amount of money on battleships as is being expended by the United States in the canal's construction, not only would Panama become its property, but in addition all those possessions that centre and are dependent on the control of the Caribbean Sea; viz., the southern half of the Western Hemisphere.

With the exception of the Monroe Doctrine, no undertaking since the formation of this Republic is more fraught with possibilities of warfare, or calls for greater military and naval expansion than the building of the Panama Canal. Unless the United States is willing to increase the military and naval strength proportionate to the dangers that at once become existent with its completion, it is a mistake to proceed with its construction.

The Isthmian Canal, by reducing the distance from Europe to the Western seaboard of North and South America, makes probable what is now impossible—the commercial and military invasion of the Eastern Pacific by Europe. In other words, it centres the attention of the world to five hundred feet of waterway.

For a European fleet to reach San Francisco or Valparaiso via the Panama Canal, the distance is only three-eighths greater than for an American fleet steaming from New York harbor. While heretofore the Western seaboards were completely removed from the sphere of European naval activities, that condition no longer exists on the completion of the canal.

The eventual control of the Panama Canal is foretold by the history of the Suez, which, diminishing the distance between Europe and the Orient to one half, became the main channel of communication between the West and the East. Built by France, it soon passed into English possession. The control of the Suez by England resulted from her masterful position in the Mediterranean and the Red Sea—the strategic possessions of Gibraltar, Malta, Egypt and Aden. That France built the canal determined in no way its final ownership. The possessions of Gibraltar, Malta, Cyprus, Egypt and Aden, together with a navy maintained on a basis of being equal to the navies of any possible coalition, determined to whom, in time of war, the canal would belong. Great Britain not only controls, by means of it, the Oriental trade, but dominates the political relationship that Europe bears to Asia. What has brought about English commercial supremacy throughout the world has been, not alone the supremacy of the English navy, but the possession of strategic bases. The existence of a great navy is entirely dependent on the ownership of strategic positions in different quarters of the globe and maintained by force.

The Panama Canal is as important to the world as the Suez, and not less so to European nations than to the American republics. The control of it is as vital to the nation that desires to command the commercial as well as political destiny of the

Eastern Pacific as the Suez is to England in the control of Asiatic hegemony.

The Caribbean Sea corresponds to the Mediterranean, and its islands and neighboring coasts to Gibraltar, Malta, Cyprus, Crete and Egypt. In the Pacific, Hawaii corresponds to Aden. At the present time the United States, England, France, as well as the Netherlands—which in the future can be considered as German—have possessions in or adjacent to the Caribbean Sea; i.e., a basis of military expansion and control. Nations possessing territory adjacent to the canal must be considered as factors in determining its future ownership.

The United States, at the present time, is strategically superior in the Caribbean to all the rest of the world, not only on account of the adjacency of its mainland, but the possession of the Canal Zone, Puerto Rico, Cuba and Hawaii, which gives it strategic possibilities that should make it the undisputed arbiter of the Western Hemisphere. But the strategic positions now held by this Republic, completely naked of defence, have for the future only one significance—that of wars for their possession.

The command of the Caribbean Sea by a European nation would not only control the Panama Canal, the Western seaboard of North and South America, the Atlantic seaboard from Cape Hatteras to Cape Horn, but it would separate the United States from the southern continent and nullify completely the Monroe Doctrine. These are the inducements to tempt European nations, singly or in coalition, to secure command of the Caribbean Sea, which, as we look into the future, is the second most important strategic sphere on the globe.

The Pacific insular possessions of the United States are also geographically so situated that they are as necessary for the command of the Pacific as are the islands of the Caribbean Sea for the command of the southern portion of the Western Hemisphere. Whatever nation possesses them controls the Pacific, upon whose seaboard dwell one half of the human race.

The consideration of the inevitable struggle for the dominion of the Pacific we have left to the concluding chapters of this work, where, in detail, will be shown the fallacies of this nation's military system, the falsity of the glamour that surrounds it, the primitiveness of its conception, its inherent elements of deterioration and incapacity to engage in successful warfare with a great power.

X

WHILE the sources of war have their origin deep down in that primitive struggle of nations and races to survive, to conquer and be supreme, the precipitating causes of international conflicts are found generally in the unreasoning vanity, acts and passions of the diverse tribes of man, as they strive along in that old and endless struggle which is Life.

The previous chapter dealt with the sources of international strife into which this Republic will, sooner or later, be plunged. In this chapter we will consider the causes that hasten and will precipitate these wars—a consideration of the diverse peoples that come under the suzerainty of the United States.

We divide these people into two classes:

(1) The inhabitants of the nation's insular possessions and the Latin republics encompassed by the Monroe Doctrine.

(2) The heterogeneity of the electoral populace of the Union, constituting the government of the nation by and for them.

Homogeneity of race has been recognized as an invariable principle in determining the stability of national institutions. The formation and execution of national ideals are possible only as this principle remains inviolable. The theorem and corollary governing, in this relation, the condition of national existence can be stated as follows:

(1) The vitality of national life, being dependent upon the harmony of its component parts, is capable of resisting temporal erosion in proportion to its racial homogeneity.

(2) The deterioration of a political entity, subject to the diversity of its constituent elements, is slow or rapid

in proportion to the fractional facets of its racial heterogeneity.

To these laws, in the past, there has been no variation, and that modification due to greater assimilativeness on account of the universality and rapidity of intercommunication is so remote that it cannot be considered; for at the present time it acts only in the closer cementation of peoples of common ancestry, and defines even more sharply the lines between races.

When a nation is composed of different peoples, its comparative stability can be said to be great or fragile as its government is in the hands of one dominant race or is diffused proportionately through the various racial and political elements that compose it.

Political history shows us again that only so long as the political and military power of a heterogeneous nation remains in the hands of a single element does it endure. As this power gradually slips away on account of the deterioration of the dominant race and becomes diffused throughout the nation, political dissension and territorial disintegration begins. Anciently, this was true of the Chaldean, Egyptian, Persian, Indian, Macedonian, Roman, the Mongol empires, and all other nations composed of variant racial elements. At the present time similar conditions are existent in a number of great nations scattered abroad over the world. The true significance of the break-up of the Chinese Empire is not other than the final passage of the Manchus and a natural reversion of the empire, if not destroyed in the dissolution of the dominant race, to the control of a single homogeneous people. For three centuries the Manchus have maintained themselves by retaining all political and military power over the entire Chinese race. This they are now about to abdicate, and, with the relinquishment of their political prerogatives heretofore guarded so zealously, the empire will pass over into the keeping of a more virile people. Soon shall the world witness their melancholy, and perhaps tragic, exit from the Palace of the Dragon and their vanishing through the sombre portals of the half-shadowed tombs that await them in the Valley of Liaoho.

In the racial dissimilarity of the Austrian and Turkish

empires are to be found similar sources of political weakness and eventual dissolution. In Russia the ruling and racially homogeneous portions of the empire, having lost their auto‹ cratic rights, the nation is being given over to a babble of ele‹ ments struggling for political supremacy, and the Russian policy of world-empire has, for the time being, come to an end.

The Marquis of Salisbury, in a few words, enunciated the future of the British Empire;

"There have been great colonial and maritime powers, four or five, but they have always fallen. . . . If we ever allow our defences at sea to fall to such a point of inefficiency that it is as easy, or nearly as easy, to cross the sea as it is to cross a land frontier, our great empire, stretching to the ends of the earth, supported by maritime force in every part of it, will come clattering to the ground when a blow at the metropolis of England is struck."

In other words, when the power of the British Empire ceases to emanate in all its absolutism from the gloom of a London street, then will it and all its greatness fall away.

Under the wide, fitful shadow of the American flag is found a heterogeneity of mankind racially, politically, religiously and geographically more divergent than has heretofore ever come under the political jurisdiction of a single nation; and in the sense of being provocative of war, a source of turmoil and struggle, there has seldom existed one more resonant with the alarums of future combat.

It is not always necessary to consider the racial elements involved, for that sinks into comparative insignificance when the political looseness governing this heterogeneity of mankind is considered; the vast geographical area over which a portion of these elements, as distinct racial and political entities, are scattered; the manner in which they have come to be subordinate or subject to the decrees of the Republic; or that other heterogeneity, through which, by the electoral franchise, is diffused the political and military integrity of this nation.

In considering the people of the insular possessions of the United States as causative of war, they must be so regarded in three different lights :

(1) The manner of their subordination; whether voluntary or due to the physical might of this Republic.

(2) Their racial character; whether it is similar to and assimilative by the people of the United States, or whether it is similar to and assimilative by a power other than this nation.

(3) The geographical location of these racially different possessions as regards their worth to other powers.

The Philippines, Puerto Rico, and in a sense Cuba, can be considered as conquered nations over whom the sovereignty of this Republic was extended in principle no different from that of Spain. The inhabitants of these countries opposed by force the dominion of Spain, and sacrificed thousands of their people that they in the end might become politically independent states. The spirit that actuated their struggles against Spain has not been lessened by a transfer of dominion. As, in the Philippines, each family paid its toll of blood to Spanish dominion, so have they to American conquest. The heroisms of the Spanish War, and the tales of valor such as speed from threshold to threshold, have now been replaced by those newer acts of self-sacrifice that tell of combats with the soldiery of this Republic.

While time mollifies the spirit of conquerors or erodes it into small dust, the spirit—which is hate—of the conquered endures on, apparently without end. As the inhabitants of these islands, both in the East and West, were continually in revolt against Spanish domination, so will they be against this nation whenever the military power over them is withdrawn or deteriorates. Moreover, by education, the United States is increasing the comprehension of their subjugation and combative ability. Nothing is more erroneous than the belief that patriotism to an alien conqueror is evolved out of general education. The education of the masses, under such conditions, only develops and gives expression to instincts and propensities already existent. Not unlike Pandora's box does it open to the hungry nature of conquered man new diseases of vanity, new epidemics of unrest, new fevers of ambition.

As these peoples forced Spain into war with the United

States to gain their ends, they will not hesitate to involve this nation in war, if by so doing its military efficiency will be destroyed or crippled to the extent of making possible a successful war of independence, the right of which this country must concede, since it owes its own origin as a sovereign state to such procedure.

That hatred of Americans exists in these islands is disputed by none but politicians. The expenditures of the United States to improve the education of the people and the administration of the government have in no way diminished the spirit of revolt. Whatever wounds have been closed have been by scarification. The hatred of the conquered is the most enduring of all human passions, and it must never be forgotten by a conquering nation that, whatever they get by force, by force they must continue to hold.

The impossibility of the American people assimilating the inhabitants of these foreign possessions is apparent.

(1) Distinct racial differences.

(2) The number of Americans who will live permanently in the possessions will be so insignificant that their presence racially will have no effect upon the inhabitants. But on the other hand, they, being numerically so inferior and unfitted by nature to withstand the erosive action of the climatic conditions, will soon vanish in the gloom of tropic depths, whither the marsh-lights of their fancied superiority led and abandoned them.

Assimilation of races is governed by the same natural law that determines the assimilation of all forms of animal life. The characteristics belonging to a race numerically predominant and physically fittest to the environment will dominate completely a race alien to the land and climate and numerically inferior.

The government of foreign possessions and conquered lands is an old task of mankind, and the empirical knowledge concerning it, co-extensive with antiquity, permits us to form more or less positive conclusions as to the means that make it possible or circumscribe the bounds beyond which the ambitions of man must not go. Knowledge gained through the devastation of so many lands and the going down of so many great empires should determine the policy of the United States in its relationship to that vast one-fourth of the world over which it has tossed with careless boldness the thirteen folds of its flag.

However confident one may feel of a greater future for this Imperial Republic, it is only possible to believe in its triumphs if it prepares for them; if not, then must one look forward to the washing-away of all that was destined to be great in it.

The difference between the political heterogeneity of empires and that of population is as wide as is their capacity to provoke war and their incapacity to wage it. A nation that is made up of various minor peoples of distinct racial characteristics is exposed to the probabilities of war in proportion to the number of nationalities that, constituting its suzerainty, possess political franchise and voice in its government. Nevertheless, such a nation might endure indefinitely, provided that the military forces are always proportionate to the possibilities of war, and the governmental and military powers securely held within the hands of a homogeneous people. When, however, the exercise of government and the command of national resources passes into the control of heterogeneous elements, the possibilities of national dissolution are correspondingly increased.

There are, within maritime countries, two latent elements of decay: the racial heterogeneity of its component states, and a heterogeneous admixture of the ruling people. This latter condition is always the resultant of the former. It is the first of that sickness which has not only dissipated national aspirations, but has been instrumental in the dissolution of dynasties and nations, whether republics or kingdoms. Of the tribes of man that have, in this manner, made their final melancholy trek across those illimitable steppes they traverse but once, they have left behind, at the most, but a crumbling tumulus of statutes and human decrees, by which they sought to nullify the simple yet imperishable laws of nature.

A nation may be kept intact only so long as the ruling element remains homogeneous. When, however, the political and military power passes from it to racial elements that are dissimilar, and politically as well as numerically constitute the main portion of the country, then the ideal of national supremacy is lost in the endless controversies of internal legislation and petty ambitions.

In the previous chapter is shown how the dependencies of this Republic, covering one-fourth of the earth, and bound together only by the fragilest of chains, are each provocative, to a greater or lesser degree, of war with the expanding nations of Europe and Asia. In this chapter will be considered the people who now rule this one-quarter of the globe, showing not only their incapacity to control dependencies, but the difficulty of controlling themselves; and that the wider this power becomes the greater are the probabilities of war.

While racial similarity is recognized as the primitive basis of all national security, it is by no means as essential in an autocratic form of government as in a republic, inasmuch as in an autocracy the ruling power, however small it may be, is generally kept free from admixture with other elements. But in a republic all participate in the government, and it is only a question of numerical superiority for an element alien in race, alien in aspiration, and alien to the spirit of the government to completely supplant the race that founded the republic, together with their ideals and ambitions.

This Republic, together with its declarations, its statutes and constitutions, was founded by men not only alike in race, but in ideals and intentions. Until the time of the Civil War the American could be considered a homogeneous people. But the statutes and declarations made at that time for conserving the national ideals were only fitted to control and direct the growth and course of the nation so long as it remained a country one in race and spirit.

At the beginning of the Civil War the foreign non-Anglo-Saxon element in this country was less than one-twelfth of the population. In 1900 this homogeneity of population had declined to less than seven-twelfths. Since that time this declination of primitive Americanism has gone on at even greater speed.

Not alone, however, must the admixture of alien races inhabiting the states of the Union be considered as provocative of war because they exceed the Anglo-Saxon race in numbers, but rather because of their peculiar geographical distribution. In a number of Southern States the negro outnumbers the white inhabitants, while in most of the other states in the South they exceed one-third the population. Of these negroes forty-four per cent. are wholly illiterate. In the Northern States ninety-four per cent of the European immigrants become domiciled, and at the present time there are in this country over thirty million persons of foreign parentage.

In the great cities of the world are to be found, more or less entire, those factors that determine the course and eventual end of nations within whose boundaries they are placed. From such cities, in proportion to their size, emanate determinate factors in the good and evil of nations. Especially is this so in republics, where the government is dependent upon the will of majorities. In cities such as Boston, Buffalo, Chicago, Hartford, Cleveland, Milwaukee and San Francisco over a third of the population is foreign-born; while in other cities, as Lowell, Fall River and New York, over half the population are foreigners. The racial character of these populations not Anglo-Saxon is exemplified in New York, where it is approximately divided as follows: three-quarters of a million German, more than a quarter of a million Russian, nearly half a million Italian, as well as half a million Poles, Austrians, and Hungarians, while another quarter of a million is made up of other nationalities. Each month the foreign population of these cities increases, and so rapidly that in a few years the Anglo-Saxon American will stand in inverse ratio to what he does now. In due time the strategic positions of this Republic, political, moral and social, will be in the hands of those who know in no manner the truth of human equality, nor the spirit of those who made it possible in seven thin and ragged years, years that tried not alone the hearts of men, but the souls of them.

If there is any such thing as patriotism, then a naturalized citizen is an anomaly. What fidelity can be attributed to a man who not only forswears the land of his birth, but that of his forefathers, their dust and their deeds? If, on the other hand, he is not an apostate in this act of naturalization, then he is a liar. But by neither one nor the other condition is it possible to expect from him other than that which impelled his immigration to this Republic—the betterment of his personal condition. He not only cannot share in national ideals, but he cannot comprehend them. If national ideals are capable of being aroused in him, then they must be for his native country. Patriotism, as ordinarily understood, does not permit the forswearing of one's nationality and the adoption of another with a concomitant display of greater virtue in adopted than in native patriotism. It is not possible that a Slav will be a better American than Slav, or that an Italian possesses more virtues in America than in Italy.

American nationalization is not a racial antiseptic.

The hereditary instincts of unnumbered generations are not erased from the fibre of men by the word of an official.

The application of American institutions to the control of the lower elements of Europeans who constitute the vast majority of immigrants has proven to be productive of crime rather than civic virtues, while the liberty given them is but a Pandorean gift of winged felonies.

Crime is an index to national character, as well as individual, and it is by this index that we make note of the character of the naturalized citizen as well as the citizen born of foreign parents. By this same index of crime, expanding in direct ratio to increasing heterogeneity of population, do we find greater incompatibility existing between their inherent character or propensities and American institutions. With the increase of individual crime is an expansion of national lawlessness that tends externally to international warfare, and internally to eventual dissolution or the introduction of a strongly centralized form of government, monarchial, autocratic, or what not, but that the homogeneous element shall rule, and shall with its great iron ladle alone stir this *potpourri* of mankind and skim off the scum that rises from it.

In considering the probabilities of war due to mixed populations, it must be understood that the morality of a nation, especially a republic, is not that morality expressed in its constitutions, its statutes, or declarations, but is, on the other hand, the composite morality of the major portion of the population which, as it becomes more immoral and criminal, hastens onward to those vaster excesses of unrestraint that are wars.

Beginning with the increase of European immigration, about fifty years ago, crime has become more multitudinous and rampant. Prior to the Civil War there were only twenty-nine prisoners to every hundred thousand of the population. From the time of the war up to the present, crime has increased more than five hundred per cent., while there has been considerably less than two hundred per cent. increase in population. That this is due to the relationship existing between the immigrant and American institutions is shown by the fact that they are less criminal in their own countries than in the United States.

In 1906 there were in England to each million of the population eight murders committed, in Germany four, in the United States one hundred and eighteen. The average number of murders during each of the last twenty years was thirty times greater than the total number of men killed on the field during the Spanish-American War. The annual number of soldiers slain in the Civil War was but slightly in excess of persons now murdered each year in these times of peace, in this land, not of liberty, but of license. The cost of crime in the United States annually exceeds the entire expenditure made necessary by any of the American wars other than the Rebellion.

The distribution of criminality in this Republic, according to nationality, is approximately as follows: twenty-four per cent. of the prisoners are born of native white parents, while seventy-six per cent. are either foreigners, born of foreign parents, or negroes. The criminality of natives born of foreign parents exceeds that of the foreign-born, while the foreign-born criminals exceed those born of native parents in ratio of 56.81 to 43.19. In this Republic the Germans exceed all other foreigners in criminality, while in their native land, under a form of government suited to them, crime is reduced to a minimum.

Denial of obedience to law may occur collectively as well as individually, if tendency to crime in the individual is prevalent. When the refusal to obey the law comes from an individual, it is a felony of some sort. When it occurs collectively, by a section of a nation as against the whole, it is rebellion; when it occurs collectively against international law and usage, it is war. The origin of a collective refusal of a nation to obey international law is very little removed, if at all, from the breaking of a local law by an individual, which is called a crime. It can be justly said that the criminality of a nation is a true index as to proportionate probabilities of war having cause in the acts and passions of people; and in ratio to the progression or retrogression of crime in a people, may war—as far as the people are productive of it—draw near or recede.

Tendencies toward crime individually, as well as nationally, increase in greater ratio when the heterogeneity of a country is of a lower moral status than the original population of the nation and exceeds it in numbers. Not only is it physiologically impossible for a superior portion of mankind to assimilate the inferior without the concomitant loss of superiority, but in this Republic there is, in addition to the deterioration by intermarriage, the infection of social contact, the erosive effect of inferior morals, a bastard patriotism, and finally the giving over into the hands of foreigners, in no manner imbued with the true spirit of American institutions, the preservation of those primitive rights upon which the great but fragile edifice of this Republic was builded.

We have already shown that ninety-four per cent. of the European immigrants settle in those very states, the Eastern and Northern, where is held the balance of political power, and that in most of the great cities from New York to San Francisco the foreign population varies from one-third to over one-half. Should the present rate of immigration continue, it is only a question of a few years when the voting majorities in all great cities will be foreign. The character of the present immigration is not rural; to them the meanest tenement in a city is preferable to the fairest field in the world.

Prior to the influx of European immigrants immediately preceding the Civil War, the ratio of urban to the total population was only twelve per cent.; in 1900 it had increased to over thirty-one per cent. In a few years it will exceed fifty per cent., and will be in an electoral sense foreign.

Republics, governed by the divine right of majorities, that illegitimate offspring of the divine right of kings, are controlled, not by rural districts nor sparsely settled states, but by centres of population, where radiate not alone political predominance, but the moral and social tendencies of the nation. Thus New York City, with one-half of its population foreign, not only in birth, but foreign in their appreciation of American institutions, has more representatives in Congress than nine Western states.

The status of morals in rural districts has no effect whatsoever on urban populations, while, on the other hand, the morality of a city, whether high or low, is, within the radius of its influence, the determining factor as regards general morality of that section of the nation.

We have pointed out four salient conditions arising from heterogeneity of population in this Republic that tend to phases of human activity other than those of peace.

(1) The precipitating causes of all future wars rest with the people.

(2) In direct ratio to the criminality of the populace are to be found concomitant probabilities of war.

(3) This Republic exceeds all other civilized nations in crime.

(4) Most of this criminality arises from its heterogeneous population, which is increasing and confining itself to cities, the strategic points morally, socially, and politically of the Republic.

Were there no other probabilities of war than those arising from the variant racial classes that make up the Republic, that alone should suffice to keep this country prepared instead of denying its possibilities. Through the excessive criminality of any nation there will always exist concomitant violation of the rights and privileges of other countries as guaranteed to them by the usage of international law, and which must, in due time, culminate in war.

XI

Heretofore, in various phases, have been considered probabilities of future wars that should be sufficient at least to turn the attention of this Republic to preparation for them rather than to continue in its present course of not only indifference, but active antagonism to any betterment of its military inefficiency.

In the last few decades the wearing down of this never over-large world into the communicable confines of what, three generations ago, would not have been considered a great state, has gone on without cessation. The shrivelling up of the political sphere of man has its corollary in the expansion of its component parts—the nations that constitute it. Man has now caught up to Time in its flight. Distance is no longer distance whole and vast, for it has been so pared down that only the shavings of it are left in the workshops of man. There are no longer oceans nor deserts nor abysses behind and beyond which nations of men can live secure. Upon this hour-encompassed world, dwindling down each decade, must nations wrestle interminably.

In Europe there is no expansion eastward; in Asia there is no westward course of empire. West must the peoples of Europe go, and eastward those of Asia, until in this hemisphere, on American continents, these two tides, inundating all before them, shall meet and struggle and subside. To prevent this the Monroe Doctrine was framed, exclusion laws enacted, new insular territory appropriated. Then—somnolent with the opiate of transitory power—this nation passes into the wild delirium of those dreams where chimeras give chase to phantoms.

In conjunction with the heterogeneity and concomitant

criminality of those who would rule the Western Hemisphere, we will consider probabilities of war from a source that is fraught with more dangers than any heretofore examined—the control of the government by the populace.

In consideration of the relationship that popular control of government bears to the causes of war, the character of the populace is more or less immaterial; the essential point to be considered is the degree of control the populace has over the central government. As the populace becomes more absolute in the control of governmental affairs, the chances of war increase accordingly; and to the degree that it is racially heterogeneous the probabilities of international strife are augmented.

In proportion to the greatness of the sphere over which a government by the people extends its sway is to be found a corresponding increase in the dangers of war. And when, in addition, the political and territorial expansion of such a nation comes in contact with similar expansion of any oligarchic or autocratic form of government, the result is contention; in defeat, dissolution or reversion to a similar form of monarchy. As is increased or decreased the number of individuals who direct the affairs of a nation, so is altered the wisdom of its acts, its stability and power of survival. Five wise men can better direct, and to superior greatness, the destiny of a nation than can fifty million of men possessed of similar wisdom. But, as the number of individuals who are in control of national affairs increases, there is a concomitant decrease of intelligence, until finally the whole nation is floundering about in the wide, shallow slough of mediocrity. Out of this there is no relief until that which is mud shall subside, and that which is clear shall again reflect the iridescence of not common—but superior—sense.

It is unfortunately true that with increasing popular control of governmental affairs, such as marks the evolution of this nation, there is not, and never will be, a proportionate increase in the intelligence of the masses to the point that they will be able to comprehend the complex obligations that constitute the international rights and duties of governments. Even if the wisdom of the masses should rise to improbable heights, there would be no diminution in the improbabilities of just observance of the rights of foreign nations.

The success of negotiations between nations, as among individuals, is in proportion to the number of negotiators, interests and prejudices involved. When the government of a country is the government of the masses, the number of negotiators is increased to the whole nation, and involves not only their mediocrity, but unending self-interests and prejudices. It was this perversion of government that confirmed John Hay in the belief that this Republic would not again be able to make an important treaty.

By treaties international affairs are governed, and inability to make such stipulations is only another way of stating the impossibility of observing treaties already made. Of the failure on the part of the United States to observe the rights and privileges due other nations, we have had many and melancholy instances.

The mind of a nation in dispute is its mob-mind, credulous and savage. It is primitive, hence brutal. It is feminine, hence without reason. It is instinctive to the degree of an animal, and is cognizant only of its own impulses and desires. It is full of hates and frivolities. While the mind of an individual is more or less constructive, the mob-mind is intelligent only in devastation. Reason roams sullenly in the dim labyrinths of its brain: a Minotaur to whom the world ever and endlessly yields up its tribute; seven Youths that are Empires; seven Maidens that are Progress. Mob-minds can be active only in a destructive sense. As the sum total of the collective efforts of man under individual direction constitutes the upbuilding of a nation, so the sum total of their collective acts uncontrolled is marked by ruin. Whenever the mob-mind rules, mankind shudders. Its voice is the evil banshee of nations.

To the divine right of majorities should be added the will of constituents—a condition that aborts nationalism and benumbs where it would rule. In Republics every office down to the pettiest of magistrates is supposedly subject to the approval of the populace. But in actuality politicians are subservient to it only in its wrath, hence they abet a popular demand for war, instead of opposing it. The will of constituents has resulted in a continual struggle to localize the efforts of government by the paramount interests of sectional legislation. Whatever may be the foreign policy of the national government, that policy must be sacrificed if it interferes with their self-interests.

As the government of a nation passes under popular control, its energies and progress are more and more consumed in the contention of internal affairs, while the nation as a whole drifts along among Scyllas and shoals innumerable. It is in this drifting that the tempests of war are encountered. A nation to withstand the tides and storms of erosive time must progress internationally; its internal affairs made subordinate to its foreign policy, and controlled to conform with its needs and vicissitudes. In republics, however, the reverse of these conditions exists, so that the nation as a derelict drifts along toward the Great Port whither others have also drifted, a port without shores or tempests.

When the inhabitants of one nation are prejudiced against the people and institutions of others, they designate this prejudice patriotism; but when such foreign antipathy is not brought in active use this kind of patriotism hibernates, and the nation gives itself over to sectional prejudices, which are strong or weak in proportion to the strength or weakness of the central government. When the national government becomes subordinate to delegates representing the will of constituencies, then the nation becomes more or less incoherent. The will of constituencies, or the mob-minds of them, has three salient characteristics: it is selfish, with a selfishness that never rises above the flattest mediocrity; improvident, with an improvidence of children; inflammable as tinder, its conflagrations are war; its embers, rebellions; while over the cinders, over the ash and slag of its going out, other nations pass or flare up.

As the government of a nation passes under the control of the populace, it passes, to a certain degree, beyond the pale of peaceful association with other nations. It enters into a condition of arrogant unrest, an isolation, insolent and impatient as to the rights of others. Out of these demeanors come wars.

An electoral populace is at its best a gigantic creation, loud like a demagogue, with the head of a tradesman, and given over to as much self-deception as a woman. It is charitable to those who tickle its vanity, brutal to those it hates, unrelenting to those it has condemned. Without capacity to reason, it has intuition, but like a child delights to be humbugged. It has laughter but no tears, and this is the brute of it.

Peaceful international relationship not only demands the highest intelligence and justice on the part of arbitrators, but a complete subjection by the people to their decision. When, however, governments are under popular control, this condition is reversed; the negotiators become only the representatives of the real arbitrators, the populace; mediocre in intelligence, violent and quick in temper, submissive to none but themselves. Should the negotiator acting for them yield in any degree their most extreme demands, he would at once be cast aside. Consequently the negotiator, knowing that the slightest variation from the wishes of the populace would mean his condemnation, acts only in accordance with popular feeling. He is but a creature of their making, and the tenure of his greatness endures only so long as he pleases them.

It was this phase of popular control that led the late Secretary of State to make the sombre prophecy that never again could this Republic, under its present form of government, conclude an important treaty. In other words, this nation's future is to be rather of war than of peace. Since it has reached that point wherein it is impossible for it to make treaties with other powers, it has fallen to that degree of incoherence that it will violate treaties already in force. The reply to such violation is battle.

The difficulty of making treaties, or respecting those already made, increases with the increase of popular control over the conduct of national government.

In this Republic almost every phase of international relationship, in which are concerned the rights and privileges of foreign nations, is indifferently regarded or directly violated with legislative acts, by powerful political sections or classes whenever it is to their interests or appeals to their passions.

The political history of the United States betrays the difficulties, not only of inaugurating, but continuing, just and friendly relations with foreign nations; while its diplomatic records lay bare the inability of the national government to constrain sectional or class legislation, though contrary to the stipulations of existing treaties. This arbitrary indifference to international obligations, and their increasing violation by sections and classes, cannot be attributed to ignorance. The unlettered savage, hidden away amid the wild thickets of the world, has been known to keep his unrecorded obligations inviolate from generation to generation. There were no laws to bind him but the law of the torrent before his wigwam, the law of the winds overhead, the law of the illimitable forests about him; yet out of this he evolved the very spirit of human obligation that this great Republic is coming to know not of. Its disregard for such pacts is not only increasing, but its violations are, in many instances, unworthy of the nation's potential greatness.

The violation of treaties, and the increasing incapacity to maintain friendly relationship with foreign countries, have their origin in the popular control of the national government: (1) by the political power of sections and classes; (2) by the subordination of legislators to the will of these sections and classes, or to such corporate interests as may control their election. As foreign nations are without votes or lobbyists, their demands are of little or no importance to the average politician. This subserviency of politicians to the will of their constituencies makes possible anti-foreign legislation. Yet, on the other hand, this subserviency is a natural but unreasonable outgrowth of governmental control by the populace, and as it is augmented the subserviency of politicians will increase, and will be followed by a concomitant increase in legislative acts originating in prejudice and arrogance or utter contempt for the rights of other nationalities.

The intelligence of a national legislator or negotiator in a nation controlled by the populace cannot, in the execution of his duties, rise above the average intelligence of his constituents. If it does, he is in conflict with them, and the tenure of his office is at an end. It is useless for a politician to possess, in such a nation, superior intelligence, for he can make use of it only to the degree that his constituency can comprehend. By this fact it is possible to account for the mediocrity of the average American politician and the refusal of the more intelligent citizens to enter into the conduct of the affairs of the Republic.

When diplomacy is unable to settle such differences as continually arise among nations, their settlement is relegated to the sphere of physical might. Whatever lessens the efficiency of diplomatic action increases the probabilities of war. And whenever there exists constitutional restriction on the freedom of diplomatic action, as is the case in a government by the populace, the possibilities of war are increased accordingly. It is only by just and comprehensive recognition of this weakness, and a corresponding increase in the armament and military efficiency of the nation, that the probabilities of war can be minimized.

In a government where the spoils of office belong to the political victor, the consular service has been relegated to awarding the cheaper class of politicians for their past services. This policy of placing transitory ignorance in positions where wide range of knowledge and long training is necessary will become more apparent as the world grows smaller and the Republic's relationship to foreign countries becomes more intimate and complex. As the internal growth of all nations forces them to external expansion, and their national needs and ambitions come in vital conflict with those of the United States, the dangers of international war—as precipitated by the ignorance of the politician diplomat—become apparent.

As the difficulties of settling international controversies increase with the augmentation of negotiators and interests involved, the inability of the negotiators is increased in proportion to the interest the people take in the controversy. If this is very great, and moves the passions of the populace, then the individual intelligence of the negotiators, or their superior knowledge of the facts, or their higher sense of justice will avail them not at all. They become subservient to the populace as soon as its angers begin to brood sullenly over the land.

Whatever intelligence and capacity the negotiators may personally possess, they are subordinate to the prejudices and hate of the mob-mind. Consequently, in the adjustment of international controversies, wisdom may be opposed by arrogance, justice by prejudice to the extent that should the negotiators, representing a government of the populace, grant the just claims of the other nations, or yield even the extreme demands of their own country, they will be bitterly arraigned by the masses that have made no effort to understand the true merits of the controversy or to consider any arguments except their own.

The diplomatic history of this Republic shows the fixed indisposition of the masses to view foreign relations except in subordination to their own sectional or class interests; hence the difficulty of a republic, in moments of stress, adjusting peaceably international disputes when they affect the vital interests or passions of the masses.

BOOK II

THE DECLINE OF MILITANCY AND THE CONTROL OF THE PACIFIC

"Regular troops alone are equal to the exigencies of modern war, as well for defence as offence, and when a substitute is attempted it must prove illusory and ruinous. No militia will ever acquire the habits necessary to resist a regular force. . . . The firmness requisite for the real business of fighting is only to be attained by a constant course of discipline and service. I have never yet been witness to a single instance that can justify a different opinion, and it is most earnestly to be wished that the liberties of America may no longer be trusted, in any material degree, to so precarious a dependence."

WASHINGTON.

I

WE NOW pass, in this portion of our work, from the exposition of conditions to the demonstration of them, to the facts and bitterness of which they are made. We pass from the contemplation of war to the combat itself.

The battlefield—that old and harrowed field—whereon this Republic has so often labored, and is destined yet through undetermined time to furrow, we have heretofore regarded from those high places where life is viewed, not in its drift and struggle of particles, but in the aggregate, as a river is perceived from a mountain-top.

We are now, however, about to transfer to the activities of actual war the conditions we have considered and the principles we have enunciated, in order to determine whether or not our deductions have been erroneous and our ideas speculative, nebulous and vain.

What has been written we realize does not readily find agreement. The average citizen holds—and fast onto them—quite the opposite beliefs. His opinions, being not other than human, are not impartial. In proportion as facts or errors have been pleasing to him have they secured firm and unmolested lodgment in his mind. None are free from this unfortunate credulity, and it is only by great effort that man can become incredulous to soothing fancies and believe in the truth of that which is painful.

We also became conscious of the fact, after writing the first portion of this work, that while the truth of it could not be gainsaid, the good we hoped it might do was liable to be nullified by that negative form of unbelief so inherent in the nature of man—his reliance on chance. Nations, as individuals, lay on the red or black, and, with the old, old credulity of luck, await serenely the shuffling of the thumbed and fateful pack.

While the past of this Republic may appear to have been under the ever-watchful and unwinking eye of Fortune, investigation shows us that the most ordinary, and by no means unnatural, conditions have been responsible for its welfare. And while we would not say that Fortune has deserted this great Tower of Babel, yet another god hath spoken—the old and material god that takes no note of the dust towers builded to-day; on the morrow pulled down and—laughed at.

While the probabilities of an international war at the present time tend more to a struggle with Japan than any other country, the chances of war are equally possible with other powers, and are existent in a modified form with still other nations. At any time an unforeseen incident, affecting the precipitating causes of war, may again transfer the immediate zone of danger from the Pacific to the Atlantic.

The political responsibilities that this Republic has so unconcernedly assumed in establishing its suzerainty over the Western Hemisphere and a tentative dominion over the Pacific are so vast and so intimately affect the nations of the world in their struggle for the potentialities of power that it is impossible to foretell whence shall come not alone alarums of war, but war itself. The smoke of unnumbered arsenals now hangs heavily on the four horizons of this nation, and the clangor of strange anvils enters even into the very heart of it.

In a war with Japan, the conflict itself and the results ensuing from such a struggle, we but exemplify what will happen, different only in time and place, when this Republic undertakes to stop the expansion of European and Asian empires, and attempts, without adequate naval and military power, to preserve intact to itself the Pacific and the Western Hemisphere, calling halt to the migration of kingdoms and that hunger-trek made from time to time by the races of man.

Japan must overcome difficulties such as would not exist in a war with Germany or other European powers. From Hamburg to the Atlantic coast is six days; from Japan to California, seventeen. But when Germany lands her forces on the

Atlantic coast they are within a few days' march of the political and financial centres of the Republic, while Japan is removed by immeasurable distance from them. By these means we give to the United States military advantages that would be impossible in a war with such a power as Germany; so that we are exaggerating, not the capacity of Japan to make war, but the capacity of the United States to defend itself. If the probabilities of victory should rest with the Asian kingdom, it will be understood how ineffectual would be the efforts of this Republic against a European power.

A war with Japan demonstrates the truth of the statement that no one can foretell from age to age, or even from decade to decade, in what quarter of the world will rise up a great military nation. This Minerva birth of militant power has always been to mankind an enigma, a dread, but never as yet a lesson. By these things he never profits. He forgets when he should remember, and scorns where he should inquire. So from time to time do warring, conquering tribes burst upon the incredulous world; sometimes from rocky places; sometimes out of wreckage; down from the alcoves of God, or up from abysses, they thunder and destroy.

So it has come about that on islands, beautiful in their poverty, terrible in their serenity, brews and rumbles another such tempest as has heretofore swept over the abodes of kingdoms that have thought naught of them.

To the over-industrial development of the United States we have the corresponding political growth of Japan; to the under-political development of the Republic, there is to be found in Japan a production of wealth unequal to its political growth. The quotient of this equation has been, throughout the entire career of the human race, war.

The American people, and not Japan, are responsible for this approaching conflict. In sacrificing the national ideal to that of the individual the expansion of this nation has been determined by his wants. All national growth, following in the wake of individual desires, has been industrial, while political development, together with its concomitant military and naval expansion, has been relegated to secondary consideration.

Man becoming paramount over the nation, legislation has, accordingly, been directed to the end most advantageous to his personal interests, while that of the nation, *per se*, in its relation to the rest of the world, has been regarded as of minor importance. Man, his welfare and ambitions, taking precedence over that of the Republic, has caused the national legislature to occupy itself with internal and petty plunderings, sectional and class legislation. The true significance of the Republic's position in the world has been put aside. It is this neglect that invites war and turns into loot the nation's treasure, the high spires of its gods, and the spangled panoply of its greatness.

Due to science and invention, international relationship, heretofore existent, has been completely revolutionized, and those lands and nations once without the sphere of conquest are wholly within it. Conquest, moreover, has ceased to be an imperial progress wherein monarchs were wont to display their greatness and crime and generosity. It has now become the conquest of peoples to gain such means of wealth as are yet unlooted in the vaults of nature. In this conquest there is little glory; nay, naught is displayed but relentless, nightless theft to appease, not the vanity of kings, but the hunger of multitudes.

The under-political development of China, and her failure to comprehend the revolution that modern science brought into international affairs within the last two decades, has laid open the empire to dismemberment. And when it is said that the realization of this change is scarcely better comprehended by the populace of the United States than by the people of China, it is stating only one of those melancholy truisms that have been uttered heretofore by American statesmen.

Vessels crossing the Atlantic in four and a half days, carrying several thousand persons and some thirty thousand tons of freight, are regarded only in an economic aspect, whereas the political and military significance is so infinitely greater that nations will vanish or grow great because of it. The Western Hemisphere has in this manner alone been brought within the demesne of Europe, while their armies of millions are now closer to the city of Washington than are the small and scattered forces of the United States.

The error of the subordination of national greatness to the material gains of the individual, concomitant with the assumption of world-wide power, with all the dangers and disasters it involves, has already been made clear. Now we are brought face to face with the actualities of a great war, in a study of which will be shown the logical consummation of this Republic's neglect.

In the consideration of a war between Japan and the United States we will make no assumptions, but will deal only with actualities. Moreover, we will not arbitrarily assume that this war will take place, but will, on the other hand, examine carefully into the chances of peace and weigh them against the probabilities of war. Likewise, before entering upon the study of the war itself, we will examine into its precipitating causes as well as its primordial sources, the armaments of the two nations, and their military potentiality. To chance, to patriotism, to prejudice, to hope, we leave nothing. Upon the airy tapestry of our desires we weave no bright threads to fade as they are woven.

We have written this work with a full knowledge of its bitterness. But we have done so because the time is now at hand when this nation must emerge from its policy of subterfuge. The national evasion of this Republic's international responsibilities must cease, as its isolation ceased when science winged the larvæ of man.

II

THERE are certain conditions that tend to the preservation of peace, just as there are other phases of national life productive of war. While the sources and causes of international conflicts might belong to conditions both basic and necessary for the future development and existence of nations, yet there may be peace factors that more than counterbalance the provocations to war. Conditions that prevent war, while numerous and peculiar to each combination of combatants, can be determined more or less accurately, and their potentiality measured against that of the causes of international conflict.

In a general sense, wars between nations are determined by certain principles already considered in the first part of this work.[1] In some instances, however, conditions demanding peace intervene. These peace factors have a relative value to the causes of war, and their potentiality must be considered in two more or less distinct phases: first, the possibility of the prevention of war; second, the probability of postponing the struggle to some indefinite period in the future.

Conditions potential enough to prevent war between two racially different nations, as Japan and the United States, can only exist when the causes of war, in either nation, are less imperative than the necessities of peace. Nations do not plunge into warfare without some comprehension of the possibilities of victory as weighed against, not only the disasters to be endured through defeat, but such losses as are incurred on account of the war *per se*.

We have shown that wars between great nations are resultant, not of passions, but of economic or political converg-

_____
[1] See Book I, chap. vii, pp. 54-56.

ence. Man may, by his passions, increase, or by forbearance decrease this convergence, but he cannot do away with war.

Before taking up the causes of war that now or in the future may exist between Japan and the United States, we will consider whether or not the necessities and tendencies for peace between these two powers are great or insignificant, and whether conditions that make for peace predominate over those that tend to war.

Two general phases of international relationship may exist between nations so as to modify hostile competition and lessen the probabilities of war.

(1) Racial relationship, with concomitant similarities in religion, ethical and sociological conditions.

(2) Economic interdependence.

Racially, there exists no relationship between the people of Japan and of the United States. And the perverse reluctance of man to forget his own tribal gods and fetiches postpones to such a remote time the assimilation of these two nations that it cannot now be considered. The ethical and sociological conditions extant in Japan, while antithetic to those existent in the United States, are nevertheless the product of two thousand years of Japanese development. To remake the Japanese racial character in order to conform with that of the Occident would require, even were it possible, a longer period of time than we can conceive. Such a racial change in Japan can no more take place than could the West alter its civilization to conform with that of the Orient. Both civilizations will, in due time, by natural but slow process, become so modified that it will be difficult to distinguish the outward forms of one from the other; but racial distinctions and antipathies will continue to remain even unto an unknown time.

A great race is like a rock in the wash of the sea, whereon, as birds of passage, transient civilizations momentarily pause in their flight ere they go on down into the dim twilight of a departed day. It is only the Undefined Sea, or the storms that come out of it, that batter, incrustate, erode, festoon, then swallow up this race-rock that seems in the eye of man made to endure forever.

No national ideals could be more antithetic than are the ethical and civic ideals of Japan to those existent in this Republic. One nation is a militant paternalism, where aught that belongs to man is first for the use of the state; the other an individualistic emporium where aught that belongs to man is for sale. In one is the complete subordination of the individual, in the other his supremacy.

When national religions differ, racial difference creates antagonism. Thus the Japanese, with their sword-girded gods and militant bonzes, are heathen in the eyes of this Republic, heathen in all the contemptuous, naked inferiority that that term in a Christian nation implies. This feeling will never decrease except with the deterioration of Christianity, since such a decadence is, as far as the Japanese are concerned, more probable than the Christianization of their country.

The ethical, sociological, or religious conditions as existent in Japan and this Republic have nothing in common, nor are their ways convergent or even parallel. Neither now nor at any time in the distant future will these nations coalesce to the extent that the sociological or religious phases of their national life will have a deterrent effect on war, or will alter in any way, other than to accentuate their racial ambitions, their perverse activities, their hates and their cries.

The only conditions that may have the power of preserving peace between Japan and the United States, or at least retarding hostilities, are to be found in the political relationship that these two nations bear to the world, and the economic interdependence they have with each other.

Political conditions that have, in an international sense, a restraining influence upon the ambitions of a nation, and are instrumental in the prevention of war, are determined by the effect that such a war would have on these interests.

In a struggle between Japan and the United States for the supremacy of the Pacific, all nations have more or less interest in the outcome, but the interests of Japan and this Republic are so paramount that the aggregate interests of the remainder of the world are less than the interests of these two nations. This condition of affairs has been brought about by Japan on three momentous occasions:

(1) The elimination of China as a Pacific power by the war of 1894.

(2) The elimination of Russia as a possible Pacific power by the war of 1904.

(3) The elimination of Great Britain and the balance of Europe by the ten-year Offensive and Defensive Alliance of 1905.

The interests of European nations in the Pacific are only tentative. Conditions that are vital to their welfare are in Europe, or in those continents upon whose shores the same sea breaks.

The centralization of power in the Pacific is impossible to any nation other than China, Japan or the United States, since such power would be without and far removed from the geographical, political, and military interests of any nation other than these three. But China, while geographically a Pacific empire, cannot be taken into consideration as a possible claimant for suzerainty over the Pacific, not only on account of her defeat by Japan, but because of the weakness and decentralization of the present system of government.

At present, and for some time to come, there are only two powers, Japan and this Republic, that can, with geographical and political conditions favorable, enter into a war for the supremacy of the Pacific. Japan's interest and inherent advantage in this struggle is due to the fact that her entire empire is not only in this ocean, but in the strategic centre of it.[2]

A second political condition that oftentimes restrains nations from entering into international war is when the strength of hostile states, on more than one frontier, exceeds the quotient of military power remaining from such forces as are necessary to successfully prosecute a war determined upon. If Japan became involved in war with the United States to the extent that her entire naval and military forces were engaged, what would prevent Russia or China, or both in coalition, from

[2] See Chart I.

attempting to recover their kingdoms lost, and their prestige —now so small in the eyes of the world?

It was the realization of this fact that led Japanese statesmen, at the conclusion of the Russian War, to enter into an Offensive and Defensive Alliance with the greatest of world powers for a period of ten years.[3] By this alliance the undefended frontiers of Japan in northern Asia are without danger of attack. She is free to divert her entire military forces upon any war that she may deem necessary to her especial interests and security. By the terms of this treaty, war-coalitions are impossible on the part of this Republic without forcing Great Britain into the field as Japan's ally.

Politically there are no conditions that can restrain Japan from entering into war with this nation. Strong in faith and in the Red Sun of her destiny, Japan began more than two decades ago her predetermined march to the Empire of the Pacific. One nation after another, by one means and another, she has removed them from her way. Nothing now remains but the overthrow of this Republic's power in the Pacific—and nothing, as far as political restrictions are concerned, prevents her from entering upon this conquest: a war that shall bring greater glory to her samurai than they have gained heretofore, and new satrapies, more vast than any now within her realm, shall be given over to her princes and daimios.

There remains to be considered but one phase of international relationship that has within itself the possibilities of preventing war, or at least prolonging the present period of peace: the economic interdependence of these two nations and their freedom from commercial competition in markets common to both.

The belief most often expressed in this Republic concerning the impossibility of war between Japan and the United States is based on a fanciful and erroneous conception of the economic interdependency of these two nations. This belief has come about through a misconception on the part of the public as to the real significance of international trade and the laws that govern it. Because of this misconception commer-

[3] Appendix, Table I.

cialism has taken unto itself the habiliments of uncrowned monarchy—a power that would scowl down from the alcove of kings.

In considering the supremacy of trade over international relationship, and especially its dominion over the destinies of Japan and the United States, we will do so by an examination into a paper on this subject by Baron Kaneko, a Privy-Councillor to the Emperor of Japan.[4]

This paper, by such an eminent economist, endeavoring to show that the economic interdependency of Japan and this Republic is such as to prohibit the possibility of war, contains most of the arguments devoted to the exposition of this belief. Hence, we feel that a consideration of Baron Kaneko's statements will tend to show clearly the wisdom or deception of such ideas.

Baron Kaneko lays down the hypothesis that the American people are so dependent upon Japanese goods, and the Japanese so dependent upon American merchandise, that war is impossible, since both nations, being deprived of these necessaries of life, will come to a plainly foreseen and miserable end.

This premise is not original with Baron Kaneko. Writing on this subject for an American magazine, he has only endeavored to exemplify the arguments of American economists and calculators. Were we not convinced of his sincerity, we might have been led to believe that, as he assembled these arguments together, he viewed them with that sarcastic nonchalance that has within itself a significance entirely its own.

"So I can fairly state," continues the Baron, with that complacency peculiarly characteristic of economists, "that no lady in the United States can get a silk dress if we stop the export of silk to that country, and that the average American citizen cannot drink tea if our tea is excluded from America. So much for the dependence of the American people on Japanese products."

This remarkable statement is followed by a list of American commodities consumed in Japan, *viz.*, flour, cotton, to-

[4] *North American Review,* March, 1907.

bacco, and petroleum. He concludes the list with the enuncia-
tion of the startling formula that "the Japanese cannot live
a single hour without American supplies."

In order to show to what degree these conclusions are
erroneous, we need but to examine one of them, since all are
based on the same hypothesis.

In modern wars, the interchange of commodities still remains governed by the law of supply and demand, much in
the same manner as in peace, owing to the diversity of trade
routes and complexity of international exchange. This condition of affairs is only affected by the destruction of the means
of production or the relative impoverishment of the consumers
or the naval command of the routes of trade emanating from
the exporting country.

Nations do not stop their own exports in the time of war,
as Baron Kaneko would lead us to believe. On the contrary,
it is essentially a part of national endeavor to protect by every
means possible their avenues of trade. If Japanese silks were
not exported from Japan during a conflict, it would not be
through their decrees.

If, in a war between these two nations, the trans-Pacific
commerce did, temporarily, cease to exist and at the same time
there continued, in both nations, a demand for their respective
commodities, the interchange would go on as before, differing
only in the route and means of transference. Neutral vessels
via the Suez would continue the trade temporarily lost to the
Pacific. This would modify the interchange of Japanese and
American goods only in time and expense of transshipment in
European ports. Whatever this additional cost of transportation might be, it would only be equivalent to a raise in price
of the merchandise, affecting the consumers in the manner of
an ad valorem tariff, but would make little or no difference to
the government or people of either nation.

Japanese tea or silk is not so essential to America that
without them the Americans can have neither tea nor silks.
The relative value of these commodities that Japan annually
exports to the United States is, to the world's total production of silk or tea, so insignificant that the entire failure of

the Japanese product would make but little difference to the consumers of such articles in the United States.

The merchandise of individual and national consumption has, in these modern times, become so general to the whole of mankind that the world has become one vast emporium, and what in the time of war cannot be gotten directly from a nation can be secured indirectly through transshipments and devious routes of neutral trade. The delusion that the intercommerce relationship between two nations is destroyed by war, and that economic interdependence is such that it prohibits war, should be put aside in the same manner as mankind has heretofore laid away some of his most cherished notions.

Japan, on the other hand, is no more dependent upon American products than is this Republic dependent on Japanese tea and silks. So long as Japan controls the trade routes to Europe, her imports will differ from what they are now only as the demands of her people for these commodities increase or decrease. Whatever American commodities Japan needs she will get in war as in peace.

It will be shown later on that the United States can never, under its present system of military and naval constraint, have any appreciable effect on the trade routes west of the Hawaiian Islands. Nor can any nation, except by blockade, affect trade on neutral bottoms. Baron Kaneko's statement that "the Japanese cannot live a single hour without American supplies" is no more true than his statement that "the average American citizen cannot drink tea if Japanese tea is excluded from America."

The second and last consideration of the economic prevention or postponement of this international conflict is the freedom from commercial competition in markets common to both Japan and the United States. In regard to this phase of commercial relationship existing between nations, Baron Kaneko observes: ". . . In the twentieth century it is the increase and expansion of international commerce that guides the policy of nations. . . . All nations are looking for new markets for their industries, and the only market now remaining which can be exploited with benefit is the continent of Asia."

American and Japanese partnership in the exploitation of the Asian continent could be possible under the reverse of existent conditions, wherein the opportunities of commercial exploitation in Asia and the Pacific were less than the interchange of commodities between the United States and Japan. But it is in the control and exploitation of those vast empires whose swagging godowns burden the shores of the Pacific that are to be found the riches of the world.

"European thought, European commerce, and European enterprise, although actually gaining in force, and European connections, although becoming more and more intimate, will nevertheless relatively sink in importance in the future, while the Pacific Ocean, its shores, its islands, and adjacent territories will become the chief theatre of human events and activities in the world's great hereafter."[5]

Among nations, coalitions in a military sense are possible, since such combinations are brought about by governments, but in the struggle for commercial supremacy there can be no such alliances; this warfare is the endless conflict of multitudinous man, the tribal swarms of them and their spawn.

Neither to Japan nor to the United States is the trade now going on between them worthy of conservation. Their efforts are directed to that vantage-point where one of them can swing the nine-knotted knout and drive to new wants nations that now sit on their heels and dream in the endless Orient dusk.

Baron Kaneko states that the United States and Japan stand, geographically, in the most advantageous position to garner the fruit of the Pacific and Asiatic trade, but he conceals the fact that they are so favorably situated that, as European nations are isolated from this trade dominion, the rivalry between them will increase proportionately until the commercial struggle for supremacy merges imperceptibly into that of political control, based on military prowess. It would be difficult to find in history an example more perfectly exemplifying the manner in which the struggle for commercial supremacy involves the competitors in warfare.

[5] William H. Seward.

In the national fabric of Japan and the United States, in their international and human relationship, conditions potential of peace are not to be found. In their racially different characters, no harmonious similarity exists, only divergent and incompatible ideals; in their international politics, no restraining influence that might, at least, postpone into the indefinite future the probabilities of war. All political restraints have been removed; one after another pulled down and thrown aside by the relentless, predetermined policy of Japan. In their economic relationship conditions that might tend to the prevention of war not only do not exist, but in this economic struggle is to be found the near source of the approaching conflict.

III

IN THE first part of this work we differentiated between precipitating causes and primordial sources of international war. We will now consider them relative to a conflict between Japan and the United States.

While the sources of this approaching war are to be found in the expansion and imperial ambitions of Japan, the causes of it, nevertheless, have their origin in the acts of this nation. In this chapter, will be considered these causes, originating as they do in this Republic, before taking up the sources of the struggle belonging to the destiny of Japan.

It has heretofore been shown that international strife results from a natural convergent expansion of two or more nations, bringing about in due time the inevitable contact of interests that culminates in a struggle for supremacy of one over the other. These angles of national convergence are seldom equal, as in the approaching war for the command of the Pacific. The angle of Japan's convergence is as much more acute than the American as their interests are more vital in the struggle for possession of this vast Empire of Waters.

The sources of war—as in this case—are existent for many decades before nations are cognizant of them, though their sullen growl falls, from time to time, ominously upon the heedless ear of their multitudes. Twenty years ago Japan recognized the inevitability of war for the suzerainty of the Pacific. It was this prescience that caused the Mikado five years later to voice solitarily his objections to the United States establishing dominion over the Hawaiian Islands.

Only when the interests of these two nations began to converge did the probabilities of war become apparent. The acuteness of the angles of this convergence was increased:

first, by the further acquisition of Pacific possessions by this Republic, thereby endangering not only Japan's commercial hegemony in the Orient, but her opportunity to become the Overlord of Asia; secondly, by Japan's success over China and Russia, with their consequent elimination from any immediate future struggle for power in the Pacific.

Since the Russian War, Japan has directed her undivided attention to that conflict which—should it end in victory—will give half the world over to the imperious barony of her daimios and samurai. Baron Kaneko, in his paper heretofore quoted, notes these ambitions concerning the Pacific.

"The United States," he writes, "occupies almost two-thirds of the whole coast of the Pacific Ocean, while the remaining one-third is held by Japan. . . . Therefore, these two nations need have no fear of any rival."

In actuality this Republic does not possess two-thirds of the Pacific littoral, nor Japan the remaining one-third. Baron Kaneko does not consider British Columbia, Mexico, Central and South America, Australia, New Zealand, the East Indies, Siam, Cochin China, the Chinese Empire, nor Siberia: these nations have no right of sovereignty in the Pacific if the United States possesses a military and naval command of two-thirds of it and Japan the other third.

But this nation does not undertake the military effort necessary to carry out this policy, and Japan, perceiving its indifference, as exemplified in the Pacific defences, the complete lack of an army, and the division of the naval forces into two widely separated oceans, has gone calmly about in her preparations for that war which will make the empire sovereign over that two-thirds of the Pacific she does not now claim to possess.

The suddenness with which the precipitating causes of war break upon public consciousness almost invariably hides the true reasons—in all probability extant many years prior—that tend to bring on the conflict; hence it happens—as is the case with this Republic—that nations go rushing blindly along acutely converging lines to that point of contact—which is war. Whenever a nation fails or scorns to differentiate between the sources and causes of war, it enters into the conflict unprepared. But those nations whose affairs of state are carried on by men fully cognizant of the difference between the trivial and the immutable are not only always prepared for battle, but they determine the time and place of the conflict; which, more often than otherwise, is an assurance of success.

Subsequent to her victory over Russia, Japan laid upon herself that labor, burdened with immeasurable grandeur, of encompassing the Pacific and becoming the Shogun of half the human race. Her preparations for war prior to her conflict with Russia were insignificant with what have gone on subsequent to that war; now equalling in military and naval preparation alone over one-half the entire revenues of the empire.

This Republic and Japan are approaching, careless on the one hand and predetermined on the other, that point of contact which is war.

It sometimes happens that both the primordial sources and the precipitating causes of war originate within one nation. When this is the case, that nation must bear the odium of preconceived, if not inexcusable, conquest. History is clangorous with wars of this kind. But at the present time the necessity of conquest, affecting in varying proportion all great nations, has brought about such conditions that conquest, *per se*, cannot be entered into. In order to pursue this policy there has been introduced into world policies an era of subterfuge, an Age of Preconceived Provocative. The tentative dismemberment of China is an example of this.

Japan, to establish herself in the sympathies of the world, rather than incur their jealous antagonism by bringing on a war that has for its ultimate object the sovereignty of the Pacific, must shape her affairs so that the precipitating causes of the conflict shall originate in this Republic. These causes do exist, and, fortunately for Japan, through no agency of her statesmen nor people; because of them the Hawk of her Valor shall scream and dart over seas and lands now unknown to it; new guests shall go into the Spirit-Invoking Temple of Shokonsha, and the prayers of a nation shall find their way to the Sacred Hillsides of Kudan.

While war between Japan and the United States originates, and primarily belongs to the natural expansion of the Japanese Empire, the responsibility for its causes will fall upon this nation, by violation of those rights, privileges and immunities heretofore granted Japan by treaty stipulations. From this relationship, as it now exists, and which will remain until war ensues, we have in these two nations antithetic conditions wherein one is not only the corollary of the other, but is subservient and controllable.

Inasmuch as the primordial sources of future conflict have their origin in Japan's predetermined intention to become supreme in the Pacific, her progress toward warfare is orderly and her preparations consistent. Not only can Japan postpone or cause a precipitation of hostilities, according to the imperfection or completion of her preparations, but she can select her successive theatres of action, as they suit her general plan for the conduct of the war. Every move is planned, every emergency taken into consideration; the American armament and preparation, or lack of it, are in all its phases tabulated; the topography of the country surveyed, climatic conditions noted, depths of streams, heights of mountains, food supplies, means of transportation and subsistence belonging to each section of possible spheres of military activity have been carefully investigated and preparations made accordingly. In this manner, years before war is declared, the most insignificant details and possibilities of hypothetical campaigns and battles have been so worked out, and all exigencies so minutely taken into consideration, that the war itself, when once begun, proceeds with invincible orderliness to a predetermined end.

In such a manner Germany overthrew the French Empire in less than two months; while the irresistibleness with which Japan converged her widely separated armies to the ultimate defeat of Russia was carried on by plans so completely prearranged that in the entire war Russia gained not a single victory.

It is in this manner that Japan prepares, not for war with this nation, but for victory over it. In response to these manifest preparations the United States has done nothing other than go on denying the possibilities of war, while it continues to pile up, one groaning on top of the other, new provocations for this very conflict over which it has no control. Now and then some one rises up against this general sophistry that is leading the country into a dismal bog of national subterfuge, but it is seldom more than a sputtering in the deadliest of marsh gases, a momentary glimmering of truth that soon vanishes into that old gloom out of which it cannot again come.

Nothing can better serve the interests of Japan, or any other nation under similar conditions, than the present characteristic indifference of this Republic to dangers threatening it. Not only indifferent to military preparation, but likewise making no effort to prevent the recurrence of acts and legislation that will serve as *casus belli* whenever Japan has determined that conditions are favorable for beginning the conflict. Moodily and at any time the Mikado may make known from his moated Castle of Yeddo his ultimatum of the wrongs and indignities laid upon his people.

In the first part of this work we showed numerous general causes that will eventually precipitate this Republic in a series of wars. In addition, there are special causes logically derived from conditions that are alone relative to the Orient and Japan. To deal with all these elements in detail is unnecessary. An exposition of one of them, in its various phases, will show the manner in which the precipitating causes of this war are inherent in the political fabric of the Republic, and in the overt acts of a portion of the people, as well as in that fatal nonchalance—itself an invitation to war—with which the entire nation regards the approach of that inevitable day when the pencilled hopes of peace and its paper prayers are cast upon the winds and the sea groans with the burden of conflict.

In considering the facts of which we are now about to take note, the reader must put aside his nationality, together with what he considers the rights of American people, in part or as a whole, and look upon these conditions as would a Samurai opportunist to whom they appear only in the double light as being derogatory to his country's honor, and potential with the possibilities of a war for which his empire now prepares or dreams of when the drooping eyelid of night stills the clangor of its arsenals and the brooding care of its council-chambers.

Where there is racial non-assimilability there is apt to be friction, but few realize that political non-assimilability in a nation where the political power rests in the hands of the masses is a source of greater friction than that coming from racial differences. Racial unlikeness does not produce inequality, but when a people are deprived of political franchise, together with its rights and privileges, which are granted to all others among whom they dwell, they are at once branded as inferior. This arbitrary determination by one class of the inferiority of another establishes that anomalous condition— caste in a Republic. The creation of an inferior caste by political disfranchisement soon permeates, by that osmose peculiar to man, every phase of daily existence. Those who are disfranchised are treated by the populace, not alone with social unconcern, but indignities. Municipalities direct restrictive ordinances against them so that they become the natural prey, not only of the lawless element, but the police. Their status being already fixed by public opinion, their voice in protesting against indignities may, in the beginning, be vehement, but their protestations soon die away in hoarse and broken whispers.

They cannot appeal to the courts where their case may be determined by a jury, for the jury, being of the people, has already decided that as heathen they cannot be believed under oath. It has come to pass on the Pacific coast that the word of one Occidental is considered more worthy of credence than the oaths of an entire colony of Orientals. They have ceased to look for justice in cases determined by juries.

State legislation further deprives them of many civil rights enjoyed by all other residents. They are segregated and participate in none of the activities common to other aliens. In some portions of the country their presence is not tolerated, and they are stoned and driven out as though unclean. They become as racial lepers whose residence in a locality is permitted only by such isolation as the citizens and European aliens consider necessary. In this manner Orientals are not alone subject to individual mistreatment, but to that of mobs. The motives, moreover, that actuate mob-lawlessness are identical with the spirit that directs municipal ordinances against them, the legislation of the state and the injustice of the judiciary.

We are making no comments concerning the right of a portion of the American people to do these things. We are alone establishing conditions that do exist, and in consequence are provocative of a legitimate *casus belli* on the part of the nation whose people have thus been treated, in variance with the rights and immunities granted them by existing treaties.

In a republic, where the political power resides in the populace, embroilments between a disfranchised class and those who possess the right do not originate in the former, but grow out of that tyranny which an empowered populace invariably directs against those whom they have ordained as inferior.

The rights of a class in a republic are determined quantitatively by the number of their votes, and qualitatively by the political acumen of their leaders. When, however, a class or race finds itself in a republic without political franchise, then as a race or class its rights are ground into broken dust. Over them the populace lifts its threatening, relentless hand. Politicians, from ward-heelers to congressmen, from mayors to governors, from police judges to supreme justices, are indifferent to the rights and justice due such aliens. They have come out of the populace that rules in this manner, and the pointing shadow of the people's forefinger marks their narrow course.

What we have here expressed are not hypothetical considerations, but a statement of facts that have for more than two decades piled up their misdemeanors against Orientals in the western portion of this Republic. What has occurred to the Chinese will—as is now being done—be directed against the Japanese, but with this difference: the oppressive acts will be as much more violent as is lacking that submission characteristic of the Chinese. To expect the Japanese to submit to indignities is to be pitifully incomprehensive of their national character. And the American people should realize that it is this cumulative memoranda of wrongs that they must, on some certain, sombre day, make answer to in a manner we will dwell upon presently.

The recognition of the fact by Japan that so long as Japanese resident in this nation were denied electoral rights they would suffer indignities and injustice led the Imperial Government to demand those rights of naturalization granted the aliens of other countries. In addition, Japan has demanded— as existing treaties give her the unquestioned right to do—that her people be accorded the same rights, privileges and immunities granted the subjects of European nations. These demands give rise to the consideration of four separate conditions:

(1) The attitude of the people of the Pacific States toward the Federal Government if the Japanese are granted these demands.

(2) Their attitude toward the Japanese; to what degree their antipathy and belligerency may be aroused against them.

(3) If the Federal Government, acquiescing to the West, refuses to grant the Japanese demands, local injustice and additional restrictions will, taking on new vigor, be directed against them throughout the states of the Pacific coast.

(4) Japan, recognizing the fact that in a republic domestic legislation takes precedence over questions involving foreign nations, will not make a positive demand for the fulfilment of these obligations until prepared for war. She can thus determine the outbreak of the war by the conservation of her demands until conditions are favorable to her for the commencement of hostilities.

The relationship that exists between the states and the Federal Government is such that, while the Federal Government makes treaties, and is held responsible by foreign nations for the inviolability of their stipulations, it has but little power to enforce these foreign agreements when their violation—as is almost invariably the case—occurs within the jurisdiction of state laws. On account of this anomalous condition, offenders against the rights of foreigners, if the popular opinion of the state is with them—as is the case on the Pacific coast in overt acts against the Japanese—are not only immune, but receive the approbation of their fellow-citizens.

Anti-Japanese sentiment may have been dormant prior to the conclusion of the Russian War, but since then it has openly manifested itself, and is not restricted, as may be supposed, to union-labor or socialistic elements, but permeates the entire social and political fabric of the West.[1]

In the wild gorges of Siskiyou, on moss-grown boulders, and half effaced by the lichens of two decades, can even now be deciphered this legend: "The Chinese must go. Vote for O'Donnell." We have seen it on the red-wood shacks of Mendocino; on the outhouses of cities and towns; on the board fences in the Valley of the Santa Clara, and from there to the Mojave Desert. Even by the border of Death Valley, in the dreariest of solitudes, the West stencilled the epitome of its racial hatred, a hatred that was taken up and put into public ordinances—into the statute-books of the state, and finally, finding its way to Washington, violated under political pressure such treaty stipulations as existed between the United States and China.

This racial antagonism has now been extended to the Japanese, and, indifferent to the rights and immunities guaranteed them by treaty, the people of the West are proceeding with the same sullen contempt of consequences as, two decades ago, they moved against the Chinese.[2]

Strangely oblivious to the militant character of the Japanese, to the vast military and naval power in their hands, to the spirit of conquest in their bosoms, to their predetermined struggle with the Republic for sovereignty over the Pacific, a portion of the American people go on indifferently, each day adding new provocations to precipitate a conflict, and yet with the utmost unconcern make no preparations for it. This indifference and lack of preparation has as much to do with

[1] Appendix, Table II.
[2] Appendix, Table III.

hastening the conflict as has the positive circumscription of Japanese rights. When Japan presents the memoranda of her wrongs to the world and declares war, the world will regard Japan's position as not only lawful, but justly taken. They also have their people in this Republic, and each year piles up in the archives of their State Departments the grim protests of their subjects.

The indiscriminate violation in different sections of the United States of the rights of aliens, and the inability of the Federal Government to protect them, is a matter of as vital concern to those nations whose subjects dwell in this Republic as a similar condition in China, where all nations, including the United States, have made war because of this very failure on the part of China to preserve inviolate such rights and immunities as are specified in the stipulations of existent treaties.

Japan, by making the cause of war the violation of treaty rights, shoulders the complaint of the world; and in giving battle to enforce the common rights of the Old World in the Western Hemisphere, Japan, and not the United States, will receive the world's approbation and sympathy.

IV

THE incomparable tranquillity with which mankind views his own immediate achievements is only equalled by the disdain with which he views the successes or failures of the human race in other ages. Yet there is no difference in these old and new works, except in the manner and place of their doing. It is only his vanity that prevents him from making use of the accumulative empirical knowledge that races have left in their flight, here and there on this great Guano Rock, fertilized with their failures and fat with their dead.

As we look backward through thirty dim centuries, we see that there existed in the Mediterranean conditions that at the present time have come up again to be determined in the Pacific Ocean. In the same manner as China and Japan maintained their exclusion from contact with Western nations, so had there existed in Egypt this same system of isolation until overthrown by Psammetichus.

Psammetichus was the predecessor of Perry.

As China and Japan have been, and in a measure still are, vast, dim regions of mysteries, so to the ancients was the Valley of the Nile.

In this analogy, however, there is a difference, a differentiation that has its own terrors. The Greeks endeavored to understand the riddle of Egypt; the West scorns the inquiry of the East.

What shall the Occident find in Asia—a slave-mart, or a master? Unanswered doubts do not alone belong to the Sphinx; nay, they are part of Time, and their apparent unsolvableness lies in the fact that the riddles of the future have all been answered and written down by the works of the Past.

The opening of the Egyptian ports thirty centuries ago gave

to Europe on the one hand its greatest intellectual impulse, but on the other it demonstrated to Egypt that, if she would continue to exist she must become a maritime power greater than the nation that forced the passage of her ports or any other that might rise on the shores of the Mediterranean. As Egypt had for so many ages recognized the principle of quietude that is inherent in national isolation, so she became at once cognizant of that other great principle determining national existence: that once the barriers are broken all future greatness depends upon militant and maritime supremacy among those countries into whose affairs and ambitions the nation may be suddenly plunged.

The difficulty in the way of Egypt becoming a naval power was a lack of timber, since there grew not enough in Egypt for those little barks that carried the dead across the Lakes of Osiris. Egypt was obliged to go into wars of foreign conquest, not with one state, but with all bordering on the Mediterranean, for possession of that which she lacked and upon which depended the continuance of her nationality.

Now, though several tens of centuries have made their predetermined passage, we find another nation, which is Japan, facing the same old problem that lay upon Egypt those years past. As the supremacy of the Mediterranean was necessary to whatever nation was to be supreme upon its shores, so to Japan is the control of the Pacific not alone vital to her mastery among nations, but to her existence.

While Egyptian power in the Mediterranean depended upon material, Japanese dominion in the Pacific is consequent upon the possession of such naval bases as will in the future prevent the establishment of a Pacific naval power by any other nation. In other words, Japan must enunciate in new form the oldest of all international doctrines—commonly known as the Monroe Doctrine—and control unto herself the Pacific.

The dissolution of Egyptian naval supremacy was followed by the desolation of the Valley of the Nile; and, though now twenty-nine centuries have passed, never again has Egypt regained her independence, never again has Egypt smiled.

It is this fate that Japan intends to avoid.

The study of maritime supremacy, ancient or modern, shows vividly among certain salient characteristics that the size of the nation is an immaterial factor. The smallest powers have, by superior naval and military force, held in check the greatest of nations.

At one time Tyre, a single city, so dominated the Mediterranean that no other country, notwithstanding its wealth and greatness of empire, could develop power or commerce upon it. In a thirteen-years war this city held off from her rock the Babylonian Empire. It was only when every head was bald and every shoulder peeled that Tyre fell, and so terrible was her going down that it is said the very islands of those seas were troubled at her departure.

It is this singular and undue power that naval and military supremacy gives to a nation possessing it that has confirmed Japan's determination to become the Shogun of the Pacific.

The greatness of Japan will depend upon naval strength. Such power, in modern times, depends primarily upon possession of widely extended and militarily protected naval bases controlling routes of trade. It might be considered as axiomatic that the worth, or even the possibility of the existence, of naval power is proportionate to the number and strategic importance of its bases.

While Japan cannot expect the immediate conquest on land, other than the sea-bordering provinces, of such vast countries as China, India, and the Americas, yet, if she is once secure in the possession of certain naval bases in the Pacific, she will be able to dominate these and other nations; and, so long as her naval and military efficiency do not deteriorate, their wealth and populations shall count as naught.

As the supremacy of the Mediterranean affected only those nations dwelling and brawling on its shores, and while the control of the Atlantic covers only a larger portion of mankind, the mastery of the Pacific will concern the entire world, for upon its waters the divided portions of the races of man have met. The Pacific Ocean consists of over thirty-four per cent. of the world's surface, and not only do more than one-half of the human race rest somewhere about upon its littoral, but two-thirds of the undeveloped resources of the earth are in the lands upon whose shores its waters break.

It is this vast combination of mankind and unsquandered riches that determine the true significance of the Pacific. Whether the world in the future is to be dominated, politically, militarily, or industrially by any one nation, or a coalition of them, in the dominion of the Pacific shall it be determined.

Japan, militarily supreme in the Pacific, becomes industrially the controlling factor in Asia. And in due time, with the mastery of the major portion of the undeveloped wealth of the earth, Asiatic militancy and industrialism shall reign supreme in this world and the Mikado shall become the Mikado of kings.

When we contrast the everlasting and huge travail of sectional and class legislation that now absorbs the energies of this Republic with the aims and progress of Japan, we are overcome with shame and bitterness. On the one hand, a *ragoût* of politicians, on the other, the grandeur of national ambition moving irresistibly to a predetermined end.

As we look back over the entire history of man since he has been gathering himself together in separate political entities, we can find no condition analogous with opportunities for world supremacy as now lie before the bushido of Japan. The statesmen of this Asian Tyre have become cognizant of this, and even so have the masses in that dim, uncertain way masses comprehend, hence has come about the expansion of that mystical word—bushido. To this ambition of Japan there shall be no end—and rightly there should not be—until her islands have been razed as bare as rocks upon which fishermen spread their nets, or until the Japanese become the samurai of the human race and the remainder of man shall toil and trade for them and their greatness.

There is no more complete surety to world-wide supremacy for Japan than for the nations of the Occident to allow the present progressive deterioration of active militancy to continue without check or end. If Japan continues in the opposite course, and holds the bushido of her people aloof from the contamination of feminism and commercialism, the spirit of her samurai unsullied in the Temple of the Forty Ronins, then shall the rest of mankind play Atlas to the Islands of the Eastern Sea.

As maritime mastery of ancient nations depended upon the possession of provinces supplying the material for naval construction, in modern times the possession of military and naval bases bears the same relation to the control of the sea. The power of nations in a comparative sense should be apportioned to the number and security of such bases.

The future of Japan depends basically upon the possession of a sufficient number of such positions, so distributed in the Pacific that they command all trade routes to and from the East and West. Failure to secure these will, in time, relegate her to the environs of her rocky islands, and, like Egypt, though twenty-nine dim centuries shall pass, she shall rise up not again forever.

Fifteen years ago Japan eliminated China from the Pacific; four years ago she crushed for all time the power of Russia in this same ocean. Her present strategic position on the north Asian coast gives her complete control of it and all the trade routes that diverge from its shores. The island of Hokkaido commands the sea of Okhotsk and the northern Siberian littoral; the island of Nippon commands the Sea of Japan, southern Russia littoral and the Amur; Port Arthur commands the Gulf of Pechili, the sea-coasts of Pechili, Manchuria, and Shantung, the Laiho, Peiho and Yalu rivers; the island of Kinshu and Korea command the Yellow Sea and the Chinese coast as far south as the mouth of the Yangtze, while the islands of Kinshu and Formosa hold dominion from the Yangtze to the southern borders of the province of Fokien.[1]

Japan is now supreme, in a military and naval sense, on the Asian coast north of Hong-Kong. China has been eliminated from these seas, as has Russia. And by Japan's alliance with Great Britain, the elimination of British power in the Pacific, as we will hereafter show, has been accomplished subtly; even with the smile of Buddha has this been done.

[1] Chart I.

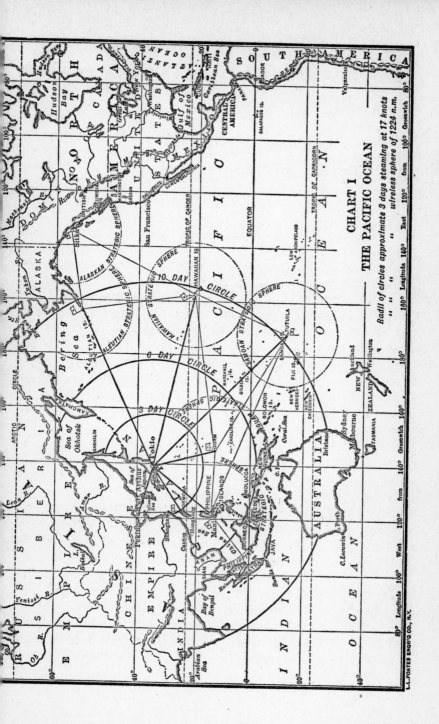

CHART I

THE PACIFIC OCEAN

Radii of circles approximate 3 days steaming at 17 knots
wireless sphere of 1224 n.m.

" " " " Longitude 140° East 120° from 100° Greenwich 80°

L.L.PONTES ENGR'G CO., N.Y.

There now remains but one power for Japan to put aside in order to make her supreme in the Pacific, with all which we have shown that term implies.

That nation is the United States.

As has been heretofore stated, Japan's future depends upon secure and widely distributed naval bases so strategically placed that they give her command over all routes of trade in the Pacific. Japan's next war will be a war for position, concerning which we have already commented upon in a previous chapter.[2]

Fortunate is it for Japan that this Republic not only possesses the very positions essential to Japan's security in the Pacific, but is sovereign over such territories as, under the dominion of Japan, will make her wholly and without doubt the Shogun of the Great Still Sea. But, more than that, Japan would, at the same time, eliminate the only rival she needs to fear in her struggle for supremacy, political or industrial, over the vast littoral of the Pacific. Should this Republic share the fate of China and Russia, then no nation or coalition of nations—as will hereafter be shown—can destroy Japan's supremacy, so long as her samurai do not wither away or bloom into feminism, and, like the *Agave Americana*, perish in florescence.

As has been shown (Chart I), the present strategic positions of Japan are, though relegated to the Asian coast, absolute in the command of those seas. By consulting the chart of the Pacific it will be seen that Japan cannot strengthen her position nor lay foundation for future supremacy by war with any country other than this Republic. The value the Pacific possessions of this nation bear to Japan is that they determine her possible supremacy of Pacific littoral. These territories consist of Alaska in the North Pacific, Hawaii in the Central, Samoa in the South, and the Philippines in the East.

To show graphically the strategic importance of these places, we have on the chart[3] circumscribed circles about them with approximate radii equal to two and a half to three days'

[2] Book I, chap. ix, pp. 72-80.
[3] Chart I.

steaming at seventeen knots an hour. The circumference of these circles, hence their value, is increased with the speed of warships or the number of hours distant from a naval base that a commander is justified in giving battle. The sphere of naval supremacy, as circumscribed by these circles, is not fixed, but is constantly expanding, concurrently with the increasing speed of warships. As each ripple wells outward their value is enhanced. Their ultimate extent or power cannot be computed, for it is correlative to the progress of invention as applied to naval warfare.

In order to show how irresistible are the incentives that force Japan to the acquisition of this Republic's insular possessions, we will consider her position as a Pacific and World Power augmented by sovereignty over those territories, singly and as a whole. These possessions have two valuations to Japan—their intrinsic wealth, and the value of their strategic position. However rich they may be in natural resources, their strategic worth is infinitely greater.

Intrinsically, the Philippines and Ladrones would more than double the territorial extent of Japan, as well as the empire's natural resources. This valuation, however great in itself, is insignificant in comparison to the strategic worth that these islands possess for Japan in their dominion over Asia and Asiatic hegemony.

We have shown that Japanese domination over the Asian coast, from the Sea of Okhotsk to the Formosan Strait, is absolute. The Philippine Islands bear the same strategic relationship to the Southern Asian coast as the Japanese islands do to the Northern, with the exception that the Philippines have the additional strategic value of commanding all ship-routes from Europe to the Far East. Their possession is more essential to Japan than either Korea or Manchuria. Without the Philippines, Japan's dominion in Asian seas will be no more than tentative, and her eventual domination or destruction will depend upon who holds these islands.

The Philippines command the Asian coast from the Formosan Strait to Cape Camao; the whole of Southern China, together with the Tsing-Kiang, the Min and West rivers; the

Gulf of Tong-King; the whole of French Indo-China, together with the China Sea, and the Sungoi and Me-Kong rivers. On the south, these islands command the entire East Indies, the Macassar and Malacca passages. Within the sphere of Philippine naval bases can be included the Gulf and Kingdom of Siam, the Malay Peninsula, Singapore, Strait of Malacca, Carimata and Sunda.

The Philippines are only three days' steaming from the main naval bases in Japan, hence Japanese bases in the Philippines would be but a continuation of her naval stations, and would allow Japan to concentrate in Philippine waters her entire navy within a comparatively few hours—lessening in time as naval invention progresses.

With the Philippines in possession of Japan, the dominion of European powers in Asia and the Pacific seas ends, and ends forever. By the time England's alliance with Japan ceases, her fortresses in the Far East will possess for her no value other than what affection may still hold for ruins and ambitions that are no more. Each of these Southern straits will become a Strait of Tsu-Shima—if there are Rojestven-skys to steam thither.

Sovereignty over the Philippines is not only imperative to Japan in her overlordship of Asia and the Pacific, but is essential to the very preservation of her national existence. The Philippines, in the possession of a great power, forms on her most vulnerable flank a point of attack that is more dangerous than would be Korea in the hands of the same power.

Possessed of the Philippines, Japan would complete her chain of island fortresses from the peninsula of Kamchatka to the Indian Ocean, by which she would bind in Asia from the West. With her castles put up on the mountain-tops of these seas, races of man could bay in vain.

The channel of Balintang is the Rubicon of Japan.

The relationship the Philippines bears to the Eastern Pacific is similarly held by Samoa in relation to the Southern Pacific. The harbor of Pago-Pago, on the island of Tutuila, is the most valuable anchorage in the South Pacific, and is equal if not superior to any in the entire ocean. This harbor can hold

twice the entire navy of Japan, and is so surrounded by towering bluffs that it cannot be reached by shell-fire from the outside, while the entrance is so narrow that two battleships
cannot enter at the same time. In such a manner has Panku,
in chiselling out this world for the wilful tribes of man, hereon
cut the perfectest of harbors in the most strategic position in
the South Pacific, a position that can be made to determine the
eventual sovereignty over Oceania, Australia, and New Zealand; and in possession of Japan would, in correlation with her
other positions, constitute the pivot of naval supremacy in the
Antipodes.

As the control of the South Pacific is determined by a proper
naval utilization of Pago-Pago, so is the naval dominion of
the North Pacific determined by the possession of Alaska,
and the strategic positions of the harbors on the peninsula. As
far as this Republic is concerned, Alaska is as insular as the
Philippines, and sovereignty over it is determined by the same
factors.

To Japan, the intrinsic value of Alaska is greater than any
other American possession. Not alone would the territorial
extent of the empire be trebled, but trebled with almost in-
exhaustible wealth. Fisheries, iron, coal, timber, copper and
gold in such abundance that the crowded coolies of that nation
could scarce indent or scratch the lid of this treasure—by which
nature has redeemed its inhospitable shores. But if, with a
single exception, Alaska were as barren as the sea-gnawed
rocks upon which the walrus lolls in the cold sunlight of the
inner Arctic, it would even then possess a determinate condition, outside of its strategic value, in the sovereignty of the
Pacific.

A navy without adequate bases is almost as useless as a navy
without guns or sailors, but a fleet without coal needs neither
bases nor guns nor men; hence the command of coal-fields on
or adjacent to the seas of naval strife does now, and in the
future more so, determine the outcome of maritime struggles.
We therefore establish this fact, that in the approaching combat for the dominion of the Pacific the control of the Alaskan

coal-fields will be eventually necessary to the victor, and without them complete supremacy cannot be maintained.

As in ancient times the possession of timber-bearing provinces was essential to naval supremacy, so the command of bordering coal-fields is imperative to the nation that would extend its dominion over the Pacific. Whether in the Eastern or Western Hemisphere, the entire littoral of the Pacific, with the exception of Japan, North China, and Alaska, is lacking in coal of good quality. As we have heretofore shown, Japan commands, so far as maritime use is concerned, the coal-fields of North China and Manchuria. With Alaska in her possession she will control the coal supply of the Pacific to the extent, and so strategically placed, that it will be impossible for any other power to carry on naval or military enterprises against her.

The harbors along the Alaskan peninsula, where vast deposits of Welsh coal are eroding in the wash of the sea, and where the winters are so modulated by the Japan current as to be no severer than in New York harbor, are three degrees nearer Japan than are the Hawaiian Islands, and command the entire ocean west of the one hundred and thirty-fifth degree of longitude and north of the fortieth degree parallel.

Had Russia not sold Alaska, her dreams for the conquest of Asia might have been realized and the battle of Tsu-Shima never fought.

Hawaii, in conjunction with the strategic positions heretofore described, can be considered the most important position in the Pacific. Not only would it be impossible for any nation to hope for sovereignty over the Pacific without being in possession of these islands, but no power could undertake without them any continuous naval operations or maritime expansion. Their great value is due to the fact that they are situated almost in the centre of the Pacific, and that the ports nearest to them are distant over two thousand miles. They sever the North Pacific from the South, the East from the West. In this segmentation lies their mastery.

The desert and the sea are in themselves the barrenest of

tenures, but while one has oases, in the other are islands, and when the caravans of man, whether by camel or ship, start across their wastes, these oases and islands determine the way of their passage.

The value of such a position is not due to its own productivity, but to the wealth of all the nations whose trade routes pass its turreted shores.

Nearly fifteen years ago the value of the Hawaiian Islands, and the necessity of their possession to any nation who would be sovereign over the Pacific, was recognized by Japan. When this Republic annexed the islands at that time, Japan alone protested and notified the American Government that she would not then, nor at any time in the future, acquiesce in the control of the Hawaiian Islands by this nation.

Years have now passed, but the protest of Japan has never been withdrawn, nor have preparations ever ceased to bring about in due time its enforcement. This Republic may forget, or after its conquests sleep, but in that Silent Pentagon[4] where rests together the sceptre of the Mikado and the sword of the samurai there is no forgetfulness, and in their slumbers—dreams.

However great may be the singular value of each of the American Pacific possessions to the future development of Japan, it is in the strategic relationship each bears to the other, and their relation in the aggregate to Japanese maritime power, that is to be found their greatest value—not the price of one, but a dozen wars.

The primary laws governing naval supremacy in an ocean surrounded, but not divided, by continents may be formulated as follows:

(1) The number of naval bases must be increased in a proportionate ratio to the increase of the navy.

(2) The efficiency of the navy is lessened whenever the number and capacity of naval bases is less than required by such fleets as conditions of warfare may force to base on them.

(3) The possession of too few or not widely spaced

[4] The Genro, or Five Elder Statesmen.

bases means the restriction of naval activity to a
defined and perhaps unimportant portion of the
theatre of war, as well as periods of complete in-
activity consequent upon undue concentration.

(4) The efficiency of the navy is correspondingly weakened where there are, within such strategic triangles
as are formed by two, three, or more of its bases,
fortified positions belonging to the enemy.

While the converse of some of the above conditions may
qualitatively determine success in maritime warfare, there are
certain positive factors that increase the value of these conditions:

(1) Success in naval warfare, as on land, is largely controlled by the number and directness of its lines of
communication to widespread and divergent bases.

(2) The greatest possible number of strategic triangles
formed by these divergent bases, in which one of
the vertices rests on the nation's main naval base
while the subordinate bases constitute the vertices of
more than one strategic triangle, independent of or
in conjunction with the main naval base.

(3) The value of these strategic triangles, outside of
their homogeneity and number, is determined by the
location and number of the enemy's bases; whether
or not they exceed or are less in number and are
within or without these strategic triangles.

In land warfare strategic positions held in the beginning of
hostilities often determine its eventual conclusion. In maritime
war this condition is even more significant, inasmuch as without a certain number of these positions war cannot be begun.
In proportion to their number, defence and strategic value can
maritime supremacy be proportionately determined prior to
hostilities.

The value of a series of naval and military bases in such
an ocean as the Pacific is determined by three positive conditions:

(1) The number of strategic triangles they form.

(2) The number of times one vertex, resting on the main

naval base of the nation, is common to the aggregate of triangles.

(3) The absence of foreign naval bases within such triangles, or the distance of their separation as determined by the number of intervening lines of offence.

It is in consideration of these principles that we will deal with Japan in the Pacific subsequent to a successful war with this Republic, to determine whether or not her future strategic position, independent of the economic and geographical advantages, will be sufficiently augmented as to warrant a war with this Republic.

If, at the end of such a struggle, Japan should retain empire over the American Pacific provinces, we know of no war between single states so significant in its results and so basic for the formation of world empire under the hegemony of one nation. By chart has been shown graphically what will be Japan's position subsequent to such a war, and its relationship to the future control of the world. Radiating from Japan, with one vertex resting therein and common to all, do eight strategic triangles spread abroad over the Pacific, while four similar triangles with vertices independent of Japan, but connected with the main vertex resting therein, surround these others with an outward sphere of defence.[5]

Within these twelve triangles there is not to be found a single stronghold belonging to another nation, while every naval base held by other powers, together with their lines of intercommunication, would be subject to Japanese attack from two to eight divergent bases. Any foreign fleet on the Pacific would always be open to attack in any part of the ocean by the whole of the Japanese navy. No power could attempt to transfer from one naval base to another, across Japan's intervening lines, a fleet less than the Japanese navy.

Anywhere on the trade routes of the Pacific Japan could fight a naval battle and always be within three days' steaming of not less than two divergent bases. Connecting Alaska and Samoa with Hawaii by submarine cable, the Mikado, within his Castle of Yeddo, could at all times be in direct and simul-

[5] Chart I.

taneous communication, not only with these widely scattered harbors, but with every Japanese warship steaming about over the Pacific. These different bases are so situated, together with subordinate isles, that no Japanese warship would ever be without the sphere of wireless communication with some one of them. Should the Mikado before dawn demand, "Where are my ships of war?" the admiral of the fleet could lay before him the chart of the Pacific and by pins in the painted ocean show whither each torpedo-boat and battleship was at that moment steaming its way through the sea and the night.

To such small space has science relegated this vast sea that the fleets of Japan could be scattered over it and yet be as much under the control of the commanding admiral in Tokio as though they were a small fleet within the vision of his eye.

Not within these twelve strategic triangles commanding the Pacific can be found a spot wherein Japan could not concentrate in ten days seven-tenths of her entire navy, free from colliers, free from supply and hospital ships, free from all the dead impedimenta of the sea. Regardless in what corner of the ocean the rendezvous might be, these fleets would at all times be within three days of one or more naval bases.[6]

By such a war Japan would be placed in a naval and military position so invulnerable that no nation or coalition of them could attack her. Calmly, from this vast Gibraltar of the ocean, she could look down upon the world and smile at its rage and trepidation—this island tribe that owns no heaven and annoys no god.

Upon this foundation of one-third the world, Japan would begin the building of a new empire; and as the militant capac-ities of the nations in the West continued to deteriorate through Hague Conferences, the crumbling diseases of femi-nism, commercialism and socialism, one by one should they go into the great tumulus upon which, in due time, shall be raised the throne of the Three-Toed Dragon.

We know not for how many years the Occident has been muttering to itself of a peril that it has called yellow. In the penumbra of its dreams it has seen indistinct shadows light-

[6] Chart I.

ened, or rather made pallid, with uncertain consciousness, in which, sicklied over with fear, phantoms have rioted. These chimeras in the fear and dreaming of Western nations are what might be called probabilities, monstrous, terrifying, but for all that only phantoms, having their origin in truth, but transferred by that strange somnolence—the public mind—to the shadowiest of realms.

To this dim region belongs the Yellow Peril.

Ever since the Occident entered into close contact with the Orient, politically as well as commercially, it has intuitively become cognizant of a peril. This intuition has been as correct as the reasons concerning its origin and consummation have been somnolently wrong. In this misplacement of the source of the Yellow Peril, the Occident has only repeated what has been done innumerable times before among all portions of mankind.

When the dread of the Orient instinctively entered and permeated the consciousness of the West, the whole Occident asked:

"Whence will it come?" The reply, based quite naturally on the old and popular misconception of what constitutes capacity to conquer, laid upon China the responsibility of the Yellow Peril because of its immensity.

The world never learns until too late what determines the militant qualities of a nation.

True militancy belongs to primitive, homogeneous peoples, wherein political control is restricted to the fewest number of persons, or even to a single individual. National militancy deteriorates in inverse ratio to the increasing complexity of social and political organisms, hence the larger a nation is and the more individualistic its inhabitants become through the multiplicity of avocations the less capable is a nation to be a conquering power. On account of this we invariably find that the conquesting period of a nation appears in the earliest portion of its career—that is, when it first enters into the comity of nations.

The Chinese: period of conquest ended with Tsin-Chi-Hoangti, twenty-one centuries ago. The building of the great wall marked its consummation.

The mistake of the Occident is an old error.

If, in the third century B.C., such great empires as Persia and Egypt were somnolently conscious of threatening peril—as no doubt they were—they committed the same error the West is making at the present time. Not one of them could imagine that out of the barren mountains of the Balkans, without wealth or numbers—nay, with nothing other than beak and talons—a young gray eagle would swoop down and destroy them as so many bleating lambs. Nor any more did the empires of the seventh century dread the wild horsemen in the barren tenure of the Arabian Desert. Not one of them; though in due time all were trampled under hoof by these same nomads.

Among the great empires of the thirteenth century not one was free from the dread of the same peril or was not haunted by the same phantoms. Yet neither China nor India, neither the empires of Central Asia nor the kingdoms of Eastern Europe, could conceive, though this ill-defined fear brooded heavily over them, of any source of danger other than from those nations whose immensity they dreaded. Upon them fell no terror of certain snout-faced marauders who roamed with their herds over the deserts of Gobi. But with the suddenness of the terrible winds that sweep across Shamo these herders fell upon the world and wagged their cowtail banners in the faces of a hundred kings.

In such a manner, in the immensity of China's shadow, four rocky islands have been overlooked.

V

IT IS difficult to make a just comparison between the naval and military capacity of one's own country and that of a nation which, through circumstances beyond the sphere of its control, has entered into a struggle for supremacy permitting of no consummation except through a conflict of arms. However sincere one's efforts may be to free himself from prejudice and exaggerated confidence in his country's prowess, yet so innumerable are the intricacies of modern warfare, and so limitless are the possibilities of self-deception, that, even in the sincerest efforts to be exact, one is apt to be unfair and his deductions unjust.

Conditions pre-eminent in peace are fondly hoped to manifest themselves in war, though they are lacking in attributes necessary to the prosecution of a modern conflict. Unfortunately or otherwise, as the case may be, those phases of warfare that are so firmly imbued in the popular mind no longer exist, except in greatly modified forms. In consequence of this, indiscriminate patriotism is almost always erroneous in its ideas concerning the conduct of modern war and the conditions necessary to its success.

These errors in popular judgment have two phases that fit one into the other, and thus complete, under the guise of discrimination, their self-beguilement. The positive factor is due to that thoughtless patriotism that exaggerates the capacity of one's own nation, and the negative factor that exaggerates the deficiencies of the enemy. While we fasten our thoughts ever on victory, we close our eyes to the difficulties of gaining it. It is in this voluntary blindness that we do not perceive our weakness nor elements of strength belonging to the enemy. Their prowess has among us no partisans, no voice.

In individual life a man who deceives himself, whether through arrogance or ignorance, as to his own ability or capacity, and in consequence ends in disaster, is regarded as a boaster, a man not only unworthy of confidence, but deserving of no compassion. His misfortunes the public regards complacently as being retributive of his vain-gloriousness and failure to take such ordinary precautions as would have laid bare the strength of his competitor.

Nations being but composite individuals, all that which moves or is part of an individual, in a larger sense, moves or is part of a nation. To free a nation from error is to enlighten the individual. And only to the degree that the individual will be receptive of truth can a nation be freed from that vanity which ends in national ruin.

The first duty a man owes his country is to realize that he cannot liquidate his indebtedness to it by vain complacency; his boasts are not only without value, but are a counterfeit of the real emotions to which he should give expression. In the survival of nations the vanity of man has no place.

In making a comparison between the naval strength of Japan and the United States, that which most commonly does service is to compare the number and tonnage of ships belonging to each navy, and then, by no other means than subtraction, determine which is the more powerful. This manner of judgment is common to man when all questions involving power are determined by visual comparison. The true criterion of naval supremacy in this epoch, when science enters into every detail of naval construction, is determined according to the efficiency of such construction, supplemented by scientific direction prior to and in battle. To this must be added strategic considerations that circumscribe or augment the opportunities of commanders, diminishing or increasing their chances of victory. Such are the conditions that must be investigated by all who wish to arrive at some just approximation of the outcome of modern war.

In recent times no means of deception are so widely employed as statistical tables. They have become in this age of calculators a fetich more potent than the wonder-working charms of a primitive people. In the beginning of 1904 these tables made the Russian navy third, and the Japanese least, of the great powers.

In a few hours, one May afternoon, the Russian navy ceased to exist.

In statistical tables to-day, we find that by vessels and tonnage the United States navy ranks third, and that of Japan fifth. Ordinarily this is as far as the casual observer goes. To him it is self-evident that a naval power of the fifth rank could not hope to compete with one that is third in naval supremacy. To determine the truth or error of this belief, and whether or not the true elements of naval superiority are proportionate to this catalogue of vessels, or are to a degree lacking, is the first duty of every citizen who wishes to arrive at a just conclusion.

In modern naval warfare there are three fighting lines, consisting of battleships, armored cruisers, and torpedo craft. According to statistical tables the United States is superior to Japan in battleships, though correspondingly inferior in armored cruisers and torpedo craft. But since the battle of Tsu-Shima a new type of battleship has been introduced into the world, that possesses a fighting capacity equal to any three battleships now in the American navy. While the American battleships exceed in number those of the Japanese,[1] yet the latter possess nearly thirty per cent. more big guns.[2]

The efficiency of the means employed in naval warfare are supposed to determine the probabilities of victory, yet these chances are great or small as the commanders are proficient or inexperienced in the duties devolving upon them, each year becoming more intricate, the strain more constant and wearing, so that the faculties and strength of men commanding these vast ships endure only so long as their vigor is unimpaired and their mentality still possesses the keen alertness of youth.

---

[1] Appendix, Table IV.

[2] "It was the powerful guns of our batteries that inflicted their casualties upon the Japanese, and it was with their large-caliber guns that they destroyed our fleet."—Admiral ROJESTVENSKY.

Never have the gods of all the tribes put upon the seas such monsters as man now sends over them. To contemplate them is to wonder; to know them is to look up to these gods and smile. That which is as soft as iron belongs in no way to them. Their steel bowels, grinding and rumbling below the splash of the sea, are fed on quarried rock. Their arteries are steel, their nerves copper, their blood red and blue flames. With the prescience of the supernatural, they peer into space. Their voices scream through gales, and they whisper together over a thousand miles of sea. They reach out and destroy that which the eye of man cannot perceive.

But all this cyclopean activity depends upon, fulfils its purpose or is worthless as is active or wearied the tiny brain of a single man. All this terribleness will vanish, returning again into the inanimate whenever the capacity and vigor of the guiding mind deteriorates or is worn down by the years that have stolen away the quick grasp of youth.

Because of this natural deterioration in man the American navy, even if it were perfect in every other phase of its construction and government, its present system of command would counteract this efficiency, and all that which had gone to make up a great navy would, in some few hours of an afternoon, vanish. For in this nation, captains are not commissioned until they reach the age of fifty-six, while in Japan the average age of such officers is thirty-eight; a difference of nearly twenty years. This is not all. While captains in the American navy have only four and a half years in this grade, the Japanese have eight, giving them twice as much experience though they are twenty years younger.[3]

As the success of armies depends primarily upon the ability of general officers, so in the great naval engagements of the future, where fleets instead of single vessels will engage in battle, success will depend upon the ability, vigor, and experience of sea-going flag-officers. In the American navy rear-admirals are not commissioned until they reach the advanced age of sixty, while in Japan officers receive this rank at forty-four. In America, sea-going flag-officers only pass one and a

[3] Appendix, Table V.

half years in this grade, while in Japan such officers are on duty for eleven years.[4]

Whatever faults exist in the American navy, the nation and not the navy is responsible. That in many of the vessels armor does not exist in vital parts,[5] that the main armor-belt itself is wrongly placed,[6] that the gun-ports are so large and the secondary batteries so placed as to expose both guns and gun-crews to destruction,[7] that the navy is without adequate torpedo protection,[8] and that the gun-decks are so low as to render useless a portion of the ship's armament under various conditions of the sea[9] are in no way the fault of the navy. For these and many other deficiencies that relegate the combative power of the American navy to a comparatively low degree, the nation is alone responsible. By its indifference, as expressed through its legislative representatives, these things have come about—to efface, in due time, all the victories of the past.

These deficiencies, however, do not affect the naval situation existing between Japan and this Republic; conditions governing their relative naval strength in the Pacific are not confined to catalogues of ships. Whether perfect or useless, these vessels last for no great period of time. Transient, fragile, these gigantic fabrications of man cannot endure for long. Their life is but a score of years, if they do not vanish in the tragedy of a single hour.

True naval comparison is, therefore, not based on naval tables nor good nor poor ships, but on conditions that shape, not only the building of navies but the destinies of nations. In such a comparison alone can we determine what naval forces are necessary for this Republic to maintain in order to be superior over Japan so long as their interests clash in the Pacific. In modern times, wherein all the phases of warfare are modified from year to year by science and invention, there must be in the army and navy of every nation a progress con-

[4] Appendix, Table V.
[5] Appendix, Table VIa.
[6] Appendix, Table VIb.
[7] Appendix, Table VIc.
[8] Appendix, Table VId.
[9] Appendix, Table VIe.

current with these changes. The old idea, still prevalent in this Republic, that armies and navies are but transitory expedients, brought into existence only in the time of war and put aside when it ends, will sooner or later plunge the nation into that abyss out of which few have come forth. Now, and in the future more so, must all preparations for war be made in time of peace, even to the extent of working out hypothetical campaigns in probable theatres of war. Whatever nation neglects these precautions is doomed to defeat.

The navy must be considered as being co-existent with the nation, and to be constantly prepared for war so long as the nation shall endure; expanding in size and efficiency as the nation expands in political greatness; progressing as science and invention progress, so that it is always ready to encounter those old storms that fall upon nations out of clear skies. In modern times there are four conditions that demand continuity in the building of a navy and a prescience in the nation's naval policy.

While a battleship endures less than a score of years, its usefulness may cease in a few months. Not only does it take years to build such ships, but the facilities for their construction are limited. A half-dozen wars could be lost and won before the destroyed fleets of a nation, or those made useless through the development of naval science, could be replaced. The potential naval strength of a nation is determined not by the products of a single year, but by the term of years that marks its duration; not by alternating cycles of renascence and deterioration, but by a continuous policy of production and excellence as determined from year to year by the increasing political importance of the nation and the progress in naval invention. To accomplish this the navy must be removed far from the sphere of politics—that state of transitory ideals, that ideal of transitory greatness. But this nation has not put aside the characteristics, so prominent in republican forms of government, of treating the army and navy as the expedients of a struggle, rather than the permanent source of a nation's safety. If this policy were possible in the past, it is no longer so, and each succeeding year diminishes its probabilities.

The present navy, being the greatest ever possessed by this Republic, is an illustration of the evils of sporadic growth upon the débris piles of deterioration. Instead of it being the result of a national ideal, it was only gained through the strenuous efforts of the executive. Should this administration be succeeded by a non-militant one, then in less than four years the American navy will be the least efficient among the navies of the great powers.

The continuity of a nation's naval policy forms, in one phase, a truer basis for naval comparison between two powers.

In Japan the army and navy are placed above and beyond the reach of politics.[10] Ministries may rise and fall, but the military and naval development goes on unhindered, co-existent with the life and greatness of the empire itself. But in this Republic, not only is there no continuity in naval development, but no freedom from political circumscription.

While the effective life of a battleship is very brief, its efficiency may be so diminished at any time as to render it practically obsolete. An example of this is seen in changes of naval architecture following the Japanese-Russian War, when, by the introduction of the *Dreadnaught* type of vessel, the fighting capacity of a single ship was trebled. Whenever, therefore, sudden and radical changes occur in naval construction, that nation which possesses a flexible naval system, freed from all political restrictions, will alter its naval policy in the shortest time, and adjust itself to new conditions before the nation whose naval department is the shuttlecock of contending political factions can even realize the necessity of such a departure. It is due to this that the Japanese navy is so superior in modern fighting capacity to that of the United States.[11]

Japan constructs a twenty-thousand-ton battleship of the new type in two years, and an armored cruiser in less time. In the United States it has required over five years to build a sixteen-thousand-ton battleship, and five years and two months to build an armored cruiser. In 1909 Japan will have four of

[10] Changes in the Japanese cabinet do not affect the ministers of war or navy. They are almost as free from political influences as the Mikado.
[11] Appendix, Table IV.

these new battleships and the United States none; in 1911 Japan will have eight and this nation two. This ratio will continue so long as the American navy remains subject to public indifference and political control: in one administration or Congress, sporadic in energy but obsolete in construction; in another, dormant, decadent, forgotten.

We now come to the consideration of the determinate factor in naval warfare wherein is to be found the true comparison of naval strength—the strategic. No nation's naval power is constant in its relation to all countries. The efficiency of a fleet decreases or is augmented as the distance from its main base to the theatre of war is lengthened or diminished. The area of naval efficiency is determined by the multiplicity, dispersion, and efficiency of its naval bases. Without these depots a navy decreases in efficiency as it increases in size.

We have, in the previous chapter,[12] made clear the strategic possibilities of the Pacific and Japan's relationship to them as well as the commanding position she already possesses. The strategic situation, concretely, is that the entire Japanese naval power, not alone her fleets, but her navy yards, docks, arsenals, people, and resources are situated in the strategic centre of the Pacific, while the naval bases and naval resources of the United States are in the Atlantic Ocean, seventeen thousand miles from the sphere of this approaching struggle. The larger the American navy becomes under these conditions the less capable is it to wage war in the Pacific.

To overcome these difficulties must be the first consideration of this Republic; hence it is the primordial basis of naval comparison between the two nations. In the previous chapter was made apparent what this nation must accomplish in order to maintain a fleet in the Pacific Ocean, viz., the establishment of naval bases in the Philippines, Hawaii, Alaska, Washington, Oregon, and California, together with their complete protection against land attack, and the maintenance in the Pacific of fleets equal to the entire navy of Japan. None of these things exist, even in an embryonic state, and, instead of preparation being made to remedy them, active opposition is

[12] Chap. IV.

manifest throughout the Republic. Unless this is done in time of peace Japan will accomplish in war what has been shown to be her ambitions.

In the succeeding chapters will be shown, step by step, the ultimate conquest of the Pacific, and the elimination of this Republic from its government and its destinies in a manner no different from the fate of China and Russia.

Were the American navy twice its tonnage, twice the number of vessels, all other conditions remaining the same, it would affect in no way nor in any degree the culmination of this approaching struggle. The conquest of the Pacific is beyond the ton weight of steel or the old, old catalogue of ships.

VI

Nations, especially republics, oftentimes go to extremes in the advocacy of some popular measure that for the time being finds favor with the masses. This has been true during the last few years in the struggle to gain a navy commensurate with the political development of the Republic. The advocates of naval expansion have, however, given a wrong impression to the public, not as to the necessity of a navy, but as to the accomplishment of enterprises that are beyond its sphere.

A nation without a navy proportionate to its political responsibilities will soon be deprived of its power beyond the sea; but a country that risks its entire dependence upon a navy places itself in a position, not only to lose the navy but its insular possessions, and, suffering defeat within its boundaries, be deprived of world significance.

Neither now nor in the future will international conflicts be determined by naval engagements. In some instances naval victories may produce conditions that will tend to hasten the conclusion of a war, but such a state of national weakness is problematical. Only those who overlook the natural laws governing international struggles fail to comprehend that victory or defeat is relative to the power or weakness of a nation as a whole.

To affect, to cripple, or destroy a nation in warfare can only be done by injuring to that degree its power of government, its resources, and its ability to defend itself against the enforcement of hostile demands. If the entire German navy were sunk in the North Sea, England could get no nearer Berlin than she is to-day, and the demands that she might then make upon the German Empire could no more be enforced than at any time prior to the destruction of that nation's navy. The multiplicity of the arteries of modern trade and interchange prevents the possibility of blockade.

If the entire American navy should suddenly be destroyed in a storm or war, it would have no effect whatsoever upon the government of the Republic, upon its resources or power. As all wars have been, so in the future will they be, determined by land warfare.

Naval engagements, being remote from a nation, affect it only as a single battle. The number of men destroyed is, compared to the nation, insignificant. Neither the political constitution of the country, nor means to wage war, nor the belligerent attitude of the people are affected. When a nation's navy is destroyed it will then assume a land defence, and only subsequent to the defeat of its armies, the passing of its territory and resources into the hands of an enemy, will it consider surrender.

The navy is but a portion of the military forces of a nation, and was originally composed of soldiers. In recent years it has the appearance of being a separate institution, but to consider it as such is to mistake the essential characteristics of warfare. A navy to-day is more dependent upon the land forces of a nation than heretofore.

Navies are not self-sustaining in any degree whatsoever. Nothing that is necessary for their maintenance can be gotten by them out of the sea. The vast theatre of war, where their campaigns are made and battles fought, is as barren as the desert. In consequence, naval bases are as necessary as fleets in every sea where nations have established or expect to extend their suzerainty.

As we have shown in a previous chapter and by chart,[1] every naval base is the centre of a naval sphere of activity, the radii of which are determined by the steaming capacity of the fleets based upon it.

The value of naval bases diminishes as the square of the distance between the extremes of their radii increases.

A nation that expects to be supreme in any ocean must be

[1] Chart I.

governed by the principle that the distance between its naval bases must never exceed the sum of the radii of any two of them.

The security of naval bases rests fundamentally with their land defence. To depend upon the navy to protect its own bases in all emergencies is to reduce naval and military science to absurdity. To attempt the protection of naval bases by permanent batteries alone is only to be ignorant of the changes modern means of transportation have made in regard to the value of harbor defences. If once the enemy gains temporary command of the sea, and at the same time possesses adequate transport fleets, it will be able to seize every naval base by land attack, unless prevented by mobile armies in their rear. Modern harbor fortifications consist of series of detached batteries, and their only defence rests on armies equal in size and efficiency to any that an enemy may land adjacent to or distant from the harbors they intend to capture.

For the United States to lose temporary possession of the Pacific Ocean, as will necessarily be the case, owing to the complete lack of protected naval bases and a navy sufficiently great to overcome the natural strategic difficulties of a naval war with Japan, means, as we will hereafter show, that it could not in the same war undertake a second naval enterprise in this sea. War between the United States and Japan will be upon land. Armies rather than navies will constitute from beginning to end the determinate factors in this approaching struggle.

To make a just comparison between the Japanese and American armies, their military systems in general, as well as their potential military power, is, in some respects, a difficult undertaking. Patriotism on the one hand and prejudice on the other are apt to circumscribe facts, though every effort has been made to avoid partisanship as well as antipathy. It is due to this cold exactitude of truth that there may come into our work another bitterness more sombre and foreboding than has heretofore been expressed.

The worth of armies is not measured by their magnitude, but by the perfection of their construction, by the spirit that inspires them, and by the skill displayed in their use.

The capacity of armies is not constant in all theatres of war nor against all nations. The maximum military strength Germany could put into the field against China would be much less than she could place in New Jersey or against the frontiers of Austria and France. As in naval comparison, it is erroneous to say that one nation is first in military power and another sixth or seventh. In armies, as in naval forces, generalizations are not permissible if a just comparison of strength between two nations is sought.

The armies of two combatants must be considered intrinsically, comparatively, then in relation to the theatre of war and the strategic conditions extant. The strategic position of one power may be so favorable as to require an excessive increase of force on the part of the other in order to overcome natural impediments. Again, that which appears in peace to be an obstacle, oftentimes in war becomes an actual aid.

The first consideration must be given to the intrinsic merits or deficiencies of the two armies. This comparison in modern times, while not exact, is possible to a greater extent than in the past. And as science enters more fully into the construction and employment of armies, the more must their training be confined to the time of peace and the longer must that training be carried on. To the degree of its thoroughness or superficiality, to its approximation of war conditions and actualities; are we able to form, in times of peace, an estimation of an army's capacity in war.

The force that Japan could almost immediately place in the field exceeds a million and a quarter of men,[2] all of whom have had three years' training in the regular army and in specific branches of service. Over eight hundred thousand have had the additional experience of from one year to a year and a half on the battlefields of Manchuria. The officers of these forces are technically trained in military science and in all the strange emergencies of actual war.

In the struggle with Russia the efficiency of the Japanese

[2] "The Japanese put into the field against us troops of various categories to the number of 1,500,000—or more than three times the estimate of our general staff." —KUROPATKIN.

forces exceeded, to the most minute details, that of any army which has heretofore taken the field. This effectiveness is due primarily to the fact that the armies of modern Japan were not organized until after the Franco-Prussian War.

Moreover, there were in Japan none of those prejudiced associations that have prevented, from time to time, the reorganization of national armies. The character of the Japanese people, in addition, permitted the development of German militarism to a high degree. It was only necessary to congeal the feudal system of old Japan into the modern feudalism of Germany, while in the Mikado was retained the first attribute of a military nation—absolute centralization of power.[3] In all phases of national life Japan is pregnant with the spirit of militarism. The religion of the nation is militant, and the empire is ridged with Hills of Kudan, within whose temples are enshrined the spirits of those who have gone down in battle. Their social organism is based upon supremacy of the samurai; the tradesman ranks below the toiler of the soil and sea. The national ideal is the bushido, the lists of the armed knight, the way of the knightly man.

The American army in time of peace is limited by Congress to one hundred thousand men, but public indifference and prejudice against military activity has reduced this force to less than fifty thousand. While Japan in modern military development came into existence subsequent to the Franco-Prussian War, the United States, in the same sense, came into being prior to the Napoleonic struggles, and the American military system of to-day was the system of Europe one hundred and fifty years ago; and there has been, not only a lack of development, but in many respects deterioration. The regular army as now constructed and stationed could not mobilize on the Pacific coast, in event of war with Japan, a field force of twenty thousand men, while six hundred thousand are necessary.

In the regular army and militia of the United States, the essentials of military organization on a war basis are absent. No staffs exist; no organization of units; no plans for mobiliza-

[3] "The strength of Japan was in the complete union of her people, army, and government, and it was this union that gave her the victory."—KUROPATKIN.

tion; no means of transportation or caring for large bodies of troops; no military equipment nor means to produce it. While Japan has over fifty thousand scientifically trained military officers, the United States has less than four thousand. A war with Japan, necessitating the mobilization of a force equal to that which Japan could put in the field, would result in placing the American armies under the command of officers, ninety-two per cent. of whom would be, not only wholly ignorant of the science of war, but, being appointed through political prefer- ence, would represent only an inferior quality of incapacity.[4] Were it possible for the rank and file of the volunteer forces to be as efficient as the Japanese line, they would only be led to disaster and slaughter through the incompetence of their civilian officers.

The efficiency of every army is determined by the efficiency of its corps of officers. Though self-evident, it is not fully understood that in great wars the genius and knowledge, the ability and experience of general officers determine more than any other factor the success or failure of campaigns. Owing to the American system, there would not be, in event of war, a single American officer who has ever handled, in peace or war, a corps of troops. Japanese generals, on the other hand, have fed, marched, cared for, placed on the field of battle, supplied with food and ammunition, manœuvred, and fought several army corps simultaneously with science and exactitude.

Success in military operations depends primarily upon the excess of rapidity that one army has over another in reaching a theatre of war and moving therein. As the theatre of war increases in distance from the main bases of the combatants and extends in area, armies become more dependent upon the rapidity and capacity of means of transportation. As an army is limited or retarded in gaining strategic positions in a theatre of war, its worth is decreased accordingly. If a theatre of war is trans-oceanic, and the means of transportation limited, then a great army at home dwindles down to the size of a single contingent, as determined by the capacity of the transport fleet per voyage.

[4] Appendix, Table VIIIa.

Modern means of transportation and communication, while shrinking in a practical sense the size of the world, have to a corresponding degree increased the area of modern and future warfare. It has become necessary for all nations having isolated possessions to defend, or a vast area of continental territory to protect, to provide in times of peace adequate means of transportation.

If, at the present time, a state of war existed between this Republic and another country which necessitated the transportation of one hundred thousand troops to the Philippines, and to this end the United States should utilize the eight American trans-Pacific steamers that constitute the entire American merchant marine in the Pacific, it would require two years to transport this number of men. To oppose their landing, a force no larger than the capacity of the transports per voyage would be necessary. The value of the American army for use in trans-oceanic warfare is determined in one phase by the capacity of its means of transportation. The complete absence of these means was recently made clear to the Republic when it witnessed that melancholy and foreboding spectacle of sixteen American battleships convoyed by twenty-eight vessels flying a foreign flag, without which they could not have steamed beyond the sphere of their Atlantic bases, and the journey to the Pacific would have been but an idle speculation.

Japan, being an Island Empire, was forced to realize early in her association with the world as a whole that her political sphere would remain circumscribed to her islands so long as she was unable to move freely over the seas. This necessity has developed, under governmental inspiration and control, a system of merchant marine, which in time of war passes, as conditions necessitate, under direct control of the government. The Japanese transport fleets consist of a hundred steamers, ranging from one thousand to fourteen thousand tons each.[5] On these fleets can be transported at one time two hundred thousand men, together with their entire equipment. These vessels, leaving the ports of Japan, would be able to reach the Philippines in five days; Hawaii in fourteen; the coast of Cali-

[5] Appendix, Table VII.

fornia in twenty-two days; the coasts of Alaska, Washington, and Oregon in less than twenty.

We have, in the first part of this work,[6] shown the worthlessness of volunteers in modern warfare, and the inefficiency of the American volunteers as demonstrated in the past wars of the nation. We will now consider the regular army of the United States, in order to determine whether or not it can be utilized in a war with Japan as a nucleus upon which to build an army of suitable proportions in the course of two or three years. In this consideration we will, by the exemplification of permanent peace conditions, show the actual state in which each branch of the army exists, so that each for himself may judge of its efficiency or inadequacy.

In an international war the harbor and coast fortifications are supposed to be the first line of a nation's defence, if the enemy has command of the sea. In Alaska, Hawaii, Samoa, and the Philippines there are no such fortifications. On the Pacific coast, San Diego, San Francisco, the Columbia River, and Puget Sound depend upon their forts for protection, with a serenity that, in light of their defencelessness and incapacity, is but a grave example of public indifference and ignorance concerning military affairs. The cry for more fortifications that from time to time goes up from different parts of the nation is, in its true significance, nothing other than the evil banshee of this Republic: the shirking of military duties, and laying upon the inanimate instruments of warfare the responsibility of this nation's safety.

The coast defences of the United States consist of sixty-seven forts, defending twenty-eight harbors. In December, 1906, Congress was informed by the Secretary of War that of the batteries then constructed two hundred and sixty-eight were out of commission, and only one hundred and twenty-four in commission. This means that of the eleven hundred guns emplaced only three hundred and ninety could be brought into action. To fully man these sixty-seven forts requires sixteen hundred and thirty-four officers, forty thousand six hundred and seventy-five men. There are now available only three hun-

[6] See Book I, chap. IV; Appendix, Table VIII.

dred and fifty-seven officers and ten thousand seven hundred men—not enough to keep the guns or machinery from rusting.

The coast artillery is one of the most highly specialized corps in the army, and requires men of superior intelligence and training. To fill their ranks with civilians recruited after a war is begun would be the same as detailing a salesman to make a topographical survey, or a tinsmith to complete a work of electrical engineering.

The Regular Army of the United States, inclusive of all branches of the service, is more than thirty per cent. below the minimum required by law, showing that it is not the fault of the government so much as it is public contempt for military enterprise that is responsible for the depleted condition of the American army, not only numerically, but in the sense of vigor and *esprit de corps*.

In the grade of second-lieutenant the army, even in its depleted condition, is almost thirty-eight per cent. short. In the Coast Artillery, thirty per cent. of the companies are without captains; sixty-three per cent. without the prescribed number of lieutenants. In the Field Artillery, comprising thirty batteries, twenty-two of them are without the prescribed number of officers. Some batteries are reduced to two guns and forty men. The infantry is in no better condition. In the Eleventh Regiment we find seven privates and four non-commissioned officers constituting a battalion.

It was said long ago by Marshal St. Cyr that every army is made up of three kinds of soldiers: one-third naturally brave, one-third naturally cowards, the other third capable of being made brave by good officers and stern discipline. If, however, the proper officers are lacking or discipline is inadequate, the middle third naturally gravitates to the cowardly third. Examples of this have been seen on many an American field of battle. Instead of this serving as a warning, the present military organization of the Republic shows, in time of peace, the total absence of the very conditions that not only Marshal St. Cyr but the experience of the whole word has shown to be necessary in the organization and conduct of armies.[7]

[7] Appendix, Table IX.

To judge, in time of peace, the worth of an army in warfare will oftentimes prove erroneous. It is only possible to judge the respective merits of national armaments, military systems and the numerical strength of the forces. By such comparisons one may come to reasonable conclusions as to the probabilities of victory. But, in addition, there must be considered the militancy of the race or nation, upon which, more than any other factor, depends the success or failure of military works. This is by no means an intangible something that the vicissitudes of war alone develop. The presence or lack of it can be determined quantitatively, and to a degree qualitatively, in all nationalities prior to war. The presence or absence of this ability is, in peace, determined by the attitude of the nation as a whole toward military activity, and by the relative position that men in the army and in civil life bear to society.

When the ideal of a nation, its religion, its aspirations, national and individual, are militant, as in Japan, then one can expect to find militancy developed to a high degree. In this country, however, there exists not only individual prejudice against military ideals, but public antipathy; the antagonism of politicians, newspapers, churches, colleges, labor unions, theorists, and organized societies. They combat the military spirit as if it were a public evil and a national crime. Under these conditions it is impossible to find the spirit of militancy other than in a most debased form, and this, terrible as is its significance, has come to be the normal condition of the Republic.

To judge the discipline, morale, and fighting capacity of troops, their loyalty and self-sacrifice, is possible in two ways: during active service, by cowardice and desertion; in peace, by disobedience and desertion. The Ten Commandments of a soldier's honor are all broken in the one act of desertion. By the lack of or prevalency of this military crime are we able to judge the degree that national non-militancy and antipathy to military ideals have on the soldier. The deserter is the product of civil life, not of militant institutions.

In Japan desertion is unknown.

In the United States during 1906 there occurred in the national army of only sixty thousand men, sixty-two hundred and eighty desertions.[8]

Whenever a recognizable deterioration exists in some portion of the government, instead of meeting this condition frankly and undertaking in a just and reasonable manner its renascence, the nation endeavors by substitution to evade responsibility. With war near at hand, public evasion is found in the formation of shooting or rifle clubs, under the delusion that to shoot constitutes the sole duty of a soldier and is the source of all military success. The fatal error of this belief is shown in a single comparison of the internal economy of the Japanese and American armies, demonstrating that in those phases of military activity least considered rests not only an army's efficiency but existence. To shoot is less important than to march; to shoot accurately less important than to obey implicitly; to kill less important than to survive.

The energy of an army, or its fighting capacity, depends primarily upon the physical vigor of the men that compose it. A body of men to fight and march and endure the hardships of war must be as physically perfect as possible. A sick man entails a greater loss than a man killed on the field, so that the ability of an army to conquer decreases geometrically as sickness and mortality increase in excessive ratio over the number killed in battle.

In the American Civil War more than four men died from preventable sickness to every one killed.[9] In the Spanish-American War fourteen men died of disease to one on the battle-field.[10] In the Japanese army during the Russian War four deaths resulted from bullets to one from sickness.[11]

In a war between Japan and the United States, should the ratio of deaths in the American army remain the same as during the Civil War, while in the Japanese forces the ratio of the Russian War should continue, the result would be that for every ten thousand American soldiers killed on the field more

[8] Appendix, Table VIIIb.
[9] Appendix, Table Xa.
[10] Appendix, Table Xb.
[11] Appendix, Table Xc.

than forty thousand would die from preventable sickness; while for every ten thousand Japanese killed only twenty-five hundred would die from disease. Should the total deaths on the battle-field during the war amount to fifty thousand for each nation, the American casualties from disease alone would be more than two hundred thousand, while the Japanese losses would only amount to twelve thousand five hundred. Should the Spanish-American War form the true basis for comparison, then the total American losses from disease would amount to seven hundred thousand, as against twelve thousand five hundred Japanese.

VII

WHENEVER a nation's attitude toward war is evasive, its conduct indecisive and its preparation an indifferent, orderless assembling of forces, it prepares for defeat.

Preparation for war must be definite in purpose, specific in application. There is no uncertainty in determining a nation's probable adversaries within such periods of time as to permit preparedness, the adaptation of armaments to specific purposes and defined theatres of war.

The objective of military activity must determine the character of its preparation. But there can be no adaptation of military means to a definite end when this preparation is purposeless and the government of it nebulous and vain. A nation's military preparedness cannot be constant nor apply equally to all countries, but must vary with each combatant, and must be determined by the strategic advantages or difficulties extant. The character of military preparation is not identical in any two wars where exist chronological, racial or topographical differences.

Whenever a nation denies the basic and evolutionary character of warfare in the development and expansion of nationalities, rigid military systems come into being. This rigidity in military science is an anomaly that has time and again brought about the defeat and eventual dissolution of nations.

The evolution of warfare is constant in cause and effect, whether we consider the time and phalanxes of Alexander, the legions of Cæsar, or the changes in armament and tactics that were introduced by Charles XII., Frederick the Great, Napoleon, Schornhorst, Von Moltke, or Yamagata. The successes of these captains were made certain by the application of new means and methods of warfare.

No phase of national activity demands so much flexibility in administration and development as the military and naval departments; no part of the government tends more quickly to deterioration if once they become subject to fixed and unalterable systems. Not only must all preparation for war be flexible as regards armament and training, but also capable of instant change, as the probabilities of war shift from one theatre of combat to another.

Conditions governing military preparedness in a conflict with Mexico have nothing to do with factors controlling military preparations for a war with Germany. Moreover, the purposes of the enemy in making war, his armaments, objective theatres of war and innumerable other conditions must determine, in variant gradations, concurrent changes in this nation's preparations; these must be approximated and prepared for in times of peace.

Whenever preparation for war is regarded only as an expedient applicable to abnormal conditions, and is postponed to the beginning of hostilities, then the nation, in modern times, is plunged into a struggle that shall terminate only in destruction.

The chances of success in modern warfare are proportionate to the rapidity with which the military and naval power of a nation can adapt itself to new conditions and diverse theatres of war. When specific preparation against a known enemy and in a predetermined theatre of war is lacking, though general preparedness has not been neglected, the difficulties of conducting the war are diminished only in a small degree. In some instances unforeseen conditions will prove so restrictive that war cannot be carried on in the enemy's principal theatre of war, though the nation is possessed of both armies and navies. Governed by these facts, it must be ascertained what preparation this nation has made for conducting a war against Japan before the conflict itself can be considered.

The theatre of this war, as a whole, will be the Pacific Ocean, divisible into six spheres of combat: the Philippines, Hawaii, Alaska, Washington, Oregon, and California. The salient characteristic that forms the determinate factor in the conduct and conclusion of this conflict is found in the vast distances that must be traversed by the armies and fleets of both nations.

In this approaching war, as in all international combats, the possession of strategic positions constitutes the main struggle of both nations, since it is in the permanent control of these that are to be found those elements of military and naval power that will determine the eventual consummation of the war. The strategic positions forming the determinate factors in a war between Japan and this Republic are entirely American, and if they were defended to the extent that an attack on them was doubtful of success, then the probabilities of war would be remote. But these territories are naked of defence, and because of this nakedness they constitute an irresistible inducement to the ambitions of a martial race.

The conditions that determine the seizure and control of the American Pacific possessions apply to this Republic as much as they do to Japan. They equalize both nations' opportunities so long as Alaska, the Pacific coast, Hawaii, Samoa, and the Philippines are not defended prior to the beginning of hostilities. Their subsequent control, whether by Japan or this Republic, will be determined by which nation first occupies them in force and makes secure their possession.

The seizure and control of these territories are determined equally to both nations by three conditions:

(1) Temporary naval supremacy in the Pacific.
(2) Rapid mobilization of trained armies.
(3) Possession of efficient means of transportation.

The disinclination of this Republic to render adequate military and naval protection to its possessions in the Pacific gives to Japan not only temporary command of the entire ocean, but time enough for the temporary character of its control to pass into permanency. Unless the United States establishes sufficient naval bases in its four quarters of the Pacific, making them militarily secure against land attack, and maintains in the Pacific fleets as much superior to the entire navy of Japan as adverse strategic conditions demand, the United States will lose in the beginning what she will never be able to regain during the continuation of the war—the entire American littoral on the Pacific.

The seizure and control of the Pacific does not alone depend upon naval supremacy. So vast is this ocean, and so widely separated are the different American possessions, that the military defence of them is of primary importance. The efficiency of navies and the sphere of their combatability is determined not only by widely spaced bases, but by their security from attack. Port Arthur was only impregnable to ships of war. This is true of all naval bases, if the command of the sea is lost to the extent of allowing the enemy an opportunity of transporting troops and making a land attack.

Temporary possession of the sea by the enemy must always be considered in military calculations as not only possible but probable. When it occurs, then all territories, harbors, and their fortifications are exposed to land attack. Their protection depends upon mobile armies sufficient in themselves to repulse any force the enemy is capable of landing—not in specific harbors, but on any portion of the sea-coast.

A war between Japan and the United States will be determined not by naval but land battles. The rapidity of mobilization and celerity with which trained armies are placed in the field at the beginning of hostilities compose the primary factors in securing and making permanent military command over these possessions.

Under the present military system this Republic could not mobilize in any one place a field army of nineteen thousand regular soldiers in the same period of time that Japan could assemble, ready to take the field, half a million veteran troops. For the United States to enlist, equip and train to the same degree of efficiency a similar force would require not less than three years.

As the determinate character of this theatre of war is its vastness, the possession of means to transport armies and to transfer them from one place to another constitutes the most vital element in determining the issue of the conflict. The movement of armies, their mobility or inertia, will be, in this war, dependent wholly upon the efficiency of their means of transportation. If Japan were without sea transports equal to the needs of her armies, the Pacific coast and the American provinces in the Pacific would be beyond the sphere of Japanese enterprise. On the other hand, if the United States possessed a standing army of two million men, but no other means of military transportation than exist at the present time, this Republic could not conduct a single campaign beyond the frontiers of the Union. Unfortunately, the United States does not possess a field army of even fifty thousand men, while Japan has such complete means of oceanic transportation that she can move her vast armies to any portion of the Pacific with greater ease than Napoleon moved similar armies from Paris across the river Elbe or beyond the Danube, or Grant across the theatre of war during the American Civil War.

This Republic is without means of military transportation. In the Spanish-American War two months elapsed before transports could be gotten together sufficient to embark a single army corps, though Havana lies only three days distant from the main centre of American commerce. In the Russian War Japanese armies had landed and were marching on the Asian continent eight days after the declaration of war. In 1907, nearly ten years after the Spanish War, the American government was obliged to charter foreign vessels to transport six thousand troops from the mainland to Cuba. The Japanese government, on the other hand, possesses sufficient transportation facilities to carry in a single voyage, if necessary, more than two hundred thousand troops.[1]

In the United States there is no nucleus upon which, in the time of war, a system of military transports can be created in the Pacific or Atlantic. At the present time so devoid is this Republic of trans-oceanic shipping that ninety-one per cent. of the entire American trade is carried on foreign vessels.

The strategic harbors in the Alaskan peninsula, commanding the North Pacific, and Samoa, capable of controlling the southern portion of the ocean, are equidistant from Japan and San Francisco. Undefended, they necessitate neither naval nor military effort to secure them, for they belong to the nation

[1] Appendix, Table VII.

that controls the ocean at large. But midway between these, likewise undefended, are the Hawaiian Islands, the portal through which Japan expects to gain the grail of her Tenro.[2] For two decades has she planned and warred toward this end. There has been no hesitancy nor doubt nor delay. Without hurry, calmly, with the inexorable certitude of a glacier, Japan has moved toward this predetermined point. At the conclusion of the Russian War her plans for taking possession of these islands assumed a positive phase.

If this Republic had created at any time a great naval and military base in Hawaii, Japan's opportunity of seizing the islands would have been lessened if not prohibited; and so long as these islands formed an invulnerable American base, the mainland of the Republic would be removed from the sphere of military enterprise. While the establishment of American naval and military power in the Pacific or Hawaii has not been attempted, yet Japan has prepared for this eventuality in so effective a manner that, notwithstanding what the naval forces of the United States may be in the future, these islands can be seized from within and converted into a Japanese naval and military base so quickly that they will be impregnable to the power of this Republic, regardless of what it may be on the mainland.

The tenure of any territory is determined primarily by military supremacy. Only when the attacking forces exceed on land those of the defence, or when a naval blockade assumes the character of a siege, does this tenure become insecure. If the military occupation of the Hawaiian Islands is in sufficient force, whether by the United States or Japan, they could not be gained or regained by naval attack. The control of these islands is a military and not a naval problem.

Japanese immigration into Hawaii has been political rather than economic, and is divided into three distinct political decades, as determined by two factors:

    (1) American Pacific Expansion:

            (a) The establishment of the Hawaiian Republic.

[2] The Elder Statesmen.

(b) The annexation of Hawaii.

(c) The conquest of the Philippines.

(2) Japanese Political Development:

(a) Protest of Japan against annexation of Hawaii.

(b) Japanese victory over China.

(c) Japanese victory over Russia.

(d) Anglo-Japanese Alliance.

In the first political decade, 1884-1896, there occurred:

(1) The overthrow of the Hawaiian monarchy and the establishment of an American republic.

(2) Japan's protest against annexation.

(3) Japan's victory over China; the elimination of that nation from the Pacific, and the beginning of Japan's political development as a Pacific power.

Simultaneous with these events the Japanese population in Hawaii increased from 116 in 1884, to 22,329 in 1896.

In the second political decade, 1896-1900, there occurred:

(1) The annexation of Hawaii.

(2) The conquest of the Philippines.

(3) The development of the Japanese army and navy.

Simultaneous with these events the Japanese population increased from 22,329 in 1896, to 61,115 in 1900.[3]

In the third political decade, 1900-1908, there occurred:

(1) Japan's victory over Russia, the elimination of that nation in the Pacific, and Japan's increased development as a Pacific power.

(2) The Anglo-Japanese Alliance, and Japan's advent as a world power.

(3) Unprecedented development of the Japanese army and navy.

Simultaneous with these events, Japanese immigration into the Hawaiian Islands, from 1900 to 1908, has been 65,708. The departures during this period were 42,313. The military unfit have in this manner been supplanted by the veterans of

[3] Total population of the Hawaiian Islands, 1900, was 154,001.

a great war, and the military occupation of Hawaii tentatively accomplished.[4]

In these islands at the present time the number of Japanese who have completed their active term of service in the imperial armies, a part of whom are veterans of the Russian War, exceeds the entire field army of the United States. Within twenty-four hours after a declaration of war the solitary American battalion that stands guard over these islands will disappear.[5] As Hawaiian sovereignty passed forever in a single day, so shall this Republic be put aside in the same manner and in no longer period of time.

The seizure of the Philippines constitutes an entirely different problem from that of Hawaii, and belongs to the sphere of military operations. In a military sense, the Philippines are closer to Japan than were the shores of Manchuria in the Russian War. There are no Port Arthurs, with guarded fleets to threaten the transportation of her troops; no armies of a quarter of a million men to oppose their landing; no rigorous winters; no tempestuous waters, such as swirl and break over the Yellow Sea; no storm-girded shores over whose billows and in the teeth of ice-laden gales landings must be made by lighters; no Liao-Yangs nor Mukdens with five hundred thousand men to drive back; no wide plains to cross in parched heat or blizzards; no half-frozen rivers to swim; no mountain-sides to clamber up, honeycombed with hidden mines; no abysses nor labyrinths; only a solitary division of troops must be overcome on these undefended islands.

The conquest of these islands by Japan will be less of a military undertaking than was the seizure of Cuba by the United States; for while Santiago de Cuba did not fall until nearly three months after the declaration of war, Manila will be forced to surrender in less than three weeks. Otherwise the occupation of Cuba portrays with reasonable exactitude the manner in which the Philippines will be taken over by Japan.

No naval force, unless equal in combative ability to the

[4] Appendix, Table XI.
[5] Twelve officers and 209 men.

entire Japanese navy, and based on the Philippines at the beginning of hostilities, could have any appreciable effect on the invasion of these islands. With the American navy no larger than at present, and the Philippines devoid of naval bases, this manner and degree of defence is recognized as impossible. Should there be a division of the American navy, the fate of the warships in Philippine waters would be but a repetition of Cervera's disaster, unless the land forces on Luzon were sufficient to prevent Manila from sharing the fate of Santiago de Cuba.

Harbor defences in the Philippines, unless they form the base of a fleet strong enough to prevent the transportation of the enemy's troops, or are in turn defended by mobile armies of sufficient strength to prevent their investment, will prove of no more defensive value than Morro Castle in the defence of Cuba. Port Arthur has again demonstrated the vulnerability of permanent fortifications and the old fallacy of their making. These stone castles of nations are but the dream castles of their vanity. Chimeras alone stand guard upon their bastions, simulacra alone throng their casements.

The fortification of Manila or Subig Bay, or any other port, will not prevent nor retard the seizure of the islands by Japan, if other elements necessary to their defence are wanting. As the conquest of Cuba was accomplished by landing forces distant from any fortified port, so will the Philippines fall. Lingayen Gulf on the north coast of Luzon, or Polillo Bight on the east coast, will form the Guantanamo Bays of the Japanese.

The conquest of the Philippines is no complex military problem, but is, on the other hand, so simple and direct that a few words will make it apparent. The American forces defending these islands do not exceed fourteen thousand, plus five thousand native troops, all of whom are based on Manila. Japan, by landing simultaneously one column of twenty thousand men at Dagupan (Chart II) and another column of the same size at Polillo Bight, would, strategically, render the American position untenable. These points of debarkation are almost

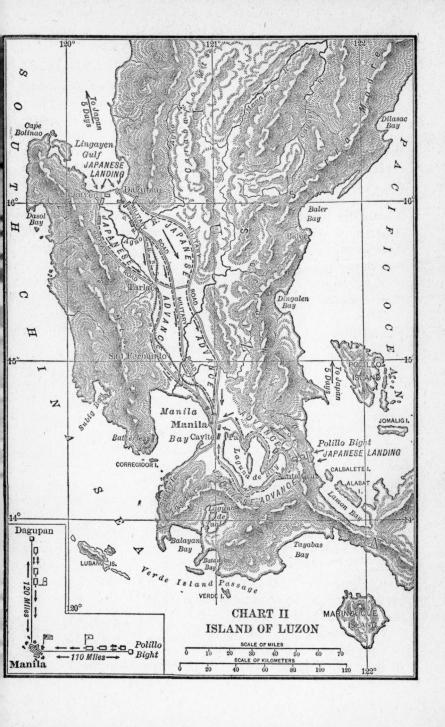

SOUTH CHINA SEA

PACIFIC OCEAN

Cape Bolinao

To Japan 5 Days

Lingayen Gulf JAPANESE LANDING

Dasol Bay

Dagupan

Lingayen

Agno R.

MILITARY R.

JAPANESE ADVANCE

Tarlac

ROAD

MILITARY ROAD

San Fernando

JAPANESE ADVANCE

ROAD

Baler Bay

Baler

Dingalen Bay

Dilasac Bay

POLILLO ISLAND

To Japan 5 Days

Agno R.

JOMALIG I.

Manila

Manila

Bay Cavite

Batteries

CORREGIDOR I.

Bataan

Laguna de Bay

ADVANCE

Polillo Bight JAPANESE LANDING

CALBALETE I.

ALABAT I.

ADVANCE

Santa Cruz

Lamon Bay

Subig Bay

Laguna de Taal

Balayan Bay

Batangas Bay

Tayabas Bay

LUBANG IS.

Verde Island Passage

VERDE I.

MARINDUQUE ISLAND

Dagupan

120 Miles

120°

Polillo Bight

Manila

110 Miles

120°

**CHART II
ISLAND OF LUZON**

SCALE OF MILES
0   10   20   30   40   50   60   70

SCALE OF KILOMETERS
0   20   40   60   80   100   120

122°

equidistant from Manila, and are connected with it by military roads, while a railroad also connects Dagupan with the capital.

The impossibility of defending Manila with the force now stationed on the islands is seen (Fig. 2, Chart II) in the strategic advantages inherent in Japan's convergent attack. These two columns, more than double the strength of the American force, converge on Manila at right angles. Advancing at equal speed, they remain at all times equidistant from the American position. Should the American force advance to meet either column, the unattacked column, being as close to Manila as the American force, could throw itself in between (Fig. 3). The Americans, separated from their base by an army equal to their own in strength, and facing a second army also as large, would be in a position wherein their capitulation could alone prevent their complete destruction.

If the American forces, on the other hand, should remain behind their lines at Manila, they would, in two weeks after the declaration of war, be surrounded by overwhelming numbers. The lines about Manila, as was demonstrated during the Spanish-American War, are incapable of prolonged defence. An aggressive enemy in control of the surrounding country can render them untenable in a short period of time.

With the occupation of the Philippines by Japan, one-fourth of the American army, which means one fourth of the trained military men of the Republic, would be eliminated from any further participation in the war; while not again could an American fleet, regardless of its size, enter the Asiatic seas during the continuation of this conflict.

If the American forces should be increased prior to the war, and no other military efforts made toward a general defence of the Philippines, it would only result in increasing proportionately the size of the enemy's advancing columns. The military and strategic conditions would not be altered nor the inevitable end retarded.

The defence of the Philippines belongs, not alone to an army or navy or fortified harbors, but to an intelligent combination of them all. This defence cannot be relegated to those expedients that are alone consequent upon sudden war, but must be inherent in the national policy of the Republic and the military preparations of prior years. It cannot be left to the shifts of unforeseen combat, but must be predetermined by existent conditions and such works as the knowledge and labor of man may evolve out of the Science of War.

VIII

WHILE the seizure of Hawaii and the Philippines includes, by the mere fact of their possession, all other insular territories of this Republic, as well as Alaska, and the naval supremacy of the Pacific, yet their occupancy is only incidental to Japan's main objective. In other words, the possession of the Pacific coast would have the same effect in establishing Japanese supremacy over these territories as would their direct seizure. As a game of chess is won by position, so, in this approaching conflict, the king's square toward which Japan moves is the Pacific coast. That Japan will in the beginning of the war take possession of these insular territories is manifest, because their occupation will cost her no appreciable effort nor detract in any degree from the naval and military power necessary for the conquest of the mainland. The occupancy of these territories will be relegated to the second line of reserves, fleets of protected cruisers and second-class battle-ships, leaving the principal naval and military forces intact.

While Japan is occupying Hawaii and the Philippines a fleet of transports carrying one hundred thousand men,[1] convoyed by battleships, armored cruisers, and torpedo craft, makes its way across the Pacific. Steaming at ten knots an hour, this fleet will reach the Pacific coast within five or possibly four weeks after the declaration of war. Then somewhere on fifteen hundred miles of sea-coast will these armies be debarked and the invasion of the United States begun.

The principal consideration that now concerns this Republic is the defence of the Pacific coast, for once it passes under the military sovereignty of Japan the Pacific and its possessions are not alone lost, but the fairest and richest portion of the Union.

[1] Appendix, Table VII.

If Japan once gains control of Washington, Oregon and California, these states will not only be segregated from the rest of the Union by her armies, but by uninhabitable deserts that moat their eastern frontiers and mountains that rampart them. No number of men nor amount of treasure, as we will hereafter show, can bring about their restoration. The defence, therefore, of the Pacific coast depends solely upon the power of the Republic to prevent Japan from gaining a foothold. To rely upon the untried hope of reconquering these coast states is but the slothful procrastination of that evasion and national vanity now so rampant in the Republic.

Primarily, the defence of the Pacific coast belongs to a navy. But so long as the necessary naval expansion of the Republic remains circumscribed by venality and ignorance, as well as public indifference, it is impossible to foresee the time when the Pacific coast will be defended by a navy powerful enough to prevent invasion by Japan. So long as it continues to be the policy of this nation to maintain a navy in its present proportion to the navies of other powers, then that navy, as has been shown, must remain united in one ocean; and, as the Atlantic constitutes the most vital naval sphere of the Republic, it will be necessary to continue it in that sea.

When Japan declares war, one of two naval conditions will be existent: either the American navy will be divided between the Pacific and Atlantic, or the whole of it will be in the latter sea. Either condition will insure instant Japanese naval supremacy. A division of the American navy means the destruction of those portions in the Pacific; while the fleets in the Atlantic will have no effect upon the conflict, whether they constitute the remaining portion or the entire navy.

In the time of peace, under the most favorable circumstances, it required four months for an American fleet to pass from the Atlantic bases to the Californian coast. But unfortunately there are many conditions in the time of war that would curtail, hinder or prohibit this transference.

During hostilities the fleets of this nation can make no use of South American ports, as was recently the case in the transference of the battleship fleet to the Pacific. International laws prohibit belligerents from sending more than three warships into a neutral port at one time. They cannot remain longer than twenty-four hours and cannot take on men, munitions nor supplies other than enough coal to proceed to the next port. The same ships cannot again enter that port within a space of three months. These prohibitions force the American navy in transit to depend entirely upon auxiliary ships for their sustenance and coal.

We have now come upon this strange paradox: that the mobility or war value of the Atlantic fleets decreases in inverse ratio to their increase in number whenever the theatre of war is in the Pacific. The size of the American navy, even, at this time, prohibits its transference to the Pacific in time of war. The recent cruise of sixteen ships necessitated the chartering of twenty-nine foreign transports, without which they could not have left the Atlantic. When this fleet is augmented by the remainder of the navy, the number of transports must be increased not only proportionately to the increase of warships, but by such additional numbers as is necessitated by this nation's inability to use neutral ports. But in the time of war belligerents cannot charter neutral vessels—a prohibition that deprives this Republic of the means upon which any extended movement of the navy must depend.

Whenever the naval defence of a nation or any portion of its territory is lacking, or when there is a measurable equality between the navies of the belligerents, the main defence of their respective possessions must be relegated to their military forces. Only when the naval superiority of one nation over another is so positive as to prohibit the hazard of battle can it be said that that nation is in a position to neglect with impunity its military forces and land defences.

In a war with Japan the defence of the Pacific coast concerns the military forces of the Republic rather than the navy, even if the policy of this government did not prevent the maintenance of adequate naval forces in the Pacific. Under present conditions the defence of Washington, Oregon and California falls upon the army as completely as though not a single American battleship existed. Notwithstanding this fact, we find that the military defence of the Pacific coast has been as completely neglected as the naval.

The defence of Washington, Oregon and California against invasion by Japan presents three obvious characteristics:

(1) The long extent of sea-coast constitutes three spheres of defence that are so widely separated as to be wholly independent of one another. Their forces cannot be shifted from one theatre of war to another, and they must maintain separate lines of communication with the Eastern States.

(2) The short period of time with which Japan is able to transport her armies to this continent—two hundred thousand men in four weeks, a half-million in four months, and more than a million in ten months —necessitates in this Republic a corresponding degree of preparedness and rapidity of mobilization.

(3) Within one month after the declaration of war this Republic must place, in each of the three defensive spheres of the Pacific coast, armies that are capable of giving battle to the maximum number of troops that Japan can transport in a single voyage. This is known to be in excess of two hundred thousand men. If the defence is restricted to any one portion of the coast, it will only have the effect of diverting the attack to one or both of the others.

At the present time there is not in any one of these defensive spheres a full regiment of regular infantry nor two regiments of militia; while in the whole of the Union are not to be found ten thousand infantry of the Federal army.

During the Spanish War a call for volunteers was issued a few days following the declaration of war, but not until after four months had two hundred and sixteen thousand men been enlisted, assigned, and their instruction begun. At the end of the war they were partially equipped, and were acquiring the rudiments of camp-life.

The first defence of the Pacific coast will fall upon such portions of the United States Army as are available, which, under the present military system and necessities, will never exceed thirty thousand men. In addition to this force it is possible that sixty thousand state militia[2] may be available for immediate service, or ninety thousand troops and one hundred and fifty guns in all. These forces are scattered over the entire Union. They must be gathered together, equipped and brigaded, as well as innumerable other contingencies met and adjusted. When this is done they must be transported by rail over a distance that is practically greater than that which separates the Golden Gate from the Inland Sea of Japan.

We have heretofore made clear that distance, in a military sense, is never measured by miles, but by the rapidity and capacity of the means of transportation. The efficiency or lack of these means correspondingly decrease or prolong the intervening spaces over which armies and their supplies must pass.

The Pacific coast has not a single point upon which the railroads crossing this continent converge. The roads that enter Washington and Oregon have no relation with those that go to California. They start from a different base and traverse another region. In a war on the Pacific coast, troops cannot be despatched to southern California by the Great Northern or Northern Pacific or the Oregon Short Line. Neither can troops be sent into Washington and Oregon by the Southern Pacific or Santa Fé. The Pacific coast is, in a military sense, restricted to the maximum of two lines of railway.

Troops for Washington and Oregon must be gathered from the various parts of the Union, together with their supplies, and taken, in all probability, to the vicinity of St. Paul, which would form the main base of all armies destined for those states. Similarly other and distinct bases must be taken for troops directed to southern and central California.

The transportation of great bodies of troops to the Pacific coast, with their vast amount of supplies and equipment, constitutes a more serious undertaking than confronted Russia in

[2] This is 67 per cent. of the organized militia. But in the Spanish War it was proven conclusively that only 40 per cent. of the militia could be counted on to enter the service. Should this continue, then only 42,000 militia could be depended upon.

the Japanese War. Russia possessed two manifest advantages denied the United States:

(1) She owned the Siberian Railroad and its equipment.
(2) It traversed a region uninhabited or possessed of a thinly scattered population, more or less primitive in its civilization, and in consequence not dependent upon the railroad for sustenance or maintenance.

When, however, the civilization of a country becomes highly developed and complex, as in this nation, the interdependence of man is increased accordingly. There is scarcely to be found in the Republic an independent and self-sustaining community. Every farmer and town and county in the western portions of the United States is dependent upon railroads, not only for their supplies, but for their funds with which to buy the necessities of life.

The distance from the Mississippi Valley to the Pacific coast is two thousand miles, and upon the few lines that traverse these Western States live a people so dependent upon them that they could not continue their livelihood if deprived of these means of communication. They must not only receive supplies, but their grain, wool, cattle, ores, timber and other products must be shipped to Eastern markets that they may purchase the means of production as well as the needs of daily existence. This traffic the government cannot stop, and it is the continuance of it during war that will make the transportation of troops and their supplies to the Pacific coast a more difficult problem than confronted Russia.

In the beginning of the war Japan possesses another advantage that is completely denied this Republic. By her vast fleets, her armies are moved in great units and are restricted to no portion of the coast. The United States, on the other hand, can only transport by train-loads. While Japan can land over two hundred thousand men on the Pacific coast in less than four weeks, it is apparent that, even if this Republic had that number of men under arms prior to the declaration of war, it would take considerably longer than four weeks to mobilize them in a single theatre of war on the Pacific coast.

In a military sense Japan is one-third closer to Washington,

Oregon and California than the military power of the United States, and will remain so until all transcontinental railways are double-tracked, one track reverting to the government in the event of war.

We will not consider the time it will take to accomplish this mobilization, organization, equipment and transportation of so many widely scattered units which constitute the American forces, but will pass on to the consideration of their destination. There are two alternatives:

(1) The mobilization of all forces, regulars and militia, in camps of instruction wherein they are to constitute the nucleus of an army of a million men; allowing the Japanese to take possession of the coast without opposition.

(2) To rush these thirty thousand regulars and sixty or forty thousand militia to the coast and dispute the landing of the Japanese.

We do not believe that the first alternative would be entertained by the Republic at large. Rather would there surge over the entire land one thought, echoed on all sides by a single cry: On to the coast!

To what portion of the coast?

If they were sent to southern California, the central part of the state, Oregon and Washington would still remain defenceless, as if these troops had never been mobilized. If they were sent to San Francisco, the same conditions would still hold in Washington, Oregon and southern California. If mobilized on Puget Sound, then all to the southward would be without protection. It is evident, moreover, that there can be no division of this force. To place thirty thousand men in each of these three spheres of defence would be to sacrifice the whole in detail, without even the ordeal of battle or delay of invasion.

The economic interests of central California approximate those of the south and north combined, while the strategic value is infinitely greater. The San Francisco peninsula is, moreover, the only position in which seventy to ninety thousand men might hold out against the great armies of Japan for any length of time. If San Francisco could be held permanently, and communication kept open with the East, the Republic might, by accumulating its military resources at that point, move in due time against the Japanese forces in southern California or those in Washington and Oregon. These considerations should, in the aggregate, influence the government as well as popular opinion in concentrating the existent military forces on the San Francisco peninsula immediately subsequent to the declaration of war. However disastrous it might prove to leave unprotected the northern and southern coasts, San Francisco constitutes, nevertheless, the true point of concentration under the military conditions now extant in this Republic.

Japan's invasion of Washington and Oregon, the conditions that circumscribe it and the manner of its accomplishment constitutes the simplest of military problems. The mouth of the Columbia River is defended by three forts. These fortifications are the entire defence of the state of Oregon against invasion, yet the combined power of all their guns is less than that of the guns on a single Japanese *Dreadnaught*.

This is not all.

To man these solitary guns requires sixty-seven officers, fourteen hundred and forty-six men. According to the Secretary of War, there are now available in these forts but ten officers and two hundred and forty-six men, which means that five-sixths of the guns emplaced could not be used. If these fortifications were not only not lacking in guns and men, but were, on the other hand, a hundredfold more powerful, they would still have no more retarding effect upon the invasion of Oregon than if they did not exist, as will, later on, become apparent.

The defence of the state of Washington is relegated to three forts on the upper reaches of Puget Sound. These fortifications are in a more impoverished condition and state of unpreparedness than those on the Columbia. While one hundred and twenty-nine officers, thirty-one hundred and eighty men are necessary to man the guns already emplaced, there are, according to the Secretary of War, only twenty-seven officers, nine hundred and two men available, which means that four-fifths of these guns could not be served.

As a defence against invasion the fortifications on Puget Sound are as valueless as those on the Columbia, and for the same reason, that they are remote from any possible base for invasion that could be selected by Japan in the debarkation of her first expedition. This landing will occur (Chart III) in Gray's and Willapa Harbors. Should these harbor entrances be mined, then debarkation will be on the open beaches between the bays, or north of the entrance to Gray's Harbor.

The first objective of the Japanese armies will not be the cities on Puget Sound nor Portland nor the cities on the Columbia, but will be directed toward Chehalis and Centralia, two small towns fifty-seven miles eastward. These places, four miles apart, constitute the strategic centre of both states, whether in relation to a defending force or invading armies. By schedule time Gray's Harbor and Willapa Harbor are but three hours westward; Seattle three hours to the north; Portland three hours and forty-five minutes to the south; the fortifications at the mouth of the Columbia seven hours and a quarter; the fortifications commanding the entrance to Puget Sound five hours and a half; Tacoma two hours; Olympia, the capital of the state, one hour and twenty-five minutes; the United States Navy Yard at Bremerton, four hours. Should it be necessary to march to any of these places, they could be made in as many days as hours are given in the railroad schedule.

Within seven hours by rail of this centre is to be found fifty-eight per cent. of the entire population of Oregon, while sixty-one per cent. of the entire population of Washington is within six hours. This strategic centre, midway between the centres of population in Oregon and Washington, is on and commands the only line of railroad that traverses these states north and south. Within three hours of this centre are eight land-locked and deep-water harbors—two on the south, two to the west, and four on the north, together with ship-yards and naval stations.

Portland, forming the right centre of the Japanese position, is connected with eastern Oregon and Washington by the Columbia River and two parallel lines of railway. Seattle and

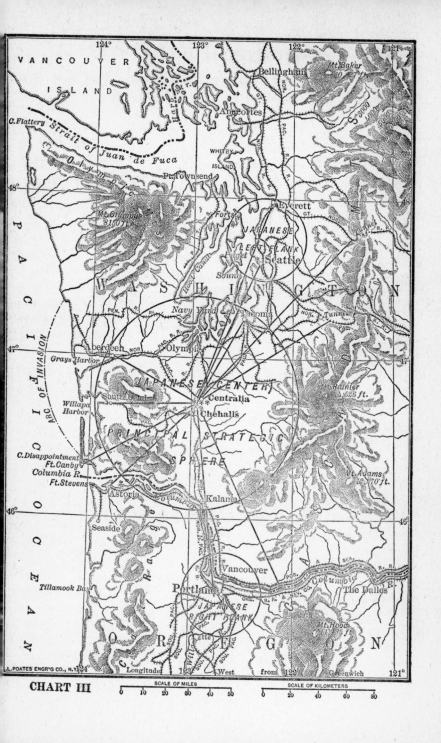

CHART III

SCALE OF MILES
0   10   20   30   40   50

SCALE OF KILOMETERS
0   20   40   60   80

Everett, forming the Japanese left centre, are connected with eastern Washington and Oregon by three parallel lines of railway.

The full significance inherent in the seizure of this strategic centre is only realized when the results are viewed in the concrete. No opposition against the landing of Japanese armies is possible unless the American forces are equal in numbers and efficiency, and are, moreover, in occupation of this position in less than four weeks subsequent to the declaration of war. The forts at the mouth of the Columbia and on Puget Sound possess no defensive value whatever when concerned with the invasion of these states.[3] The cities which they are supposed to protect will be occupied by the Japanese without the invading forces coming within fifty or a hundred miles of either fortification. As Portland and the cities on Puget Sound are possessed by the Japanese, these ports will pass into their control without the firing of a shot.

By this single movement Japan not alone possesses these states in a military sense, but economically and politically as well. She commands all lines of communication, all harbors, and practically the entire personal wealth of a territory that is larger and richer than the Japanese Empire. By the occupation of this position she segregates and dominates the inhabitants, controls them and their activities, their productions and industries, to a degree of unity and absolutism now unknown in this Republic. With the seizure and fortification of the Bitter Root Mountains east of Spokane, together with the Blue Mountains in eastern Oregon,[4] the dominion of Japan over these two American states becomes complete.

[3] See Chart III.
[4] See Chart IV.

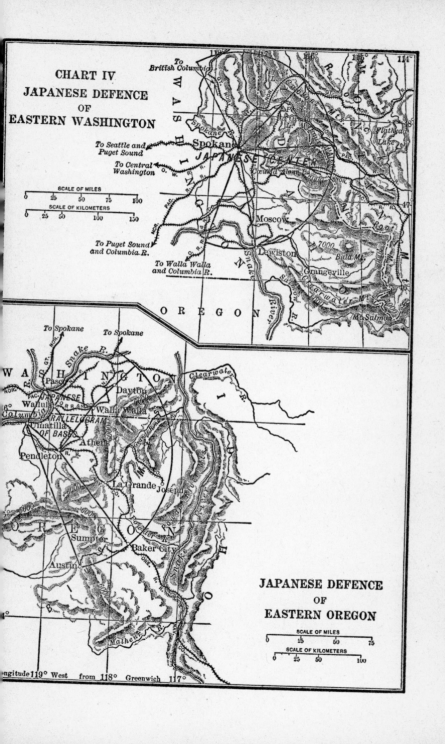

CHART IV
JAPANESE DEFENCE
OF
EASTERN WASHINGTON

To British Columbia

To Seattle and Puget Sound

To Central Washington

SCALE OF MILES
0   25   50   75   100

SCALE OF KILOMETERS
0   25   50   100   150

To Puget Sound and Columbia R.

To Walla Walla and Columbia R.

WASHINGTON

Spokane

JAPANESE CENTER

Moscow

Lewiston

7000
Bald Mt.

Grangeville

Mt. Salmon

Flathead Lake

OREGON

Snake River

Clearwater Mt.

To Spokane   To Spokane

WASHINGTON

Pasco

Wallula
Columbia
JAPANESE
PARALLELOGRAM
OF BASES

Umatilla

Athena

Pendleton

Dayton

Walla Walla

Clearwater R.

La Grande   Joseph

Sumpter

Baker City

Austin

OREGON

Malheur R.

JAPANESE DEFENCE
OF
EASTERN OREGON

SCALE OF MILES
0   25   50   75

SCALE OF KILOMETERS
0   25   50   100

Longitude 119° West   from 118°   Greenwich 117°

IX

As the defencelessness of Washington and Oregon is due
primarily to the failure on the part of this Republic to
recognize the changes that modern science and invention have
brought about in increasing the possibilities of invasion, and
in altering to a corresponding degree the manner and means of
defending seaboard states, so is the undefended condition of
southern California due to the same general reasons.

These two localities, forming the extreme flanks of the
Pacific coast, are equally remote from the main centres of the
Republic, separated therefrom by deserts and mountain-chains.
And while the forts of the north are without value, not only on
account of their worthlessness, but because of their remoteness
from any avenue of invasion, southern California is without
even the delusive dependence of such fortifications.

We have shown how simple, and yet how decisive, is the conquest of Washington and Oregon, how quickly it can be accomplished by Japan without even the probability of a battle; yet
the seizure of southern California presents less difficulties than
are to be found in the Northern States.

Southern California is less in area than one-half of the state
of Oregon, but of this area three-fourths belong to deserts and
mountains, while only a portion of the remaining one-fourth
is inhabited. The cities and cultivated areas are all adjacent to
the sea, so that over ninety per cent. of the entire population
dwells within thirty miles of the ocean, while 94.25 per cent.
of the total wealth lies within this same distance of the sea.[1]

The seizure of southern California is simplified by an increased concentration of wealth and population in a single
seaboard county, where is to be found two-thirds of the entire

[1] Chart V.

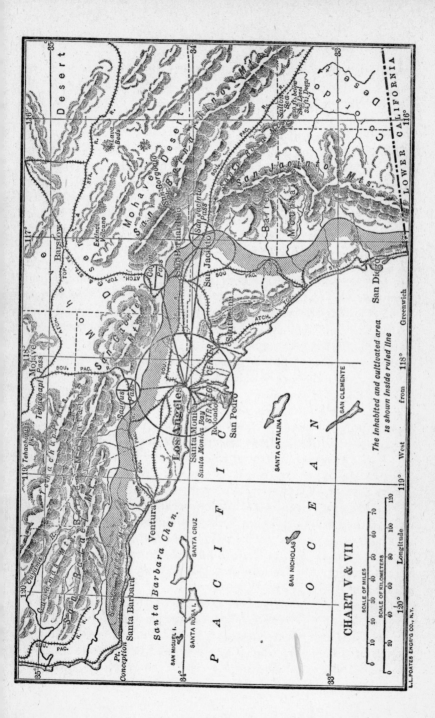

CHART V & VII

The inhabited and cultivated area is shown inside ruled line

L.L. POATES ENGR'G CO., N.Y.

SCALE OF MILES

SCALE OF KILOMETERS

West   from 118°   Greenwich

Longitude

population of this territory and more than two-thirds of its wealth. This delimitation of the strategic area is finally reduced to the environs of a single city, so that the conquest of the southern flank of the Pacific coast is relegated to and depends upon the seizure of the city of Los Angeles. Within this city alone is to be found more than half of the entire population and wealth of southern California. It constitutes the political, economic and railroad centre of this entire territory. All other cities, communities and industries are dependent upon it. If every city in this region except Los Angeles were seized by the enemy, southern California would still remain, militarily, politically and economically a part of the Republic; but if Los Angeles passed into possession of an invading force, the whole of southern California would fall though not another blow were struck. There is not a city nor community in this region that can exist for any portion of time after Los Angeles is in the possession of the enemy, though no hostile demonstrations were made against them. There is not a town, nor even a rural community, that is self-dependent nor interdependent, but are, as a whole, suburban to Los Angeles.

San Diego in a military sense, politically and economically, is without relative importance. This city, as all other towns in southern California, is but a distant suburb of Los Angeles, connected to it by a single strand of railway. With the severance of this artery of trade, whether it occurs a mile north of San Diego or at Los Angeles, one hundred and twenty-seven miles distant, is immaterial—the fate of that city is the same. With the enemy in control of the ocean, the isolation of San Diego is complete. Like ancient Carthage, it is built where the sea and desert meet. Westward is the ocean; eastward, southward and northeastward, just beyond its environs, reclaimed from the deserts, rise hillsides as barren as those that are beyond the Valley of the Tombs.

The single line of railroad, which is this city's means of communication, runs northward along the coast for a distance of seventy-four miles, within four hundred to nine hundred yards of tide-water. Thus a single vessel can blockade this city by land and by sea. So complete is the geographical and strategic isolation of San Diego that a rampart of Gibraltars would not increase its military significance nor add a single element to the defence of southern California. Its capitulation will be brought about by ignoring its existence. This, under similar conditions, has happened many times before in the wars of man.

Though Los Angeles constitutes, as will be seen, the single strategic point upon which depends the security of southern California, no effort, up to the present time, has been made to render it secure from attack. One regiment can now occupy the city with impunity. The only effort made toward its defence has been the advocacy of fortifying Point Fermin at the entrance of San Pedro Harbor. This proposal but demonstrates that to which we have already called attention, the prevailing ignorance concerning modern warfare.

We have heretofore shown the general state of deterioration inherent in the existent fortifications of the Republic, together with the depleted condition of the Coast Artillery, a state of decadence that has resulted in rendering useless four-fifths of the guns already emplaced. Until there is a complete reorganization of the Republic's military system, it is not only useless to construct new fortifications, but in so doing the nation is involved in new dangers to which we have already called attention.

Fortifications for the entrance of San Pedro Harbor possess no intrinsic or relative importance as regards the defence of Los Angeles. They belong, not to the land defences of this region, but to the naval, and their erection presupposes the presence of an active fleet in these waters. San Pedro may be made a naval base, but beyond that it possesses no defensive value whatsoever. The purpose of such fortifications are specific—the defence of the harbor itself, or a fleet based upon it. The sphere of actual defence belonging to such fortifications is determined by a semicircle, the radii of which are the effective range of their guns. Modern harbor fortifications are not self-defensive. Their protection depends upon either a fleet of sufficient strength to prevent the transportation and landing of the enemy's forces, or mobile armies able to prevent the enemy from gaining a foothold on any portion of the coast, whether adjacent to or distant from the fortifications to be attacked.

We have already shown the impossibility of naval defence for the Pacific coast whenever the American navy is in the Atlantic prior to the beginning of hostilities, or whenever the American fleets in the Pacific are inferior to the entire Japanese navy. The fortification of San Pedro presupposes a navy many times larger than at present; the size of the fleets in the Pacific, and their efficiency, being determined by Japanese naval development.

Fortifications at San Pedro, without a fleet relatively as strong as that of the enemy, are useless. As Los Angeles is the objective point, landings will be made upon the closest available seaboard. And in a military sense San Pedro is twice as far from Los Angeles as Santa Monica Bay.[2] This harbor, moreover, is so contracted that the danger of submarine mines and torpedoes would, under all circumstances, prohibit its utilization by the Japanese until the harbor itself and the surrounding country passed into their control. Santa Monica Bay, on the other hand, gives a free seaboard of over twenty miles in extent—adjacent to the environs of Los Angeles.

So long as this city forms the objective of invading armies their forces will not, under any circumstances, land within twenty miles of San Pedro Harbor, and the forts at that point must, regardless of their strength, capitulate whenever Los Angeles is seized. To hold these proposed fortifications against a land attack would require as great an army as might, in the beginning, delay the invasion of southern California. Once an enemy gains the shores of Santa Monica Bay, San Pedro must, owing to the peculiar topographical features of the peninsula, either fall to an inferior force or be defended on a continuous front of a number of miles.

Extending across the San Pedro peninsula almost east and west is a range of barren hills, similar to those north of Port Arthur, with an irregular crest exceeding a thousand feet in

[2] Fig. 2, Chart VI.

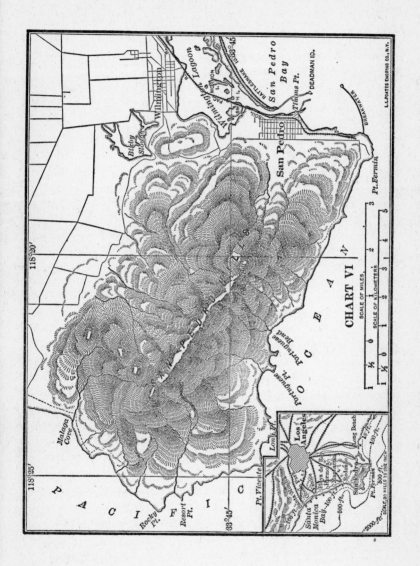

CHART VI

SCALE OF MILES.

SCALE OF KILOMETERS.

San Pedro
Bay

Wilmington

Lagoon

RATTLESNAKE ISLD.

Timms Pt.

DEADMAN ID.

BREAKWATER

Pt. Fermin

San Pedro

Biby Slough

O C E A N

Portuguese Bend

Portuguese Pt.

Pt. Vicente

Lomb Pt.

Malaga Cove

P A C I F I C

Rocky Pt.

Resort Pt.

Los Angeles

Santa Monica Bay

Santa Ana

Long Beach

118°25′

118°20′

33°45′

height and nearly twelve miles in length.[3] Sixteen hundred yards north of the proposed fortifications the contour rises to two hundred and eighty feet; at three thousand yards the elevation is five hundred feet; at five thousand yards the elevation increases to nine hundred feet; while at six thousand five hundred yards is the crest of the ridge, fourteen hundred feet above the proposed batteries. This ridge continues westward to Santa Monica Bay, so that any attack upon the forts defending San Pedro would be by that bay, the enemy moving eastward and occupying this range of hills. Once these heights are seized the harbor and forts would be rendered untenable. The base of an attack on San Pedro is identical with that of an advance on Los Angeles—the Bay of Santa Monica.

As the whole of southern California will pass into the hands of an invading force once Los Angeles is occupied, all means employed for the defence of this region must be directed toward the security of this city, its environs and communications.

So extensive is the seaboard by which Los Angeles can be attacked, and so close is the city to the sea, that the only means —once command of the sea is lost—which can insure it from capture is to prepare before war systematically and thoroughly such means for the defence of the entire seaboard by mobile armies as modern warfare demands. Isolated fortifications, small and inefficient forces, will not only not hinder nor even delay the conquest of this region a single day, but will, on the other hand, result in useless destruction of life and devastation of the country.

We have called attention to the brevity of modern wars in general and naval movements in particular; how, within a few weeks after war is declared, concurrent with the seizure of the Philippines, Hawaii, and Alaska, will the conquest of Washington and Oregon be consummated. In the same manner and within three months after hostilities have been begun other armies will land upon the seaboard of southern California.

The question that now rises naturally in the thoughts of the reader is, What will the United States be doing during

[3] Chart VI.

these three months? Instantly the mind is crowded, not alone with the speculations of victory, but with the vague grandeur of a nation's hope. The Old Lamp is rubbed and vast armies are suddenly mobilized; armaments are brought out of hidden recesses; great generals are made in the twinkling of an eye; then winged, these legions take their flight across the mountains and deserts of the West. But what will actually take place in the Republic after war is declared is so well known as to make it unnecessary to again refer to the confusion, ignorance, peculation and complete lack of every form of military preparation, armaments, supplies, or means of securing them.

To conduct a war on the Pacific coast against the forces of Japan, this Republic is at present less prepared and less capable than it has ever been prior to any war undertaken by it in the past. Due to the scorn of consequence, to the vanity of ignorance and indifference toward military preparation, no force can be placed on the seaboard of southern California either within three months or nine months that would delay the advance of the Japanese armies a single day.

Irrespective of armament and ante-bellum preparation, however, we find other conditions that would prevent the mobilization of an army in southern California capable of defending it against invasion and conquest.

The maximum force that can be mobilized in the Republic immediately following a declaration of war is less than one hundred thousand men, of whom two-thirds are militia. This force, made up of more than forty miniature armies, is scattered, each under separate military and civil jurisdiction, over the entire nation. By the time these heterogeneous elements are gathered together, organized into proper military units and made ready for transportation to the front, the states of Washington and Oregon will have been invaded and their conquest made complete by a vastly superior force.

At this stage the nation is brought face to face with the weakness inherent in republican forms of government during war—the supremacy of popular control over military movements. With the seizure of the Philippines, Hawaii and Alaska, the excitement and clangor in the nation would be very great;

but with the invasion and conquest of two states forming an
integral part of the Union, the tide of patriotism and of wrath
would well still higher, and the populace would be satisfied
with nothing less than an immediate advance against the
Japanese. Being ignorant or indifferent as to the military efficiency of Japan or what even constitutes it, vain in their
valor and in the victories of the past, the entire country, from
the most remote hamlet to the Congress of the nation, would
urge the diversion of the mobilized forces against the Japanese occupying Washington and Oregon.

Whether popular demand would succeed in diverting the
American forces in the direction of these states or not is immaterial as far as the present strategic situation is concerned,
for it is certain that they would not be turned to the extreme
southern flank of the Pacific coast, placing them in a position
almost as remote from the invading armies as if they had not
been moved west of the Mississippi, still leaving the whole
coast, except a small area, exposed to invasion. If popular
opinion did not prevail or the forces were not retained in the
East, the only point upon which they could concentrate, as
stated before, would be San Francisco. If mobilized there prior
to the invasion of southern California, this flank would still
remain defenceless, inasmuch as these forces could not move
five hundred miles to the southward without diverting the
Japanese attack upon San Francisco and exposing the most
strategic point on the Pacific coast to capture. This would permit the union of the Japanese armies seizing San Francisco
with those occupying Washington and Oregon, relegating the
American position to an extreme and strategically unimportant
flank.

The probabilities of the American armies being directed
against the Japanese forces in Washington and Oregon through
the force of popular agitation presents this apparently anomalous condition, that the larger the American armies are at
the time of invasion—regardless of what portion of the coast
it may be—the more certain are these forces to be directed
against that point. Two factors determine this:

(1) The numerical equality or superiority of the first

Japanese expedition over the entire American land forces, preventing an American army of corresponding strength from being sent against it simultaneously with the despatch of similar forces against other probable points of invasion.

(2) The power of popular opinion to direct the available military establishment against the invading forces, regardless of the general military situation or strategic considerations.

Japan, to make this condition constant, needs but to have the strength of her first column proportionate to that of the entire American forces, which would be relatively small as regards her military establishment, even if the American standing army were five times its present size. So long as the existent military system continues in the Republic there can be no adequate defence of any single portion of the Pacific coast within a year after a declaration of war, nor the three spheres within as many years.

Three or four months after war is declared will find Japan in occupation of all insular possessions, Washington and Oregon with an American army of less than one hundred thousand men either assembling in the East, moving against the Japanese in the North or concentrating at San Francisco.

Japan, landing an army on the shores of southern California at this time, would occupy, without opposition, the strategic centre of this region on the following day, and the conquest of southern California would be, in a practical sense, complete.

We now come to the consideration of the most important phase of the military occupancy of southern California by Japan. It has nothing to do with the intrinsic worth of this region, neither its economic nor political significance, but appertains alone to its strategic value, its necessity for and capacity of defence against subsequent efforts on the part of this Republic to reconquer the Pacific States.

There are only three avenues by which armies can gain entrance to the Pacific coast from the eastern portion of the United States, and southern California constitutes one of these avenues, hence the possession of this region early in the war is essential to Japanese control and security.

The conformation of this section[4] is peculiarly adapted to effective defence from the Pacific side. The sea-coast from Mexico to Point Concepcion is an elongated, irregular crescent, and with but isolated exceptions—as the valley holding the towns and orange orchards of San Bernardino, Riverside and Redlands—the inhabitable area follows the sealine and extends back but a comparatively few miles. North and eastward of this oasis region are four principal mountain ranges: the San Jacinto, San Bernardino, San Gabriel and Tehachapi, with the crest-line ranging from five to eleven thousand feet. Beyond these mountains are deserts, lava beds and Valleys of Death.

Entrance into southern California is gained by three passes —the San Jacinto, Cajon and Saugus, while access to the San Joaquin Valley and central California is by the Tehachapi. It is in control of these passes that determines Japanese supremacy on the southern flank of the Pacific coast, and it is in their adaptability to defence that determines the true strategic value of southern California to the Japanese.

Los Angeles forms the main centre of these three passes,[5] and lies within three hours by rail of each of them, while San Bernardino, forming the immediate base of forces defending Cajon and San Jacinto passes, is within one hour by rail of both passes.

The mountain-chains encompassing the inhabited regions of southern California might be compared to a great wall thousands of feet in height, within whose enclosures are those fertile regions which have made the name of this state synonymous with all that is abundant in nature. These mountains, rugged and inaccessible to armies from the desert side, form an impregnable barrier except by the three gateways mentioned.

Standing upon Mt. San Gorgonio or San Antonio one can look westward and southward down upon an endless succession

[4] Chart VII.
[5] Chart VII.

of cultivated fields, towns and hamlets, orchards, vineyards and orange groves; upon wealth amounting to hundreds of millions; upon as fair and luxuriant a region as is ever given man to contemplate; a region wherein shall be based the Japanese forces defending these passes. To the north and east across the top of this mountain-wall are forests, innumerable streams, and abundance of forage. But suddenly at the outward rim all vegetation ceases; there is a drop—the desert begins.

The Mojave is not a desert in the ordinary sense of the word, but a region with all the characteristics of other lands, only here Nature is dead or in the last struggle against death. Its hills are volcanic scoria and cinders, its plains bleak with red dust; its meadows covered with a desiccated and seared vegetation; its springs, sweet with arsenic, are rimmed, not by verdure, but with the bones of beast and man. Its gaunt forests of yucca bristle and twist in its winds and brazen gloom. Its mountains, abrupt and bare as sun-dried skulls, are broken with cañons that are furnaces and gorges that are catacombs. Man has taken cognizance of this deadness in his nomenclature. There are Coffin Mountains, Funeral Ranges, Death Valley, Dead Men's Cañons, dead beds of lava, dead lakes, and dead seas. All here is dead. This is the ossuary of Nature; yet American armies must traverse it and be based upon it whenever they undertake to regain southern California. To attack these fortified places from the desert side is a military undertaking pregnant with greater difficulties than any ever attempted in all the wars of the world.[6]

The value of Japan's strategic position in southern California is not alone determined by the limited area of the inhabitable region and its adjacency to the sea, nor the concentration into a single sea-board county of two-thirds of its wealth and population, but is due to the strategic advantages afforded by the location of the Cajon, San Jacinto, and Saugus passes, their proximity to Los Angeles and to one another, the shortness of their interior lines, and the location of their fortified positions in mountains not only inaccessible to armies

[6] Appendix, Table XII.

from the east, but, while their redans point out upon a desert, their rear rests immediately upon one of the most fertile sections of the Republic.

The strategic position of the American forces attacking these passes presents the reverse of these conditions. While the Japanese fortifications are built among and enclose an abundance of resources of every kind, the American armies must attack these positions with forces resting upon a desert that is not only without resources, but is without water sufficient to supply a single regiment within striking distance of these passes.

If an attempt were made to force the San Jacinto Pass, the nearest water adequate for the needs of an army is in the Imperial Valley, one hundred and thirty miles distant. If the Cajon were to be attacked, the nearest water available for the use of an army is the Colorado River, two hundred and twenty miles distant. If an attempt were made to force the Tehachapi, the nearest water-supply is two hundred and sixty miles away.

In modern warfare the increased effective use of gun-fire gives forces established in semi-permanent fortifications the advantage to the extent that the attacking force must be several times stronger, according to the character of the defences and the efficiency of the troops manning them. Considering the opposing forces equally efficient, there would be to every hundred thousand Japanese a minimum force of several hundred thousand Americans. But the Japanese would possess still another strategic advantage that would increase this disproportion to an almost exaggerated degree. Their interior lines, connecting these passes and uniting them on the main base at Los Angeles, are so contracted that a small force can accomplish, on account of the rapidity of transportation, what would otherwise require a great army.

For the Japanese to transfer a train of troops or munitions from Cajon to the San Jacinto Pass would require but two hours, while a change on the same front by the attacking forces would necessitate several days. Only forty-odd miles separate the Japanese forces defending the Cajon from those in the

San Jacinto, while nearly fourteen hundred miles must be traversed by the American forces in changing from one front to the other.

This shortness of the Japanese lines and the excessive length of the American would of necessity restrict the main attack to one pass. Neither the Saugus Cañon nor the Tehachapi could be attacked with the enemy in possession of the Cajon unless the American forces were vast enough to mask Cajon while attempting to force these positions. But the desert not only minimizes the number of troops resting upon it, but these two latter passes are of secondary importance, their value and possession being determined entirely by the control of the Cajon and the San Jacinto. Hence the reconquest of southern California will be by one or both of these main passes.

If the American advance is directed against San Jacinto, not only must they make their assaults on fortified positions one hundred and thirty miles from water, but their communications with the first base of supply would be restricted to a single line of desert railway one thousand miles long. If, on the other hand, the main advance is directed against the Cajon, the American forces would have two lines of railway. This advantage of increased means of communication is, however, nullified by the fact that the nearest available water supply sufficient for a single brigade is two hundred and twenty miles distant.

Such are the conditions that render southern California impregnable against attack once these passes are fortified and held in force. No fortitude, no vastness of numbers, no amount of patriotism, no human ingenuity can overcome these inaccessible ramparts and desert glacis once an enemy militarily as efficient as the Japanese occupies the three gateways through which alone armies may pass.

In a later chapter we will show how other conditions increase—if it were possible—the impregnability of this position to such a degree that not even the contemplation of an attack is possible.

X

THE duration and causes of war are never constant, although the factors that determine the length or brevity of wars are invariable in their application. These determinate conditions may, in modern wars, be divided into three general principles:

(1) Whenever the state of military preparedness among nations is proportionately developed and continues constant in peace, ensuing wars are medium in duration and minimum in destruction of life and property.

(2) Whenever the state of military unpreparedness among nations is proportionately the same in peace, ensuing wars are longest in duration and maximum in destruction of life and property.

(3) Whenever the state of military preparedness is highly developed in one nation and lacking in another, ensuing wars are short in duration and one-sided in destruction of life and property.

As the art of war passes from the brutish valor of the individual to the calm, angerless domain of science, the more absolute becomes the application of these principles in the consummation of modern conflicts.

The relative state of preparedness for war in Japan and the United States is such that, unless there is an immediate military renascence in this Republic, the approaching struggle will be relegated to that class of conflicts exemplified in the Chinese-Japanese War of 1894, the Franco-Prussian War of 1870, the German-Austrian War of 1866, and the Japanese-Russian War of 1904, the determinate conditions of which are the inherent factors of the third principle.

In a war with Japan there are other conditions of preparedness that will augment the rapidity of her conquest—*viz.*, the movement of her troops and naval forces to positions adjacent to the theatre of war prior to a formal declaration of hostilities.

This initiative is characteristic of Japanese military activity; and though naturally condemned in this Republic on account of military unpreparedness, the initiation of war without the formality of a declaration does not alone adhere to Japan. Of the hundred and twenty wars that were fought in the Occident between 1790 and 1870, one hundred and ten were begun without notification. A formal declaration of war is not other than a survival of the age of chivalry, when challenges were sent ceremoniously by a herald to the camp of the enemy. All such formality in modern conflicts has been and is considered by nations prepared for war as superfluous. Only those countries unprepared groan at such activity, and the overpowering advantage this initiative gives to their adversaries.

It will therefore be found that the rapidity of Japanese movements against the possessions of the United States will be greater than we have in this work set down.

In considering the seizure of this nation's insular possessions, as well as Washington, Oregon and southern California, we have minimized the military efficiency of the Japanese and the capacity of their transportation. By this minimization we have increased unduly the defensive capacity of the Republic. Yet we are forced to witness, in spite of this, its complete and utter helplessness.

There now remains but the seizure of San Francisco to bring about the final dissolution of American power upon the Pacific and complete the victory of Japan. That the seizure of San Francisco would occur earlier in the war than we state is admitted by all strategicians conversant with conditions. But in order to permit the maximum defence possible to San Francisco under present military conditions, we have postponed any attack until the entire available military forces of the Republic have been concentrated in its immediate vicinity—an improbable, if not impossible, mobilization as regards time.

San Francisco is the most important point on the Pacific coast, commercially, politically and strategically. Its proximity to the Central Pacific, together with its great harbor, makes it the centre of American Pacific trade.

From the standpoint of naval strategy, San Francisco is the most essential position on the Pacific littoral. With the enemy in control of this bay, in addition to the territories already considered, no American fleet, regardless of its size and efficiency, could enter upon the Pacific so long as war continued. San Francisco Bay is the main naval base of the Republic on the Pacific, and with its loss all hope of regaining naval control over this ocean will be gone forever.

Militarily its strategic importance also exceeds that of any other locality of the Pacific slope. Midway between the northern and southern flanks of the coast, it makes them both, when in possession of an enemy, vulnerable to a rear attack. It not only divides the enemy's forces occupying these territories, but by holding this position their union is made impossible. San Francisco, commanding the San Joaquin, Sacramento and Santa Clara Valleys, controls the whole of central and northern California to nearly the same degree as Los Angeles dominates southern California. Once San Francisco Bay is seized by the Japanese, this entire region passes into their hands.

Should Japan occupy in force both flanks of the coast, as we have heretofore described, and the United States should retain command of San Francisco and its lines of communication with the East, this nation would still be possessed of a position strategically equal to that of Japan, provided:

(1) That the military establishment of the Republic permitted the immediate mobilization in the environs of San Francisco Bay of armies capable of defending it against attack.

(2) That additional military forces existed in the Republic adequate in numbers and efficiency to counterbalance any attempt on the part of Japan to gain a preponderance of strength north and south of this locality.

If these conditions, determined by ante-bellum preparation,

were possible, then the American position, piercing the Japanese centre and segregating their flanks, would equalize the strategic situation and permit the consummation of the war to be determined by battles. But, unfortunately, the issuance of these problematical combats concerns us in no way, for we are forced to deal alone with facts, not fancies nor hopes nor delusions.

It is generally believed that the defences of San Francisco are not only effective, but are particularly well adapted to ward off any attack that may be made upon it; the truth, however, is that this city, under existent military conditions, is defenceless. And so long as the armies of this Republic are so inadequate as to relegate the defence of San Francisco to the peninsula on which it is situated its capitulation will be without even the trial of battle.

The defence of San Francisco does not depend upon holding fortified positions, but in maintaining military control of the entire region surrounding San Francisco Bay. Because of its peculiar situation, the weakness of this city is strategic and not tactical, and its fate depends upon the issuance of battles fought many miles from its present fortifications.

The existing defences of San Francisco are restricted to several forts commanding the entrance to the bay. These forts, situated partly on the north side of the channel and partly on the south, are neither self-protective nor inter-protective from any attack except naval. To man them and serve the guns already emplaced requires one hundred and seventy-five officers, and forty-two hundred and sixty-two men. But there are available only forty-two officers and fourteen hundred men. Due to this depletion, two-thirds of the guns cannot be served while the fire-power of the remaining one-third is less than that of two Japanese battleships.

The general public does not comprehend the limitations of permanent fortifications in modern warfare. They not only do not force an attack, but, on the other hand, serve to divert the direction of the enemy's advance. This freedom of movement and attack was at one time restricted to small bodies of troops in the nature of raids, the general advance or occupation first necessitating the naval seizure of fortified harbors. But modern means of sea transportation have changed this, and raids or landings upon sequestered shores are now possible to armies of two hundred thousand men.

There are, however, other factors inherent in modern warfare that serve to prevent the naval seizure of any harbor regardless of its fortifications:

(1) The development and extensive use of submarine mines.

(2) The increased effective range of torpedoes.

These two means of marine warfare alone prohibit the naval occupancy of any land-locked harbor until the surrounding territory has been possessed. The defence or seizure of San Francisco is unaffected by its harbor fortifications, as no Japanese fleet would approach the Golden Gate until the bay and its entire environs were in possession of their armies.

The defence of San Francisco is only insured by the use of mobile armies, and is concerned with three distinct theatres of action, separate from its present system of fortifications:

(1) The defence of the San Francisco peninsula.

(2) The defence of the Sausalito peninsula.

(3) The defence of its inland lines of communication.

To defend the San Francisco peninsula belongs to an army stationed, not on the peninsula, but in the Santa Clara Valley, fifty miles southward. This position also shields the inland lines south and east of the bay. Whichever combatant gains command of this valley is in a position to attack or hold the San Francisco peninsula and seize or command all southern lines of communication.

To defend the Sausalito peninsula, on the other hand, belongs to an army stationed, not adjacent to forts Barry and Baker, but fifty miles northward in the county of Sonoma. Whichever combatant gains control of this region is also so strategically placed as to attack or hold the Sausalito peninsula and to seize or command the northern lines of communication.[1]

The mobilization of American forces in the vicinity of San

[1] Chart VIII.

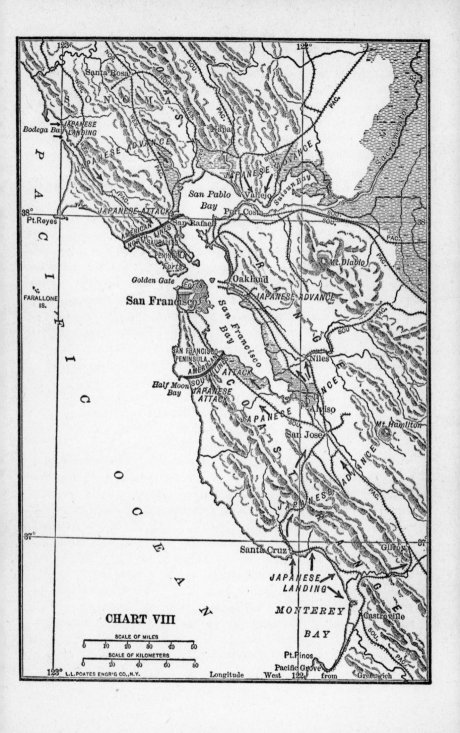

CHART VIII

SCALE OF MILES

0   10   20   30   40   50

SCALE OF KILOMETERS

0   20   40   60   80

L.L.POATES ENGR'G CO., N.Y.   Longitude   West 122° from Greenwich

Francisco must be for the defence of the entire territory adjacent to the bay, since no one part can be defended to the exclusion of the others. The topographical features of this region are such that its inherent strategic difficulties cannot be overcome except by the operation of two quasi-independent forces; one restricted to operations north of the bay and the other to the south. If these armies are not self-sustaining, nor in size adequate to the defence of their respective theatres of action, they become as a whole incapable of effective defence of San Francisco. Should the Japanese column moving northward from Monterey Bay be materially larger than the American forces in the Santa Clara Valley, it will either necessitate this army's reinforcement from the forces defending the northern shores of the bay, or its retirement in that direction, or the destruction in detail of both forces. If reinforced, then the north shores of the bay and San Francisco would be open to attack by the Japanese column advancing southward from Bodega. If the southern army, on the other hand, retired north, then the southern shores of the bay, the peninsula, and city of San Francisco would be undefended.

Reversing this hypothesis so as to deal with the Japanese column advancing east and south from Bodega, we have practically the same conditions in Sonoma, and so north of the bay, as existed southward:

(1) Reinforcements drawn from the Santa Clara Valley, exposing that region to attack by the Japanese column advancing northward from Monterey and leaving San Francisco open to capture, or

(2) Retirement to the south or east shores, leaving Sausalito open to seizure and San Francisco to bombardment.

(3) The destruction of both forces in detail.

The security, therefore, of the American position rests on the superiority of both armies over the Japanese columns advancing simultaneously north and south.[2]

Under present military conditions the maximum number of troops that this Republic, by denuding every fort and post in

[2] Chart VIII.

the nation, and by utilizing the available militia, can mobilize in the vicinity of San Francisco in five months after hostilities have been begun is less than one hundred thousand, two-thirds being state militia.

In this entire force neither the regular infantry nor cavalry would exceed twelve thousand men, while the field artillery would consist of less than four regiments. It is evident, therefore, that the size and elements composing this army would prevent any division of it into the two independent forces mentioned: one in Sonoma County, fifty miles north of San Francisco, and the other fifty miles southward in Santa Clara. Moreover, the smallness of this force would not only forbid its separation into two independent theatres of action, but would prohibit its giving battle to a numerically superior enemy upon a field that did not provide protection to its contracted flanks.

The specific *raison d'être* of this army is the defence of San Francisco, and if it is not possessed of numerical equality to either act on the offensive or, separated, to remain on the defensive, there is but one alternative—the selection of a single main defensive position. This main position cannot be north of the bay nor east nor southeast without leaving open to attack the objective point of the enemy—the city and peninsula of San Francisco. This leaves but two positions to select from—the San Francisco Peninsula or the Santa Clara Valley. While this latter locality constitutes the true defence of San Francisco from an attack by armies landing on the southern coast, the smallness of the American force prevents it from taking a position where it can be flanked at will and cut off from its base by armies numerically superior. This consideration, therefore, relegates the army to its final main position south of San Francisco, with lines thrown across the peninsula, one flank resting on the shores of the Pacific and the other on San Francisco Bay.

That which most vitally concerns a beleaguered city and the armies defending it is the water supply. In former ages this was usually found within the environs of the city itself in the shape of wells and cisterns; but in modern times, especially in the United States, the sources of a city's water supply are generally situated at some distance from it. Whenever this is the case the main line of defence must always include the city's water-works and reservoirs.

The sources of the water supply of San Francisco are in the San Mateo Mountains, between thirty and forty miles to the south, consisting principally of the San Mateo Creek, Alameda Creek, Pilarcitos Creek, and Crystal Springs Lake. There are three reservoirs: the Pilarcitos, thirty-two miles from San Francisco, holding one billion gallons of water; the San Andreas reservoir, with a capacity of six billion gallons, and the Crystal Springs reservoir, storing nineteen billion gallons. If these reservoirs and watershed fall into possession of the enemy, San Francisco must capitulate.

To protect the Andreas and Pilarcitos reservoirs, consisting of less than a third of the water supply, the line of defence must extend across the peninsula south of these reservoirs, a distance, as determined by the contours of probable fortified positions, of nearly thirty miles of front. The centre of this line would be thirty-five miles from San Francisco. If the entire water supply were to be protected, the line of fortified positions and intrenchments would have to extend across the peninsula, south of the Crystal Springs Lake, which would greatly lengthen the line as the peninsula widens toward its base.[3]

The difficulties of defending this peninsula at such a distance from San Francisco by a limited and inexperienced force are very great. The east side of the peninsula consists of a very narrow valley running parallel with the San Francisco Bay on the east and the mountains on the west. The eastern and lower slopes of these mountains consist of rolling hills with contours free from woods, except scattering oak and thickets in the ravines. But higher up, on the top of the ridges and on the western slopes, the contours are broken, irregular and rugged. They are covered with a dense chaparral, heavy thickets of scrub and poison oak, redwood and manzanita.

The American lines, as a whole, must be constructed at right angles to the ridges and contours of these mountains. And

[3] Chart IX.

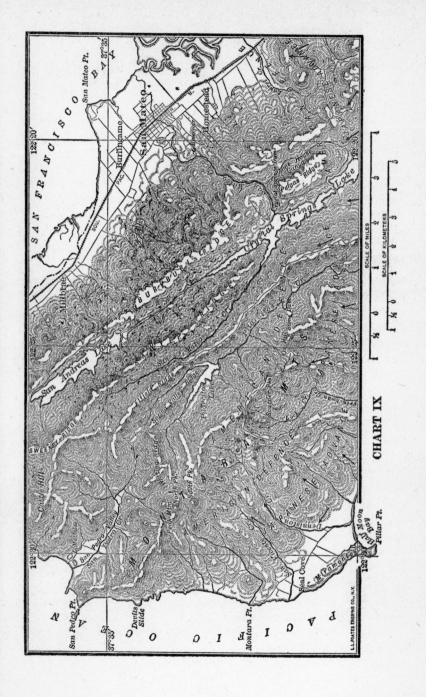

CHART IX

with the exception of the narrow valley along the bay and rolling east slopes, the rugged, thicket-masked character of this peninsula deprives the defence of those essential advantages that modern weapons give to intrenched positions.

Outside of the valley hills there are no slopes with bare glacis such as make possible the defence of an intrenched army. There are no wide zones of fire which the veldt and kopjes of South Africa gave to the Boers, rendering possible the maximum effectiveness of modern armaments. On the other hand, in these mountains, except on the east slopes, it is rare to find exposed fronts of a few hundred yards. Declivities and thickets in endless succession so cut up and screen the topography that modern artillery would be comparatively useless and the effect of infantry fire reduced to a minimum. The defenders, their positions being known, will be in many respects at a greater disadvantage than the attacking forces. In the assaults and repulses that must characterize the fighting in these mountains, discipline will constitute the necessary element of success.

The defence of San Francisco is not, however, restricted to such lines as may be thrown across the peninsula south of the city, but is subject to bombardment whenever the enemy gains possession of the Sausalito peninsula. So, in considering the final intrenched defence of San Francisco, the lines thrown across the northern peninsula must be considered of not less importance than the lines south of the city.

Forts Barry and Baker, situated at the extremity of the peninsula, are in themselves defenceless against a land attack. This is due to the fact that they are backed by a continuous series of ascending heights (see diagram), until Mt. Tamalpais is reached at the northern end of the peninsula. The last defence of San Francisco from the north cannot be made south of a line running westward from a point east of the town of San Rafael, across the north end of the peninsula, to the ocean. This line is approximately from twelve to fifteen miles in length, and, should the Japanese break through it, San Francisco is doomed.[4]

[4] Charts X and XI.

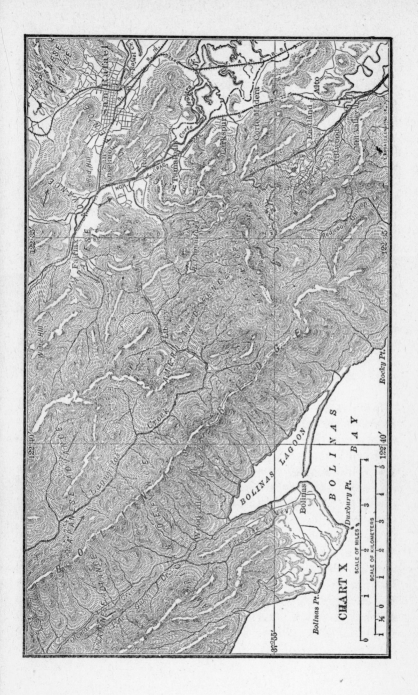

CHART X

We have now considered the conditions governing the final defence of San Francisco, by no means the true one, but the only one that is possible so long as the indifference of this nation restricts its immediate defence to less than a hundred thousand men, composed principally of undisciplined militia under the command of political appointees, or relegates it to forts that are useless.

As one-fourth of the Regular Army is lost in the seizure of the Philippines, these seventy to ninety thousand men would constitute the entire available military establishment of the Republic, and yet, irrespective of its heterogeneity and military worthlessness, this force is so inadequate in numbers that the only position it can occupy for the defence of San Francisco, without meeting destruction on an open field of battle, is the one just considered—the last line of intrenched defence. This means—as must every defence of San Francisco—a division north and south of the bay:

(1) Across the base of the Sausalito peninsula, with a front of nearly fifteen miles.

(2) Adjacent to the base of the San Francisco peninsula, with a front exceeding thirty miles.

This is an aggregate of approximately forty-five miles of front to be defended by less than three divisions of regular troops and three corps of militia. A defence of such a length of front against superior forces for any length of time is manifestly impossible, even if the positions were contiguous. In this case, however, one-third of the line bears no more relationship to the other two-thirds, and vice versa, than if they were one-third in Oregon and two-thirds in southern California.[5]

Japan, after seizing the American insular possessions, Washington, Oregon and southern California, can, within five months after war is declared, land simultaneously at Monterey and Bodega bays a total force exceeding one hundred and seventy thousand veteran troops. Debarking fifty thousand at or above Bodega Bay, from three to five days' march north of the Sausalito defences, and the balance at Monterey Bay,

[5] Chart VIII.

six days' march south of the American defences across the San Francisco peninsula, the Japanese have the alternative of five strategic moves to bring about the seizure or capitulation of the American forces, together with San Francisco and central California.

The southern Japanese army of one hundred and twenty thousand men move north and front the American lines across the San Francisco peninsula simultaneously as the northern Japanese army of fifty thousand move south and front the American force extending westward from San Rafael. Allowing two thousand men per mile in the defensive works, the American forces would approximate seventy thousand on the south line and thirty thousand on the north. The Japanese could:

(1) Simultaneously attack both positions—on the north, fifty thousand Japanese regulars against less than ten thousand American regulars and twenty thousand militia on lines fifteen miles in extent; on the south, one hundred and twenty thousand Japanese regulars against less than twenty-five thousand American regulars and forty-five thousand militia on lines over thirty miles in extent.

(2) Leaving a sufficient force before the American north line, so as to prevent any aggressive action and to take advantage of any retrograde movement, the balance of the northern Japanese army to reinforce the southern army by Point Costa, Oakland, and Niles, their combined forces assaulting the American defences on the south.[6]

(3) Leaving a sufficient force before the American southern lines, so as to prevent any aggressive action and to take advantage of any retrograde movement, the balance of the southern army to reinforce the northern army, their combined forces assaulting the American north line. In this movement the Japanese would have one hundred thousand regulars to ten thousand American regulars and twenty thousand militia.

[6] Chart VIII.

American defeat would give the Sausalito peninsula into the hands of the Japanese and expose the city of San Francisco to a more complete destruction by bombardment than was recently brought about by earthquake and fire.[7]

(4) The Japanese northern army remaining before the American north line, and the southern Japanese army, with the exception of one corps, remaining before the south lines. This detached corps, with siege batteries to occupy Oakland and vicinity; and, if the Oakland Mole has been destroyed, to seize Goat Island under cover of batteries placed on Point Gibbon. Establishing batteries on Goat Island, the entire city is again exposed to destruction by bombardment.[8]

(5) The Japanese northern army to remain before the American north lines, with the exception of one division. The southern Japanese army to remain before the American south lines, except two corps. One corps to occupy the east shores of the bay, one flank joining the left flank of the northern army at Vallejo Junction, the other forming a junction with the right flank of the southern army at Alviso, thus completely surrounding the bay and cutting off all American communications. The second corps to occupy the Sacramento Valley, one division at Sacramento and the other at Stockton. The detached division from the northern army to move eastward over the Union Pacific and establish a fortified position in the Truckee Valley on the east slopes of the Sierras, thus completing the isolation of California and the Pacific coast.

The destruction and demoralization consequent upon the recent earthquake and fire shows that if San Francisco were bombarded from either Goat Island or Sausalito that it would be destroyed within a single day. But whatever course the

[7] Chart XI.
[8] Chart XI.

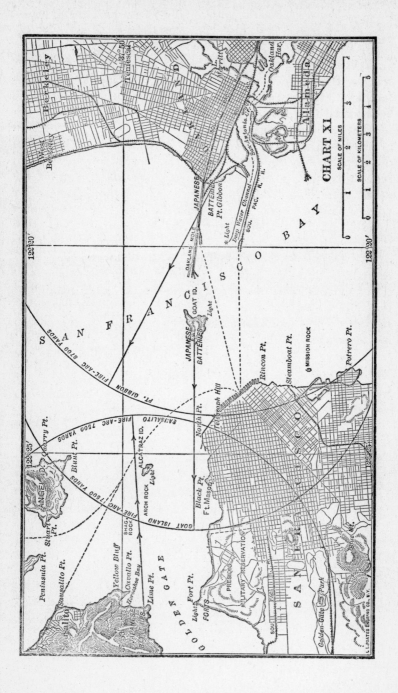

CHART XI

Japanese pursue, whether by battle, by bombardment or by seizure, San Francisco will be forced to capitulate within a fortnight after its investment is completed, though defended by the entire military establishment of the Republic.

The inevitable consummation that follows the investment of San Francisco becomes apparent in the utter helplessness of the Republic. In the entire nation is not another regiment of regular troops; no generals, no corporals. Not months, but years, must elapse before armies equal to the Japanese are able to pass in parade. These must then make their way over deserts such as no armies have ever heretofore crossed; scale the intrenched and stupendous heights that form the redoubts of the desert moats; attempting, in the valor of their ignorance, the militarily impossible; turning mountain-gorges into the ossuaries of their dead, and burdening the desert winds with the spirits of their slain. The repulsed and distracted forces to scatter, as heretofore, dissension throughout the Union, brood rebellions, class and sectional insurrections, until this heterogeneous Republic, in its principles, shall disintegrate, and again into the palm of re-established monarchy pay the toll of its vanity and its scorn.

APPENDIX

TABLE I

SECOND ANGLO-JAPANESE ALLIANCE

THE governments of Great Britain and Japan, being desirous of replacing the agreement concluded between them on January 30, 1902, by fresh stipulations, have agreed upon the following articles, which have for their object:

A. The consolidation and maintenance of general peace in the regions of Eastern Asia and India.

B. The preservation of the common interests of all the powers in China by insuring the independence and integrity of the Chinese Empire, and the principle of equal opportunities for the commerce and industry of all nations in China.

C. The maintenance of the territorial rights of the high contracting parties in the regions of Eastern Asia and of India, and defence of their special interests in the said regions.

ARTICLE I.—It is agreed that whenever in the opinion of either Great Britain or Japan any of the rights and interests referred to in the preamble to this agreement are in jeopardy, the two governments will communicate with one another fully and frankly, and will consider in common the measures which should be taken to safeguard those menaced rights or interests.

ARTICLE II.—Should either of the high contracting parties be involved in war in defence of its territorial rights or special interests, the other party will at once come to the assistance of its ally, and both parties will conduct a war in common and make peace in mutual agreement with any power or powers involved in such war.

ARTICLE III.—Japan, possessing paramount political, military and economic interests in Korea, Great Britain recognizes Japan's right to take such measures for the guidance, control and protection of Korea as she may deem proper and necessary to safeguard and advance those interests, providing the measures so taken are not contrary to the principle of equal opportunities for the commerce and industry of all nations.

ARTICLE IV.—Great Britain having a special interest in all that concerns the security of the Indian frontier, Japan recognizes her right to take such measures in the proximity of that frontier as she may find necessary for the safeguarding of her Indian possessions.

ARTICLE V.—The high contracting parties agree that neither will, without consulting the other, enter into a separate arrangement with another power to the prejudice of the objects described in the preamble.

ARTICLE VI.—As regards the present war between Japan and Russia, Great Britain will continue to maintain strict neutrality unless some other power or powers join in hostilities against Japan, in which case Great Britain will come to the assistance of Japan, will conduct war in common, and will make peace in mutual agreement with Japan.

ARTICLE VII.—The conditions under which armed assistance shall be offered by either power to the other in the circumstances mentioned in the present agreement, and the means by which such assistance shall be made available, will be arranged by the naval and military authorities of the high contracting parties, who will from time to time consult one another fully and freely on all questions of mutual interest.

ARTICLE VIII.—The present agreement shall be subject to the provisions of Article VI, and come into effect immediately after the date of signature and remain in force for ten years from that date. In case neither of the parties shall have been notified twelve months before the expiration of the said ten years of an intention of terminating it, it shall remain binding until the expiration of one year from the day on which either of the parties shall have renounced it; but if, when the date for the expiration arrives, either ally is actually engaged in war, the alliance shall *ipso facto* continue until peace shall be concluded.

Signed, August 12, 1905, by Lord Lansdowne, on behalf of Great Britain, and by Baron Hayashi, on behalf of Japan.

TABLE II

The first expression of anti-Japanese sentiment did not occur until 1900, when a mass-meeting was held in San Francisco.

In 1904, at the twenty-fourth annual session of the American Federation of Labor (2,500,000 members), resolutions were passed to permanently exclude the Japanese from the United States and its insular territories. These resolutions were reaffirmed at the annual sessions in 1905 and 1906. During 1905, twelve great national conventions endorsed and adopted the same resolutions, as did 539 other organizations, comprising civic, fraternal, political and labor associations.

In 1906 the Japanese-Korean Exclusion League was organized. The membership of this league in California numbers about one hundred and twenty-five thousand, composed as follows:

Labor bodies	169
Fraternal societies	18
Civic bodies	12
Benevolent societies	3
Political and military	3
Total	232

This number does not include branch leagues, with their affiliated organizations, outside of San Francisco.

In 1908 there was established, in general convention, the Asiatic Exclusion League of North America, the outgrowth of the Japanese-Korean Exclusion League of 1906. This league has branches in all of the Western States.

The demands of this league are expressed in their following Memorial to Congress, and is expressive of the general sentiment in the West to act, on this question, in direct contravention of treaty stipulations:

MEMORIAL

The first annual convention of the Asiatic Exclusion League of North America, in regular session, Seattle, Washington, February, 1908, do hereby most respectfully

REQUEST, The immediate passage of a law which will exclude, absolutely and emphatically, all Asiatics from the mainland and insular possessions of the United States, and your memorialists do hereby emphatically

PROTEST, Against the administrative and executive officers of the United States entering into any agreement which will permit the ruler of any foreign country to make stipulations as to what class of persons and in what numbers shall leave said foreign country for the purpose of immigrating to the United States and your memorialists

DECLARE, That any such agreement with a foreign power is a subversion of the traditions and policies of the United States, and a betrayal of the rights of American citizens. Your memorialists further

PROTEST, Against the employment of Asiatics on board vessels flying the American flag, to the exclusion of American seamen, and in violation of American law; therefore, your memorialists pray for the speedy enactment of a law which will prohibit the employment of Asiatics upon all vessels flying the American flag, or in any branch or department of the public service. Your memorialists again emphatically

PROTEST, Against the continuance of Asiatic immigration upon the exalted grounds of American patriotism, for the reasons:

FIRST, That these Asiatics come to the United States entirely ignorant of our sentiments of nativity and patriotism, and utterly unfit and incapable of discharging the duties of American citizenship.

SECOND, The introduction of this incongruous and non-assimilable element into our national life will inevitably impair and degrade, if not effectually destroy, our cherished institutions and our American life.

THIRD, These Asiatics are alien to our ideas of patriotism, morality, loyalty and the highest conceptions of Christian civilization.

FOURTH, Their presence here is a degrading and contaminating influence to the best phases of American life.

FIFTH, With their low standard of living, immoral surroundings and cheap labor, they constitute a formidable and fierce competition against our American system, the pride and glory of our civilization, and unless prohibited by effective legislation will result in the irreparable deterioration of American labor.

SIXTH, The living in our midst of a large body of Asiatics, the greatest number of whom are armed, loyal to their governments, entertaining feelings of distrust, if not of hostility, to our people, without any allegiance to our government or our institutions, not sustaining American life in times of peace, and ever ready to respond to the cause of their own nations in times of war, make these Asiatics an appalling menace to the

American Republic, the splendid achievements wrought by the strong arms and loyal hearts of Caucasian toilers, patriots and heroes in every walk of life.

Senator Lodge, in commenting upon this movement to exclude the Japanese from the United States, in a speech given at Boston, said:

"Such a movement of people as this is, in itself, a historic event of great magnitude, deserving the most careful consideration; but what we are concerned with is its effect upon and its meaning to the people of the United States and the future of our country," etc.

Careful investigation shows that on the Pacific slope the people are not only anti-Japanese in sentiment as regards economic competition, but they are becoming more subject to racial antipathies. They may, in regard to Japanese immigration and naturalization, be divided into four classes,

8 per cent.	of whom	are			pro-Japanese
22 "	"	"	"	"	indifferent
30 "	"	"	"	"	hostile
40 "	"	"	"	"	belligerently hostile

TABLE III

THE first official act directed toward the exclusion of the Japanese from the United States was that of Governor Henry T. Gage, in his biennial message to the Legislature of California in 1900. Pursuant to his suggestions, a joint resolution was adopted by the Legislature and forwarded to the National Congress in which the exclusion of the Japanese was urged. Concurrent resolutions were again adopted by the California Legislature on March 22, 1905, and by unanimous vote both the Senate and the Assembly declared that "unrestricted Japanese immigration is a menace to the state."

A similar resolution was unanimously adopted by the Senate and Assembly of the Nevada Legislature. Since that time, over the entire Pacific Slope, like action has been taken in state, county and municipal bodies, culminating in the act of the San Francisco Board of Education in excluding the Japanese from the public schools, and which so nearly caused serious international complications. While these acts are clearly contrary to all treaty stipulations, yet the California Supreme Court declared them constitutional, thus showing the difficulties of maintaining just and peaceful relationship with foreign powers when the popular sentiment of the state is opposed to the policy of the Federal Government.

In reply to President Roosevelt's message to Congress, December, 1906, relative to the Japanese trouble, Governor Pardee addressed a message to the California Legislature, January, 1907, expressing, in part, the sentiment of the people as follows:

"It is safe to say that the President, when he penned that portion of his annual message in which he referred to the treatment of the Japanese in the San Francisco schools, was not aware of the conditions on this coast, especially in California. . . . The President does not understand the racial differences between the Japanese and Chinese and people of Caucasian blood. . . . Our laws and customs regard intermarriage with them miscegenation. . . . Were the racial differences in civilization, thought, manners and customs not inseparable between these Asiatics and Caucasians, whatever inhospitableness our people might show toward them would insensibly disappear. . . . It is useless to expect that people with such different racial characteristics and such different civilization can ever mix with our people and become absorbed into our body politic. They cannot become good American citizens; it is useless to attempt to make them such."

It is only to be expected that such popular sentiments and official acts would soon become incorporated in the aspirations of the political parties of the Pacific Slope, and in due time, as these sentiments merged into the politics of the West, becoming inherent in a fixed and settled policy, they would be incorporated in the national platforms of the great political parties. This has accordingly come about, showing the development of this sentiment from a sectional to a national issue. Subsequent to 1900, increasing in number and intensity, municipal conventions, county and state conventions of all political parties, and in all portions of the Pacific Slope, have incorporated in their resolutions declarations for the absolute exclusion of Japanese. So thoroughly has this sentiment permeated the political fabric of the West that it has been incorporated into the platforms of two of the national parties.

INDEPENDENCE PLATFORM

Adopted in National Convention, July 28, 1908.

We oppose Asiatic immigration, which does not amalgamate with our population, creates race issues and un-American conditions, and which reduces wages and tends to lower the high standard of living and the high standard of morality which the American civilization has established.

We demand the passage of an exclusion act which shall protect American workingmen from competition with Asiatic cheap labor, and which shall protect American civilization from the contamination of Asiatic conditions.

DEMOCRATIC PLATFORM

Adopted in National Convention, July 10, 1908.

We favor full protection, by both national and state governments within their respective spheres, of all foreigners residing in the United States under treaty, but we are opposed to Asiatic immigrants who cannot be amalgamated with our population, or whose presence among us would raise a race issue and involve us in diplomatic controversies with Oriental powers.

In 1907, Baron Hayashi, Minister of Foreign Affairs, replied to this government, relative to the proposed Japanese exclusion and anti-naturalization legislation, that the Imperial Government would continue its demand (in accordance with treaty stipulations) for the same rights, privileges and immunities for the Japanese going to and resident in the United States as are granted the aliens of other nations.

TENTATIVE ANTI-JAPANESE LEGISLATION—1908-09

California Legislature
Oregon Legislature
Washington Legislature
Nevada Legislature
Arizona Legislature
Colorado Legislature
Wyoming Legislature
Idaho Legislature
Hawaiian Legislature

TABLE IV

IT HAS been difficult heretofore to find a true basis for comparison of the strength of the various navies. A statement of the total number of ships in each navy means nothing, because these ships and their *personnel* vary so widely as to make any such comparison useless. A comparison on the basis of armor protection is likewise worthless, since a fleet powerful only in defensive qualities, as a fleet of monitors, would be of no use under modern conditions; so a comparison by speed is also erroneous, since a fleet of exceedingly swift but moderately armed and armored cruisers would possess no combative qualities if engaged with a fleet of battleships. Moreover, in all comparisons between ships the question must be considered: War-ships built to-day have four times the fighting value of those constructed a few years ago.

Since the naval battle of Tsu Shima new conditions were brought to light that make possible a more accurate comparison between the fighting qualities of two fleets. The victory of future naval engagements will go to the fleet that is able to bring the greatest number of heavy guns within the shortest line of battle. In this comparison the guns included are those that can pierce heavy armor at 5000 yards: *i. e.,* the 50-caliber 9.2-in., the 45-caliber 10-in., the 40-caliber 11-in., the 35-caliber 12-in., and the 35-caliber 13-in. and 13½-in.

The Japanese battleships built prior to the Russian War and the vessels captured from Russia have, in accordance with these ideas, been reconstructed and the armaments altered so as to double their fighting strength. The vessels of the Mikasa type, which have heretofore carried four 12-in. guns and fourteen 6-in., will carry four 10-in. instead of the 6-in. guns, so that their main armament will be brought up to eight guns of heavy caliber. The Russian battleships have likewise been re-armed with eight guns of heavy caliber.

The following tables show the fighting qualities of the two fleets.

By these tables it is seen that the Japanese navy, in its battleships, possesses nearly thirty per cent. more big guns than the American navy, while its battle-line is only slightly over one half as long.

TABLE OF JAPANESE BATTLESHIPS (FIRST-CLASS), 1909

Ship	Displacement, tons	Number of big guns		Speed, knots
Shikishima........	15,000	4 12-in.,	4 10-in.	18.3
Asahi.............	15,000	4 "	4 "	18
Iwami............	13,566	4 "	4 "	18
Hizen............	12,700	4 "	4 "	18
Suwo............	12,674	4 "	4 "	19
Sagami..........	12,674	4 "	4 "	19
Fuji.............	12,300	4 "	4 "	18.5
Tango...........	11,000	4 "	4 "	18
Mikasa...........	15,200	4 "	4 "	18
Katori...........	16,400	4 "	4 "	19.5
Kashima.........	16,400	4 "	4 "	19.2
Satsuma.........	19,200	4 "	12 "	20.5
Aki..............	19,800	4 "	12 "	21.5
Huki............	21,000	12 "		21.5
	14 ships	132 heavy guns		

TABLE OF AMERICAN BATTLESHIPS (FIRST-CLASS), 1909

Ship	Displacement, tons	Number of big guns		Speed, knots
New Hampshire........	16,000	4 12-inch		18
Alabama..............	11,552	4 13 "		17
Connecticut..........	16,000	4 12 "		18
Georgia..............	14,948	4 12 "		19
Idaho................	13,000	4 12 "		17
Illinois..............	11,552	4 13 "		17
Iowa................	11,348	4 12 "		17
Kansas..............	16,000	4 12 "		18
Kearsarge...........	11,520	4 13 "		17
Kentucky...........	11,520	4 13 "		17
Louisiana...........	16,000	4 12 "		18
Maine...............	12,500	4 12 "		18
Michigan............	16,000	8 12 "		18
Minnesota...........	16,000	4 12 "		18
Mississippi..........	13,000	4 12 "		17
Missouri............	12,500	4 12 "		18
Nebraska............	14,948	4 12 "		19
New Jersey..........	14,948	4 12 "		19
Ohio................	12,500	4 12 "		18
Rhode Island........	14,948	4 12 "		19
South Carolina.......	16,000	8 12 "		18
Vermont............	16,000	4 12 "		18
Virginia............	14,948	4 12 "		19
Wisconsin...........	11,552	4 13 "		17
	24 ships	104 heavy guns		

JAPANESE ARMORED CRUISERS
1909

Cruiser	Displacement, tons	Number of big guns		Speed, knots
Tokiwa..........	9,700			23
Asama...........	9,700			22.1
Idzuma..........	9,750			22
Iwate............	9,750			22
Yakumo.........	9,850			20
Adzuma..........	9,436			20
Aso.............	7,726			22
Kasuga.........	7,229	1 10-inch		22
Nisshin..........	7,700			20
Tsukuba.........	13,750	4 12-inch		21
Ikoma...........	13,750	4 12 ”		20.43
Kurama..........	14,600	4 12 ”		20
Ibuki	14,600	4 12 ”		23
....	18,000	4 12 ”	8 10-inch	25
	14 cruisers	29 heavy guns		

AMERICAN ARMORED CRUISERS
1909

Cruiser	Displacement, tons	Number of big guns	Speed, knots
Brooklyn..............	9,215		22
California.............	13,680		22
Colorado.............	13,680		22
Maryland.............	13,680		22
Montana.............	14,500	4 10-inch	22
New York.............	8,150		21
North Carolina.......	14,500	4 10-inch	22
Pennsylvania.........	13,680		22
South Dakota.........	13,680		22
Tennessee............	14,500	4 10-inch	22
Washington...........	14,500	4 ”	22
West Virginia.........	13,680		22
	12 cruisers	16 heavy guns	

	United States	Japan
Torpedo-boats.....................................	36	79
Torpedo-boat destroyers............................	16	54

TABLE V

THE following table shows the ages of the captains and flag officers, with their average years in the two grades, in the navies of Great Britain, France, Germany, Japan, and the United States:

	Captains		Sea-going flag officers	
	Age	Average years in grade	Age	Average years in grade
Great Britain.................	35	11.2	45	8
France.......................	47	9.5	53	14.2
Germany.....................	42	6.2	51	6
Japan........................	38	8	44	11
United States................	55	4.5	59	1.5

PERSONNEL OF THE AMERICAN AND JAPANESE NAVIES

	United States	Japan
Flag officers..	18	49
Captains and commanders.........................	182	185
Other line officers and engineers..................	697	1,451
Medical officers....................................	254	311
Pay officers..	188	240
Warrant officers...................................	624	1,064
Enlisted men.......................................	32,000	35,312

TABLE VI

A

"In twelve of the American battleships there is to be found in the after-end of the superstructure a section that is entirely unarmored. Being just in front of the after-turret, this unprotected portion of some fifty square feet exposes the shafts that pass down into the auxiliary magazines of the vessels."

B

"In all the American battleships the main armor belt does not extend more than six inches above water when the vessel is fully equipped and ready for sea. It was this sunken condition of the main armor that resulted in the sinking of so many Russian warships in the battle of Tsu Shima. This belt of armor should extend several feet above the water-line, as is the case in the principal foreign navies. In France it reaches from five to eight feet above the water, while in the modern British war-ships it extends eight feet below and five above the water-line."

C

"In twelve of the American battleships the gun-ports are so large that the guns and gun-crews are exposed to destruction. The turret-ports in the *Kearsarge* and the *Kentucky* are so large that a number of twelve-inch shells could enter them at the same time. The open spaces above and below the guns in these turrets are ten feet square. In some of the battleships the broadside guns are in exposed openings as wide as six feet. While foreign navies observe the principle of isolating the guns of the secondary armament by pairs in turrets, or singly in casements, it is not done in the American navy, except the last five ships. In the *Kearsarge* and *Kentucky* there are fourteen guns in one compartment. A shell exploding in this compartment would not only put all of the guns out of commission, but would probably kill or wound the one hundred and forty men stationed there."

D

"In the evolutions of the Atlantic fleet recently it was found that sea-going torpedo-boats or destroyers, when directed against the fleet of battleships, could get into a position to destroy them. To protect this one fleet it was made apparent at that time that it would be necessary to have a cordon of forty-eight torpedo-destroyers to defend the fleet from the destroyers of the enemy."[1]

E

As was shown in Admiral Evans' report concerning the cruise of the battleship fleet to the Pacific, the lowness of the American ships affects seriously their fighting qualities. Three of the battleships have their bows but eleven feet above water; two others, thirteen feet. The latest battleships have their bows only eighteen feet over the water-line, and the latest cruiser but twenty. In foreign navies modern battleships have their forward decks from twenty-two to twenty-eight feet above water, while the forward decks of armored cruisers are from twenty-five to thirty-two feet high.

In a naval battle, where high speed is essential, the disasters that may ensue on account of this lowness of the gun-decks are vividly portrayed in the trial trip of one of the latest American battleships, the *Virginia*. Steaming at 19.04 knots, the bow wave of solid water reached the height of fifteen feet, while an impenetrable spray rose forty feet above the water level. This battleship, with all her ports closed by steel bucklers, shipped one hundred and twenty tons of water into her forward turret while making the trip from Cuba to Hampton Roads. Had the ports of this ship been open for action, immense quantities of water would have poured through them and rendered the guns of the forward turret useless. During the cruise to the Pacific it was demonstrated that if the battleships steamed at high speed in a moderate sea, or at medium speed in a rough sea, the guns of the forward turret could not be used. This would reduce, under such conditions, the main armament of big guns to one half, since two of the four heavy guns on the American ships are carried in the forward turret.

The broadside guns, constituting the secondary armament of the American ships, are on even lower gun decks. In twelve of the latest battleships—the *New Hampshire, Connecticut, Kansas, Idaho, Louisiana, Minnesota, Vermont, Georgia, Mississippi, Virginia, Nebraska, New Jersey*—they are only about eleven feet above water. In each of the new

[1] See Table IV, last paragraph.

TABLE VII

VESSELS CONSTITUTING JAPANESE TRANSPORT SYSTEM IN TIME OF WAR

MAJOR FLEET, 1909

Steamer	Gross tonnage	Troop capacity, officers and men
Tenyo Maru	14,000	4,600
Chiyo Maru	14,000	4,600
....	14,000	4,600
Kamo Maru	8,600	3,594
Hirano Maru	8,600	3,594
Miyazaka Maru	8,600	3,594
Atsuta Maru	8,600	3,594
Kitano Maru	8,600	3,594
Mishima Maru	8,600	3,594
Tango Maru	7,463	3,168
Hitachi Maru	6,716	2,886
Aki Maru	6,444	2,842
Shinano Maru	6,388	2,916
Iyo Maru	6,320	2,965
Awa Maru	6,309	2,854
Kaga Maru	6,301	2,872
Wakasa Maru	6,265	2,717
Bingo Maru	6,247	2,805
Sado Maru	6,227	2,740
Inaba Maru	6,189	2,816
Kanagawa Maru	6,170	2,832
Hakata Maru	6,161	2,415
Tamba Maru	6,134	2,794
Kamakura Maru	6,126	2,670
Sanuki Maru	6,112	2,700
Kawachi Maru	6,101	2,532
Hong-Kong Maru	6,000	2,600
America Maru	6,000	2,600
Nippon Maru	6,000	2,600
Tosa Maru	5,823	2,885
Nikko Maru	5,539	2,400
Kumano Maru	5,076	2,396
Ceylon Maru	5,068	2,300
Riojun Maru	4,806	2,840
Takasaki Maru	4,747	2,176
Wakamiya Maru	4,723	2,292
Kageshima Maru	4,687	2,070
Yetorofu Maru	4,166	2,185
Colombo Maru[1]	4,709	1,000
Bombay Maru[1]	4,629	1,000

40 Steamers   Troop capacity, 114,235

MINOR FLEET NO. I

Steamer	Gross tonnage	Troop capacity, officers and men
Kagoshima Maru........................	4,405	1,726
Tenshin Maru..........................	4,173	1,670
Yeboshi Maru..........................	4,098	2,140
Kasuga Maru...........................	3,820	1,800
Yawata Maru...........................	3,817	1,900
Moyori Maru...........................	3,773	1,790
Shiokubi Maru.........................	3,755	1,842
Benten Maru...........................	3,668	1,680
Totomi Maru[1]........................	3,412	900
Miike Maru............................	3,365	1,790
Yamaguchi Maru........................	3,321	1,845
Hiroshima Maru........................	3,283	1,500
Matsuyama Maru........................	3,099	2,010
Mikawa Maru[1]........................	2,932	800
Saiko Maru............................	2,904	2,400
Kobe Maru.............................	2,877	1,680
Tategami Maru.........................	2,703	1,640
Takeshima Maru........................	2,673	2,372
Hakuai Maru...........................	2,636	1,750
Kosai Maru............................	2,635	1,909
Kokura Maru...........................	2,596	1,520
Yamashiro Maru........................	2,581	2,480
Chikuzem Maru[1]......................	2,578	700
Chiugo Maru[1]........................	2,563	700
Wakanoura Maru........................	2,527	1,500
Yeijo Maru............................	2,506	2,260
Omi Maru..............................	2,501	1,800
Yokohama Maru.........................	2,373	2,560
Niigata Maru[1].......................	2,184	650
Awaji Maru[1].........................	2,045	600
Santo Maru............................	2,032	1,800
Yeiko Maru............................	1,966	1,640
Sakata Maru...........................	1,963	1,944
Satsuma Maru..........................	1,939	2,168
Sagami Maru...........................	1,934	1,600
Chefoo Maru...........................	1,934	1,670
Nagato Maru...........................	1,884	1,718
Fushiki Maru[1].......................	1,839	600
Takasago Maru.........................	1,789	1,477
Otaru Maru............................	1,571	1,822
Hanasaki Maru.........................	1,570	1,822
Kamikawa Maru[1]......................	1,465	550
Hirosaki Maru[1]......................	1,460	550
Genkai Maru...........................	1,447	1,952

Steamer	Gross tonnage	Troop capacity, officers and men
Hiogo Maru............................	1,438	1,890
Suminoye Maru.........................	1,425	1,990
Higo Maru.............................	1,420	1,735
Takamatsu Maru[1].....................	1,335	500
Osumi Maru[1].........................	1,335	500
Ishikari Maru[1]......................	1,312	500
Yechigo Maru..........................	1,280	1,000
Ise Maru.............................	1,250	1,480
Tokachi Maru..........................	1,110	1,642
Kushiro Maru..........................	1,076	1,190
Saishu Maru...........................	2,117	1,637

55 Steamers   Troop capacity 85,291

[1] Steamers built primarily for carrying freight, hence low troop capacity.

	Steamers	Troop capacity
Total, Major Fleet...............	40	114,235
Total, Minor Fleet No. 1.........	55	85,291
Grand Total...................	95	199,526

We have not the data of Minor Fleet No. 2.

cruisers ten of the fourteen medium guns are at the same height. These guns could not be fired to the windward while the ships were steaming at battle speed in a moderate sea, or at medium speed in a rough sea. The broadside guns of foreign warships are, in a general sense, twice as high as the American, and in some instances three times as high.

While it is true that four or five, or even more, Japanese can get along comfortably in the same space that an American deems necessary for one person, this condition has not been taken advantage of to a very marked degree, as a comparison of the American and Japanese transports, with their relative troop capacity proportionate to their tonnage, will show.

In comparing one of the largest American transports, the *Meade*, 5641 gross tonnage and troop capacity of 2075 officers and men, with one of the *Tenyo Maru* class of Japanese transports, of 14,000 gross tonnage and troop capacity of 4600 officers and men, it is seen that while the American transport carries one man to every 2.95 tons, in the Japa-

COMPARATIVE TABLE

AMERICAN TRANSPORTS IN 1898–1900

Steamer	Gross tonnage	Troop capacity, officers and men
Knickerbocker............................	1,642	945
Buford..................................	3,039	1,052
Cherokee................................	2,557	1,000
Grant...................................	5,590	1,909
Logan...................................	5,672	1,796
Warren..................................	4,375	1,292
Thomas..................................	5,796	1,781
Sherman.................................	5,780	1,888
Sheridan................................	5,673	2,000
Meade...................................	5,641	2,075

nese vessel 3.04 tons is utilized; showing that the American ship is carrying not less but more troops to her tonnage than the Japanese.

In the next largest class is the American transport *Warren*, 4375 gross tonnage and troop capacity of 1292 officers and men. Comparing this to the next largest Japanese transports of the *Kamo* class, 8600 gross tonnage and troop capacity of 3594 officers and men, we find that in the American vessel one man is carried to every (approximately) 3.38 tons, while in the Japanese ship approximately 2.4 tons is utilized to each man; showing in this case that the Japanese vessel is carrying more men to her tonnage than the American, though the difference is slight.

In the next highest class is the American transport *Buford*, 3039 gross tonnage and troop capacity of 1052 officers and men as compared to the Japanese third largest class exceeding 6000 gross tonnage. In this instance the American transport carries one man to 2.8 tons, while the average for the Japanese vessels is approximately 2.44 tons, or nearly the equivalent.

In the Japanese vessels of lower tonnage we find, however, that the tonnage proportion to the troop capacity grows less, until, in some instances, one soldier is carried to each ton or less of the gross tonnage. This is due to the fact that these smaller vessels were built almost exclusively for the use of Orientals, whose characteristics in domicile permit the maximum passenger capacity with the minimum of space and tonnage.

Should Japan embark on these two fleets an average of two Japanese to the space and tonnage ordinarily deemed necessary for one American, then the troop capacity on a single voyage of these fleets would exceed three hundred thousand officers and men, together with their equipment and supplies. That this would be easily possible and would work no hardship on the men was demonstrated by the Japanese winter-quarters in Manchuria during the Russian War. We have, however, not taken this possibility into consideration, but have given the troop capacity of the Japanese vessels per European measurement.

TABLE VIII

A

THE following table shows the number of officers who were obliged to leave the Union Army during the Civil War.

Arms of service	Discharged			Cashiered	Resigned
	With dis-honor	For incapacity	Without stated reasons		
REGULARS					
Cavalry...............		1	25	1	97
Artillery...............			18		50
Infantry..............		1	79	5	253
Total...............		2	122	6	400
VOLUNTEERS					
Cavalry...............	12	330	394	38	3,055
Artillery...............	15	159	163	14	999
Infantry..............	159	2,569	1,586	200	17,036
Total...............	186	3,058	2,143	252	21,090
COLORED TROOPS					
Cavalry...............			5		34
Artillery...............		8	9		68
Infantry..............	18	158	144	16	679
Total...............	18	166	158	16	781
Grand totals.........	204	3,226	2,423	274	22,271

Grand total, 28,398

The resignations tabulated in the last column are in character very little removed, if at all, in the vast majority of cases, from the factors tabulated in the other columns. These resignations were almost always the product of two conditions: (1) to escape being discharged under the other four heads; (2) after every disaster or defeat great numbers of resignations were sent in. Carl Schurz, in his *Memoirs*, especially mentions the great number of regimental officers that left the Union Army immediately after the defeat at Fredericksburg.

Allowing incompetent officers to resign, instead of cashiering them, was only characteristic of official leniency practised during this war against military offenders. This was most vividly portrayed relative to

TABLE OF DESERTIONS IN THE
AMERICAN CIVIL WAR

Arms of service	Number of deserters	
	Officers	Enlisted men
REGULARS		
Cavalry..............................	2	1,866
Artillery.............................		3,162
Infantry.............................	3	11,332
Total.............................	5	16,360
VOLUNTEERS		
Cavalry..............................	34	31,856
Artillery.............................	4	11,942
Infantry.............................	149	126,231
Total.............................	187	170,029
COLORED TROOPS		
Cavalry..............................	4	674
Artillery.............................	2	1,843
Infantry.............................	18	923
Total.............................	24	3,440
Grand totals.........................	216	189,829

Grand total, 190,045

desertion, which in the time of war is punishable by death, yet in this conflict there occurred nearly two hundred thousand desertions from the Union Army and only seven executions.

B

Within a short time after the defeat at Fredericksburg 85,000 men deserted. This fact shows, to a certain extent, the actuating motive in the desertion of short-term volunteers and the disasters that ensue to the nation whenever its forces meet defeat on the field. See table on preceding page.

All confederated forms of government are only durable in prosperity and success; in disasters the tendency is not to greater cohesion and unity, but to disintegration. Should the armies of this Republic meet with a continuous series of defeats, as characterized the Japanese-Russian War or the Franco-Prussian War of 1870, the probable culmination would be the dissolution of the present form of confederated government.

MILITIA, RAN AWAY OR DESERTED

Battle	Date		Organization or Expedition
Long Island.............	Aug. 27,	1776	Parsons' brigade
Evacuation of New York	Sept. 15,	1776	Parsons' and Fellows' brigades
Brandywine.............	Sept. 11,	1777	Sullivan's division
Camden, S. C.	Aug. 16,	1780	Virginia and South Carolina brigades
Guilford Court House, N.C.	March 15,	1781	North Carolina regiment
Indian village near Fort Wayne, Ind.	Oct. 22,	1790	Harmar's Miami expedition
Darke County, Ohio......	Nov. 4,	1791	St. Clair's expedition
Frenchtown and Raisin River, Mich.	Jan. 18-20,	1813	Winchester's column
Sackett's Harbor.........	May 29,	1813	General Brown's command
French Creek, N. Y.	Nov. 1-5,	1813	General Hampton's column
Chrysler's Field, Canada ..	Nov. 11,	1813	General Wilkinson's column
Evacuation of Fort George, Niagara River.........	Dec. 10,	1813	Gen. McClure's N. Y. militia
Burning of Buffalo and Black Rock, N. Y.	Dec. 30,	1813	Gen. McClure's N. Y. militia
Bladensburg, Md.	Aug. 24,	1814	Maryland, Virginia, and District of Columbia Militia and Volunteers under General Winder
New Orleans, La.	Jan. 8,	1815	800 militia under Gen. Morgan, posted on the left bank of the Mississippi
Lake Okeechobee, Fla.	Dec. 25,	1837	Missouri volunteers and spies
Bull Run, Virginia........	July 21,	1861	Gen. McDowell's entire force of militia

While the Civil War shows, in its various activities, the fallacy of
militia and volunteers, the Spanish-American War and Philippine Insurrection portray a progressive deterioration. The worthlessness of the
American military system, however, does not alone adhere to these late
wars, but has been co-existent with the Republic from its inception, as
the three tables on pages 242, 243, and 244, published by F. L. Huide-
koper in the *North American Review*, show.

This partial list shows the character of the wholesale desertions and
flights up to the time of the Civil War. Subsequent affairs are too well
known to necessitate repetition. In the Civil War it must always be
remembered, when the valorous deeds done there come to the mind, that

MILITIA MUTINIED

Place	Date		Mutineers
Morristown, N. J.	Jan. 1,	1781	Pennsylvania line (6 regiments), 1300 men
Pompton, N. J.	Jan. 24-28, 1781		New Jersey line
Lancaster, Pa.	June,	1783	80 recruits, joined by two hundred other malcontents, marched to Philadelphia, demanded their pay, and held Congress prisoner on June 21, 1783
On the march from Urbana, Ohio, to Detroit, Mich. .	June,	1812	General Hull's militia
Detroit, Mich.	July,	1812	180 Ohio militia of Hull's command
On the march from Fort Harrison, Ind., to the Wabash and Illinois rivers	Oct. 19,	1812	4000 Kentucky mounted militia under General Hopkins
En route to the rapids of the Maumee River.	Oct.,	1812	Kentucky, Virginia, and Ohio militia under Gen. W. H. Harrison
En route from Plattsburg, N. Y., to Canada.	Nov.,	1812	Nearly all the 3,000 militia under General Dearborn
Battle of Queenstown	Oct. 13,	1813	New York militia under Generals Rensselaer and Wadsworth
Fort Strother, Fla.	Nov.,	1813	Tennessee militia and volunteers
Retreat to Buffalo after evacuation of Fort George.	Dec.,	1813	General McClure's New York militia
Withlacoochee River, Fla.	Dec. 31,	1835	Florida militia and volunteers under Gov. Call, Clinch's expedition
Charlestown, W. Va.	July 16-18, 1861		Militia of the Army of the Shenandoah

in due time, after two or three years' service, militia ceased to be militia and volunteers had become regulars.

Even as early as the American War of Independence, when science and invention had entered very little into the conduct of war, the worthlessness of militia and volunteers was fully recognized by the military leaders of that period. Washington expressed himself as follows:

"Regular troops alone are equal to the exigencies of modern war, as well for defence as offence, and when a substitute is attempted it must prove illusory and ruinous. No militia will ever acquire the habits necessary to resist a regular force. . . . The firmness requisite for the real business of fighting is only to be attained by a constant course of discipline and service. I have never yet been witness to a single instance that can justify a different opinion, and it is most earnestly to be wished that the liberties of America may no longer be trusted, in any material degree, to so precarious a dependence."

STATES DEFY THE U. S. GOVERNMENT BY REFUSING TO FURNISH THEIR MILITIA TO ITS SERVICE

State	Governor	Date	Cause and Reason for Refusal
Massachusetts.	Strong.....	April, 1812	Denied right of President or Congress to determine when such exigencies arise as to require calling out of militia. Claimed that "this right is vested in the commanders-in-chief of the militia of the several states"
Connecticut...	Griswold ..	April, 1812	Substantially the same contention as the above
Vermont......	Chittenden	Nov. 10, 1813	Declared that "the military strength and resources of this state must be reserved for its own defence and protection exclusively"
Vermont......	Chittenden	Sept., 1814	Refused to order militia to support Gen. Macomb in repelling the enemy
Virginia	Letcher....		
North Carolina	Ellis......		
Kentucky.....	Magoffin ..	April, 1861	Rebellion
Tennessee.....	Harris.....		
Missouri......	Jackson ...		
Arkansas......	Rector....		

TABLE IX

LETTER to the President of Congress, September 24, 1776:

"To place any dependence upon militia is assuredly resting upon a broken staff. Men just dragged from the tender scenes of domestic life, unaccustomed to the din of arms, totally unacquainted with every kind of military skill (which is followed by want of confidence in themselves when opposed by troops regularly trained, disciplined, and appointed, superior in knowledge and superior in arms), are timid and ready to fly from their own shadows.

"Besides, the sudden change in their manner of living, particularly in their lodging, brings on sickness in many, impatience in all, and such an unconquerable desire of returning to their respective homes that it not only produces shameful and scandalous desertions among themselves, but infuses a like spirit in others. Again, men accustomed to unbounded freedom and no control cannot brook the restraint which is indispensably necessary to the good order and government of an army, without which licentiousness and every kind of disorder triumphantly reign. To bring men to a proper degree of subordination is not the work of a day, a month, or even a year. . . . Certain I am that it would be cheaper to keep fifty thousand or one hundred thousand in constant pay than to depend upon half the number and supply the other half occasionally by militia. The time the latter are in pay before and after they are in camp, assembling and marching, the waste of ammunition, the consumption of stores, which, in spite of every resolution or requisition of Congress, they must be furnished with or sent home, added to other incidental expenses consequent upon their coming and conduct in camp, surpass all idea and destroy every kind of regularity and economy which you could establish among fixed and settled troops, and will, in my opinion, prove, if the scheme is adhered to, the ruin of our cause."

TABLE X

A

THE number of deaths from disease in the American Civil War cannot be positively ascertained, on account of the great numbers who died subsequent to discharge due to disability. Careful investigation demonstrates that an equal, if not greater, number died after leaving the field and base hospitals than died therein.

Deaths from disease while still in the ranks:

Officers and men.................... 199,720

B

The casualties in the Spanish-American War were as follows:

	Battle	Disease
In the Philippines.......................................	17	203
In Puerto Rico...	3	262
In Cuba...	273	567
In U. S. camps..		2649
Total...	293	3681

The mean strength of the American army during this war was approximately 170,000. The number of admissions to hospital on September 10, 1898, was over 158,000, *i. e.,* 90 per cent. of the entire force.

These men were, but a few months prior, selected, after examination by surgeons, on account of their physical perfectness, so that this vast amount of disease and death was not due to the physical weakness and incapacity of the American volunteer, but to the worthlessness of the military system of the Republic. While only about 38,000 men participated in the military operations of the Spanish-American War, and while the casualties in battle were very few, yet 43,000 pension claims have been issued or are pending in the Pension Office of the United States.

C

JAPANESE-RUSSIAN WAR

A statement of the Japanese casualties from disease by Baron Takaki, Surgeon-General (Reserve) Imperial Japanese Navy:

"To be sure, we did lose men from disease, but in all human history there has never been a record like ours. We established a record of four deaths from bullets to one from disease. In the Spanish-American War fourteen men died from preventable sickness to one man killed on the field of battle. The following table gives a comparison of the mortality from disease per one thousand men in the Japanese-Chinese War and the Japanese-Russian War:

Japanese-Chinese War			Japanese-Russian War		
Cases		*Deaths*	*Cases*		*Deaths*
	Cholera			Cholera	
82.87		50.96	None		None
	Typhoid			Typhoid	
37.14		10.98	9.26		5.16
	Malaria			Malaria	
102.58		5.29	1.96		0.07

"While Japan put into the field, during the Russian War, 1,500,000 troops of various categories, the total number of typhoid cases amounted to only 9722, resulting in 4073 deaths. Dysentery cases amounted to only 7642, resulting in 1804 deaths."

TABLE XI

JAPANESE immigration to the United States (mainland) has been governed by the same considerations.

Immigration by political decades:

1891–1900	24,806
1901–1905	64,102
1905–1906	14,243
1906–1907	30,226
Total	133,377

During the last six years there have come to the United States (Report of Bureau of Immigration) 90,123 Japanese male adults.

In California the Japanese constitute more than one-seventh of the male adults of military age:

Caucasian males of military age	262,694
Japanese males of military age	45,725

In Washington the Japanese constitute nearly one-ninth of the male population of military age:

Caucasian males of military age	163,682
Japanese males of military age	17,000

TABLE XII

THE author spent nearly seven months exploring, from a military viewpoint, the San Jacinto, San Bernardino, San Gabriel, and Tehachapi mountains, the Mojave and its adjacent deserts, traversing between one and two thousand miles. The results are embodied in the text.

THE END